WHAT DOES IT MEAN TO BE CATHOLIC?

What Does It Mean to Be Catholic?

Jack Mulder Jr.

WILLIAM B. EERDMANS PUBLISHING COMPANY
GRAND RAPIDS, MICHIGAN / CAMBRIDGE, U.K.

Nihil obstat: Rev. Charles R. Dautremont, S.T.L.
              Censor Deputatus
              April 8, 2014

Imprimatur: Most Rev. David J. Walkowiak, J.C.D.
             Bishop of Grand Rapids
             April 25, 2014

Note: The *nihil obstat* and *imprimatur* are official declarations that a book or pamphlet is free
of doctrinal or moral error. No implication is contained therein that those who have granted
the *nihil obstat* and *imprimatur* agree with the content, opinions, or statements expressed.

Published 2015 by
Wm. B. Eerdmans Publishing Co.
2140 Oak Industrial Drive N.E., Grand Rapids, Michigan 49505 /
P.O. Box 163, Cambridge CB3 9PU U.K.
www.eerdmans.com

Printed in the United States of America

21 20 19 18 17 16 15   7 6 5 4 3 2 1

Library of Congress Cataloging-in-Publication Data

Mulder, Jack, author.
What does it mean to be Catholic?: a guide for the curious / Jack Mulder Jr.
pages   cm
ISBN 978-0-8028-7266-1 (pbk.: alk. paper)
1. Catholic Church — Doctrines.   I. Title.

BX1754.M74   2015
282 — dc23

2015004726

For our children, Maria and Lucas,

our godchildren,

and the students of Hope College,

that they may grow in grace and in the knowledge

of our Lord and Savior Jesus Christ (2 Pet. 3:18).

Contents

Acknowledgments

The work in this book, it will be quickly discovered, is very meaningful to me personally. Perhaps some people find it important to write without invoking their own lives, but I just don't. I hope that isn't self-indulgent. I simply find it helpful to approach topics as someone who cares about the answer. When I joined the Catholic Church ten years ago, I would have found something like this book to be helpful, and that is why I wrote it. It is not intended as an encyclopedia of Catholicism, but it is intended to give some help on what the Catholic Church has taught through the years. If adult Catholics have an experience like mine, they are unlikely to learn anything like the full spectrum of Catholic teaching before they actually become Catholic. Because of this, few non-Catholics will get an accurate representation of Catholic beliefs. So I thought it might be good to explain some important beliefs in a way that I thought could be approached by people who might be curious. The result, with a generous helping of grace, is the modest book you're reading.

I like to say I didn't really receive a catechesis, but this isn't true. My best teachers were my parents, who taught me the Christian faith and nurtured in me a love of Jesus. I still remember my dad's high-school Sunday school class on the *Heidelberg Catechism*. Without this, the best kind of catechesis, I could not have learned how to follow the same Lord Jesus into a new tradition, that of the Catholic Church. I also learned a great deal from my wife, Melissa, and her family. Some of the best teaching of the Catholic faith happens through the Mass, and so many faithful Catholics know their faith through prayer and worship before they ever bother to articulate it to themselves and others. I have learned a lot this way, and continue to do so.

Another way I learned the Catholic faith is by being challenged to explain it, both to myself, which I had to do anyway as a theologically inclined philosopher, and to others. This has happened in countless conversations since I became Catholic, but it has particularly been true of my time teaching at Hope College. Hope is a wonderful place and it has been truly providential in my life. Since I returned to teach at Hope, many of my colleagues and students have been both gracious and inquisitive, and it has pushed me to investigate more deeply and articulate my Catholic faith more clearly. For this I am truly grateful. It is not always easy to explain how the Catholic faith is distinctive when distinctiveness is sometimes felt to tear at the unity we so deeply desire. My hope is that we can continue to inquire together in ways that show concern for one another and for the truth. My colleagues in philosophy (especially Carol Simon, now of Whitworth University) have been extremely helpful in this process, as have other friends around campus. In particular, two students who helped me develop this book were extraordinary dialogue partners, namely, Andrew Peterson and Chikara Saito. Without their work the book is almost unimaginable. It has also been enjoyable, and invigorating, to talk with Catholic friends who share a commitment to exploring the teachings of the faith, and to seeking truth together, especially Louis Mancha, Joe LaPorte, Lyra Pitstick, and Jared Ortiz. I also wish to thank Fr. Charlie Brown and Msgr. William Duncan for helping me obtain an imprimatur for this work, and His Excellency Bishop David Walkowiak for granting it. Thanks also to the helpful people at Eerdmans, especially William B. Eerdmans Jr., Linda Bieze, and Mary Hietbrink.

I pray this little book will help the reader come to know and love Jesus more.

Abbreviations and Frequently Cited Works

LW   *Luther's Works*. Ed. Jaroslav Pelikan and Helmut Lehmann. St. Louis: Concordia, 1955-1986. Cited by volume and page number.

DH   Heinrich Denzinger and Peter Hünermann. *Enchiridion Symbolorum, definitionum et declarationum de rebus fidei et morum*. 43rd edition. Ed. for English edition by Robert Fastiggi and Anne Englund Nash (San Francisco: Ignatius Press, 2012). Cited by paragraph number.

CCC   *Catechism of the Catholic Church*. 2nd edition. Washington, DC: United States Catholic Conference, 1994. Cited by paragraph number. See http://www.vatican.va/archive/ccc/index.htm.

ST   St. Thomas Aquinas. *Summa Theologica*. 5 vols. Translated by the Fathers of the English Dominican Province. 1948, repr. Allen, TX: Christian Classics, 1981. Cited by part, question, and article.

CCL   *Code of Canon Law*. Vatican: Libreria Editrice Vaticana, 1983. Cited by canon number. See http://www.vatican.va/archive/ENG1104/_INDEX.HTM.

For Vatican documents appearing after 1950 or otherwise not included in available editions or translations of Denzinger, refer to the following URLs:

Papal documents:
http://www.vatican.va/holy_father/index.htm

Documents from the International Theological Commission (unless another source is given):
http://www.vatican.va/roman_curia/congregations/cfaith/cti_index.htm

Documents from the Congregation for the Doctrine of Faith:
http://www.vatican.va/roman_curia/congregations/cfaith/doc_doc
_index.htm

Documents from Vatican II:
http://www.vatican.va/archive/hist_councils/ii_vatican_council/index
.htm

**Documents from the Pontifical Council for Promoting
Christian Unity:**
http://www.vatican.va/roman_curia/pontifical_councils/chrstuni/index
.htm

Compendium of the Social Doctrine of the Church:
http://www.vatican.va/roman_curia/pontifical_councils/justpeace/
documents/rc_pc_justpeace_doc_20060526_compendio-dott-soc_en
.html

Introduction

As I write this sentence, I am sitting in a huge convention center having just met a man who told me he had never been around so many Catholics who cared so deeply about their faith. Neither had I. There can be little question that in recent years Catholics have not done a very good job of educating their own about the Catholic faith. Consequently, Catholics have not done a very good job of educating others about the Catholic faith. There are signs of encouragement. Recent popes, beginning with Pope Paul VI (pope from 1963 to 1978), called for a "new period of evangelization" of both those who have not heard the Gospel as well as those who have heard the Gospel but need to return to the faith with fresh eyes.[1] This book is really for three groups, namely, new Catholics who want to know more about their faith; non-Catholics who want to understand Catholic distinctives better; and lifelong Catholics who would like to be reacquainted with what they believe. The purpose of this book is to describe and explain a Catholic worldview to a contemporary audience. My purpose is not to convert the reader, but I do want lay Catholics and especially other Christians to consider what a coherent Catholic faith could look like. I cannot attempt to explain everything, nor can anyone claim to know everything, but I am captivated with the Catholic faith, and I want to explain why. Other Christians will find me interacting with thinkers from lots of Christian traditions and showing how and why Catholic teaching differs from their views on various points. I hope that such Christians consult their own traditions first in an effort to think through how to love Jesus Christ with their minds, as he himself commands us (Luke 10:27).

One of the earliest issues which I can remember earnestly strug-

1. Paul VI, *Evangelii Nuntiandi*, 2.

1

gling with in my childhood denomination was the issue of whether non-Christians might attain salvation. I can remember disagreeing with my youth leader about the salvation of non-Christians. I wasn't trying to be theologically rebellious, and I wasn't upset with our kind youth leader. I just didn't understand why God would reject certain people simply because they were not Christians. That was about the time in high school when I was writing a paper on Gandhi, whom I really admired. I had difficulty understanding why a figure as righteous as Gandhi would be denied entry into God's kingdom. Our youth leader at the time was doing the best she could probably do, but I don't remember being particularly reassured.

Since that time, my views evolved, and I became comfortable with the idea that one would need to leave it up to the justice and power of God to determine whether and how non-Christians would find salvation. In the meantime, I thought, I had better take St. Paul's advice and "work out [my] salvation with fear and trembling" (Phil. 2:12). Years later, I would read Pope St. John Paul II's (pope from 1978 to 2005) claim that it would be wrong to expect Gandhi immediately to convert to the very religion of India's British oppressors,[2] and the Second Vatican Council's (1962-65) claim that "those who, through no fault of their own, do not know the Gospel of Christ or his church, but who nevertheless seek God with a sincere heart, and, moved by grace, try in their actions to do his will as they know it through the dictates of their conscience — those too may achieve eternal salvation."[3] When I read such things, I found myself being welcomed into a community I had already begun to enter.

So it would be wrong to get the impression that I am starting this book on Catholicism by writing about my struggles with the salvation of non-Christians because I was so repelled by the position of the Reformed tradition in which I had been raised that I needed to seek refuge in the Catholic Church. Despite the evangelical bent of the Reformed community on this point, I had already gotten some sense that my hope for the salvation of non-Christians was nothing new or unwelcome in the Reformed tradition. My movement to the Catholic Church came about because I came to love the Catholic Church, not because I came to detest some other Christian community.

Rather, I begin with this episode because I want to make my aims in this book clear. This book is not intended primarily as an apologetic

---

2. See St. John Paul, *Crossing the Threshold of Hope*, trans. Jenny McPhee and Martha McPhee, ed. Vittorio Messori (New York: Alfred A. Knopf, 2003), pp. 79-80.

3. Vatican II, *Lumen Gentium*, 16.

argument for why anyone reading it should be Catholic, though I will be discussing the reasons for why Catholics think the way they do. It is also not a detached scholarly introduction to Catholicism, though I do aim to give readers some information that may be helpful. It is something more like an open letter, addressed primarily to other Christians, explaining why the Catholic story captivated, and still captivates, me. My goal is to enhance dialogue within the Christian community, not to convert anyone. As Metropolitan Kallistos Ware of the Orthodox Church once noted in an interview, conversion is to Christ.[4] The Christ we encounter in the pages of the Scriptures is the real Christ. There is not another. When I became Catholic, I did not "find" Jesus. Readers from other Christian traditions should not believe that they are being given a map to a new hidden Christ. I am not claiming that this work is astonishingly new; rather, I hope that it is astonishingly old. I hope that the work is true to the message of Jesus, even if I hope to explore his message in some new and interesting ways.

On Catholic Truth

I am a Catholic and I believe that Catholicism is true. That means, of course, that I think beliefs that conflict with my Catholic faith are false. Nothing could be more natural. In 2007, when the Catholic Church reaffirmed that the church of Christ subsists in the Catholic Church, even while elements of Christian truth and salvation exist in the Orthodox Church and the Protestant traditions, many in the media rushed to condemn this as arrogance. But Charles Colson, who had been involved in Catholic-Protestant dialogue for years, said that it was "much ado about nothing." He wrote, "As a Baptist, I believe that the Baptist understanding of ecclesiology is biblically correct, that it is the true expression of the Church. The pope, of course, makes the statement that his view is the true expression of the Church. But we will keep seeking common ground."[5]

Real faith commitments always commit you to saying some ideas are true and some ideas are false. We should, however, search for ways to be charitable and to find common ground even amid disagreement. Christians disagree with Muslims about whether Jesus died on a cross. This does not

---

4. See http://www.youtube.com/watch?v=pOC5MaCNqeY. Accessed 10 July 2014.

5. This was from a 2007 *Washington Post* blog that is no longer active. Colson's contribution was called "Much Ado about Nothing."

mean that Islam has nothing to offer us; on the contrary, Islam's emphasis on the one God is a powerful witness to God's undivided Lordship over our world. Buddhism, though it is not usually thought of as a theistic religion, is a powerful witness against materialism and our tendency to remain content with what cannot ultimately satisfy. At Vatican II, the Catholic Church emphasized that all of our great religious traditions have something important to teach us and that "the Catholic Church rejects nothing that is true and holy in these religions."[6] In fact, since Jesus himself is, for Christians, the truth (John 14:6), any tradition and any person upon whom a light of truth has shone is participating in some degree in the light that is Christ.[7]

Judaism has a special place among non-Christian religions because it is already a faithful response to God's revelation in the Scriptures. Christians have much to learn from the Jewish people about how to meditate on God's law both day and night (see Ps. 1:2). Nor are Christians at liberty to believe that somehow the Jewish approach to the law is totally obsolete, as if Jesus came to abolish it, for we know that he did not (Matt. 5:17). The great twentieth-century rabbi and theologian Abraham Joshua Heschel wrote that a mitzvah (a good deed, or fulfilling of a commandment) is the place where God and humanity meet.[8] Christians often stand in need of reminding that deeds make a life, and our lives are our responses to God's love for us.

Of course, we're not only our deeds, and we must remember that our own ability to meet God is always outstripped by God's ability to meet us, as the Protestant Reformation thinkers remind us. Furthermore, it is always God who works within us, moving us closer to him. God's grace works within people as they come to Christ, no matter what stage of that journey, however long, they are on. That does not mean that people cannot resist this movement of God within them. Certainly we can do this in sin, and we do it far too often. But, with God's assistance, we are capable of much that is good as well. Yet even the good that we find within ourselves to do what is right through conscience is always an echo of our Creator.

6. Vatican II, *Nostra Aetate*, 2.

7. Vatican II, *Nostra Aetate*, 2, and St. John Paul, *Crossing the Threshold of Hope*, pp. 80-81.

8. Abraham Joshua Heschel, *God in Search of Man: A Philosophy of Judaism* (New York: Farrar, Straus, & Giroux, 2000), p. 287.

The Church as an Ark of Salvation

The Christian faith holds that the world has sunk very low, and that we bear the marks of this fall at least as much as anything in God's creation. While we feel a tug-of-war within us between good and evil, we also know that the pull toward evil is stronger than it should be. Left to our own devices, without the God who made us, knows us, and gives us the self we are truly meant to be, we will make a mess of our lives. This is not a recent development; it is an overarching theme of the Scriptures. But it can be glimpsed in an especially poignant way in the story of Noah, whose willingness to build an ark at God's command, so that he and his family could withstand the long storm to follow, serves as a warning and offers hope that God will reach out to us to rescue us when we turn to him.

The early church saw herself as an ark of salvation. St. Cyprian of Carthage (c. 200-258), a prominent bishop in North Africa under the Decian persecution of Christianity, used the imagery of Noah's ark to explain how, on his view, there could be no salvation outside the church.[9] Now, I've already said that I do not believe, and that the contemporary Catholic Church does not believe, that God's hands are tied concerning the salvation of those who are not visibly and noticeably Christian. Of course God can reach out to such people in ways we might not fully understand. But salvation is nevertheless an accomplishment of Christ's. So why not just say that the early church, which, when it sometimes claimed that there could be no salvation outside the church, got it wrong and be done with it? To understand why this is a legacy that the contemporary Catholic Church cannot pass over entirely, we need to understand what was happening in the church at the time of Cyprian.

At the time of the Decian persecution, everyone who claimed to be Christian was likely to be asked to offer a sacrifice to the Roman gods, since doing so was thought to be important for the success of the emperor's rule. What really bothered the Romans was not that Christians worshiped the Christian God, but that they would not worship the Roman gods as well. That is, what bothered the Romans was precisely what we would call the exclusivism of Christianity. Christians took idolatry very seriously, both because they inherited the Jewish prohibition of it and because they felt

---

9. *The Unity of the Catholic Church*, 6, in *The Lapsed and On the Unity of the Catholic Church* (both works in one volume), trans. and ed. Maurice Bévenot (New York: Newman Press, 1956), p. 49.

the weight of Jesus' words that "whoever denies me before others I will deny before my heavenly Father" (Matt. 10:33). Since many Christians had bravely resisted the persecution and had suffered torture and in some cases died for their obedience, what the martyrs and "confessors" (those who suffered but did not die for their faith) were saying is that what they had found in Christ's church was not available anywhere else. Suggesting that it was available elsewhere would not only disobey the first commandment, but it would suggest that the deaths of the martyrs and sufferings of the confessors were in vain. So the church insisted that fleeing to a pretended Christian community that allowed Christians to sacrifice to the Roman gods (and there were such communities) would mean treating idolatry as a small matter and thereby committing a serious sin against Christ and his church.

So what changed? Part of what changed is that the church continued to come to grips with the reality of persecution by treasuring her martyrs. Now the sacrament that initiated people into the church and was the vehicle for entry on the ark of salvation was baptism. Joining the church was a much more difficult business in the early days of the church than it is now, particularly in *some* forms of American evangelical Christianity. I certainly experienced many worship services in which there was what is known as an "altar call" issued, and anyone who wished could come forward and profess an acceptance of the Lordship of Jesus. Some talk about this experience as one in which they were "saved." It is important to understand that, from a Catholic point of view, there has been a loss in appreciation for the sacraments of the church in these communities. After all, Jesus suggests that baptism is extremely important in this connection (John 3:5), and the early church took it from this that baptism was necessary for salvation. There was also a good deal of preparation for baptism in the early church to prevent impetuous conversions, and Catholics still baptize new members, after a process of initiation, on Easter Vigil.

But what if, during a persecution, you were taken captive before you could be baptized and you were killed as a result? John 12:25 certainly suggests that losing one's life in persecution can be a gateway into a new life. But even apart from this Scripture, what is known in the Catholic Church as the "baptism of blood" makes good sense.[10] If someone is willing to give her life for Christ, surely Christ means to welcome her into the future he

10. *CCC*, 1258.

has prepared for her. In a related concern, the church asked what might happen if a person were to be part of the catechumenate (those preparing for baptism) and die before she could be baptized. To take the formal step of joining the catechumenate and preparing to join the church is a bold step. It means stepping away from one's former life and readying oneself for a new life. If one were to die before experiencing the sacrament of baptism while on this path, surely God would smile upon this, just as a loving father might whose son gives him a birthday card before he has quite learned to spell the words. This is called a "baptism of desire."[11]

Of course, baptism is not a guaranteed ticket to heaven. Someone could say all the right things and still be a fraud. Or someone could mean all the right things and fall deeply into unrepentant sin sometime later in life. But this just raises another variation on the question. How explicit does this desire need to be in order to be a "baptism of desire"? Does one have to formally join the catechumenate? On this point, we should remember that God always knows us better than we know ourselves. Indeed, sometimes others know us better than we know ourselves, especially when it comes to something for which we have a kind of blind spot. Before my wife and I were dating, we were close friends for some years in college. Toward the end of our college careers, we were working very closely together for our campus chapter of Habitat for Humanity. We would often exchange calls late into the night, and our friendship began to deepen. Since we were reluctant to set aside a deep friendship in exchange for what we worried could become an ill-fated college relationship, we claimed that we were "just friends." While this farce lasted some months, our friends didn't buy it. Before long, we realized that our friends were right, and we ultimately got married. The reason I use this example is that sometimes our "hearts" take us places our "heads" won't. God can see through to the heart of a deeply pious man like Gandhi and find that, despite his disavowals of Christianity as a particular religion, his heart might very well have been, as we say, in the right place. This, I think, is something like what it can mean to have "implicit" faith, or an "implicit" desire for baptism. It is also a way of reconciling the inclusive way that the Catholic Church still understands how we are saved only through Jesus Christ and his church.

---

11. See International Theological Commission, *The Hope of Salvation for Infants Who Die without Being Baptized,* 29.

The Dialogue of Salvation

Of course, many will find it troubling that all of this comes back to the centrality of Christ as the author of our salvation. Certainly no one wants to be told that, while she understands herself to be worshiping, say, the Hindu god Vishnu, what she is actually doing is worshiping Christ. At this point, a dose of humility is important for all of us. We must take a step back and realize that it is often difficult to separate oneself from one's religious heritage. Being brought up in a particular religion does not make that religion true. That is the case for Christianity as much as it is for any other religious tradition. What makes a religion true is reality. If Christianity is true, it is because things really are the way Christianity says they are. Christians are persuaded that Jesus is God in the flesh, the Lord of life and death, and the one through whom all things were made. We are not the authors of creation, but Christians cannot stand idly by when Christ beckons to us. I can certainly recall God's work in my life as it seemed to call me to join the Christian community of my youth by making a profession of faith. At that time it would not have been realistic to expect me to spontaneously join the Catholic Church, about which I knew very little. But I believe that God's hand was at work in that decision, and I think I can believe the same thing about many others in different religious traditions. All of what the Catholic Church sees as true in other religious traditions is ultimately a preparation of hearts for the Gospel. I have no difficulty with the idea that Muslims might believe that my Catholic faith is a preparation for a Muslim faith. Indeed, I hope they believe this about me, and there is a great deal of room for dialogue between us, but I remain bound to my Lord.

What can be said, then, about other Christians who do not share my Catholic faith? The first thing to note is the way I have phrased that question. I am asking what I as a Catholic should say about other *Christians*. I believe that the historic Christian church did well when she determined the most fundamental doctrines on Christ and the Trinity. These doctrines are so fundamental that when they are rejected, it is difficult to join in worship as one throng. When we speak of Jesus as the Lord and we acknowledge that there are three divine persons existing as one undivided and eternal God, then our liturgy is Christian. People who share this faith with me are my brothers and sisters in the Lord. I honor them with the name "Christian," and I expect the same favor from them.[12]

12. See Vatican II, *Unitatis Redintegratio*, 3.

Still, there remain significant divisions between non-Catholic Christians and Catholics. In the chapters that follow, I will be discussing these often with a view to what is distinctive about the Catholic faith. The Catholic views of Mary, the saints, the pope, and purgatory are just a few of the things that are often posed as questions for Catholics. What I hope to develop is the reason these things make sense to a Catholic understanding. I do not deny that there are other Christian visions that have a certain coherence of their own, but I do hope that what I can provide here is a small glimpse of the internal coherence, the beauty, and the depth of the Catholic faith.

Pope Paul VI once wrote of the circles of the dialogue of salvation, a theme also taken up by St. John Paul. As Paul VI puts it, there are four concentric circles of people: first, all humanity; second, the worshipers of the one God; third, all Christians; and fourth, Catholics themselves.[13] This, of course, does not mean that anyone included in the dialogue is saved without further ado, but it does mean that Christ, in drawing all to himself (John 12:32), draws people toward himself through deepening stages that emphasize our common humanity, our Creator, our Savior Jesus, and the church as his body.

I am a professor at a predominantly Protestant Christian college. I'd like to think I understand the Christian mission of the college and play my own role in helping us execute that mission. Our Christian college would not be as effective as it is if I did not have colleagues from various denominations to serve our students and give them a vision of the diversity of the Christian faith. When I came back to teach at my current school, I came back as a Catholic to an institution I had left as a Reformed Christian. I was also given the opportunity to teach a course on contemporary Catholicism, and I tried to reinforce what I want to reinforce here: we are all to grow in grace and advance in the knowledge of the Lord Jesus Christ (2 Pet. 3:18). Jesus is the truth, but he is also a person. I have no trouble believing that many of my non-Catholic brothers and sisters know him better than I do, but I have found my way with the help of his Catholic Church, and in this book I offer you my loving reflections on it.

13. Paul VI, *Ecclesiam Suam*, 97-113.

Chapter 1

Scripture and Tradition

The purpose of this book is to give an introduction to the way Catholics think about some important matters, and to do it in a spirit of open and honest dialogue with others and especially with other Christians. In my experience, the way to start such a dialogue is to begin by talking about the Catholic views of revelation and the Bible. Although the truth is that the Catholic tradition and other Christian traditions now agree on more with regard to the Bible than is commonly thought, vestiges of the popular view that they are deeply opposed remain. To be sure, there are differences among Christians on Scripture, the most obvious of which is that the Catholic Old Testament has more books in it than the Protestant Old Testament, and one fewer than the Orthodox Old Testament (3 Maccabees). Yet, the differences that still divide Christians on the Scriptures are not as fundamental as the conviction that the task of the Bible is to communicate the one revelation whose entire content is Jesus Christ.[1] The purpose of this chapter is to discuss the way Scripture is understood in the Catholic Church, and to discuss the relationship it bears to tradition. Though I intend everything here to be faithful to the Catholic understanding of the topics I discuss, I will sometimes quote writers from other Christian traditions. Except where I note divergence from the Catholic tradition, I will be doing this to show where there are some significant points of agreement across Christian traditions.

---

1. Vatican II, *Dei Verbum*, 2.

What Is Scripture?

In my wallet I carry a little card with a picture of St. Thomas Aquinas (1225-1274) and a tiny piece of cloth laminated to it. Next to the cloth it reads: "This piece of cloth has been touched by his relics." This is not something I would have been carrying years ago. At that time I would have either regarded it simply as idolatry or as one more strange "religious" practice that only serves to get in the way of a real relationship with Jesus. The shift in my thinking, however, did not come about because I began to turn my attention away from Scripture and Jesus, but because I began to reflect more deeply on Scripture and the Lord it reveals. Let me explain.

For a Catholic, the written record of Scripture attests to Christ and how to follow the Gospel. In the Catholic community there will never be another testament of Jesus such as the Latter-day Saints (or Mormon) community sees in *The Book of Mormon*.[2] Holy Scripture is unrepeatable and definitive; its words attest to the saving work of God in Jesus Christ and they will never be surpassed. Not everything that is authentically Christian, however, can be read right off the face of the scriptural record. In some cases, a longstanding practice of the early church is referenced, or an insight is recorded, that is something like a seed sown in the Scriptures, and only later, through centuries of reflection, does it manifest itself as a practice or a doctrine. That doesn't mean that it is not an authentic way to live the faith of Jesus. What it means is that we still discern that faith through time. Thus, in Acts 5:15-16, people sought to have those who were sick near Peter so that even his shadow might fall on them, as he was curing others. These people were making a good inference. People crowded in on Jesus and one woman was healed just by touching his cloak in faith (Mark 5:25-34), and Jesus himself said that "whoever believes in me will do the works that I do, and will do greater ones than these, because I am going to the Father" (John 14:12). If Peter has the power, from Christ, to heal in his name, then it's reasonable to suppose that coming into contact with him, with faith in Christ's power to heal through him, could actually heal you. But then why not others who follow in Christ's footsteps? Why indeed wouldn't we attach special significance to holy people and things associated with them? If done in the right spirit, this can serve to bring to mind their example as heroes of the faith and, if God should will, even be a source of encouragement and healing.

Christ is a Christian's life, and we draw our understanding of how to

---

2. Vatican II, *Dei Verbum*, 4.

live the Christian life from his example. Thomas Merton, a Catholic Trappist monk, once wrote that "[t]he whole truth of Christianity has been fully revealed: it has not yet been fully understood or fully lived."[3] As the Gospel of John has it, the "Word" of God is Christ himself (John 1:1), and it is this communication of God to us that is the fundamental revelation to which the church is always attending. This does not mean that Jesus, in his earthly life, had a kind of "to-do list" in seeing to it that the whole content of God's message was revealed and that he just managed to accomplish everything at his death. No, Jesus' very person just is God's self-communication. Of course, there is general revelation in nature, and there is special revelation in Scripture, but God is one, and Jesus Christ the God-man is the whole content of God's revelation to human beings. The apostles, as they wrote and taught, were communicating, in ways that we are still discerning, God's fundamental revelation in Jesus Christ.[4] Thus, while Christianity looks to the Bible as a permanent source of revelation, the Catholic Church does not see Christianity as a "religion of the book" but as a religion of the living word of God.[5]

This is why I will not be spending much time in this book on the scholarly questions concerning what Jesus "really" said or did not say. While I agree that when a claim by Jesus occurs in, say, all four Gospels (or even in Matthew, Mark, and Luke, the "Synoptic" Gospels), this should enhance our confidence that it was said by Jesus in much the way it is recorded, I am nervous about the opposite conclusion, namely, that my confidence that Jesus "really" said something should diminish just because only one Gospel reports a particular saying. As a believing Christian, the way in which I receive the apostolic testimony about Jesus reflects the way I receive Jesus himself. Even if Jesus did not utter exactly the words one Gospel reports, I must have faith that the Gospels accurately reflect his message and that I will do no better as a Christian than by following the earliest memories of the church and its apostolic communities, as they converge on the central message of Jesus. That message may need to be shepherded down through time and interpreted, but that claim itself reflects a very Catholic understanding of Scripture.

The claim of the Christian church is that the texts in which the apostles, prophets, and other inspired writers testified to God's revelation in

---

3. Thomas Merton, *New Seeds of Contemplation* (New York: New Directions, 1972), p. 143.

4. Gerald O'Collins, SJ, and Mario Farrugia, SJ, *Catholicism: The Story of Catholic Christianity* (Oxford: Oxford University Press, 2003), p. 101.

5. Pope Benedict XVI, *Verbum Domini*, 7.

Jesus are inspired texts. Inspiration is a gift of the Holy Spirit to individuals who are then moved to give a written account of God's revelation.[6] While divine revelation is primarily God's communication of himself and the way of salvation for human beings,[7] "inspiration" can be taken to refer to the messages of the entire texts. Now if God inspires human beings to communicate his revelation through written accounts, we should expect that these authors are right when they definitively claim something about how human beings attain salvation. We should not, however, necessarily expect that the authors of the biblical texts would stand altogether outside of their cultural environment and the literary customs of their ages.

In contrast to an important current that has run through some modern American evangelical and fundamentalist communities, the contemporary Catholic Church has not generally concerned itself much with whether Scripture is "inerrant" in the way that word is often understood in those traditions.[8] A good example is the Southern Baptist Convention, which, in its dialogue with the Catholic Church, claimed that in Scripture, "every inflection, . . . tense of the verb, . . . number of the noun and every little particle are regarded as coming from God," and this meant for this group that every assertion is true in the text, down to "the attributed authors and the historical narratives."[9]

Instead of claiming that each word of the Bible is individually inspired, it would be more accurate to characterize the approach taken by Catholics after the Second Vatican Council as saying that "[t]he Scriptures are verbally inspired but in the limited sense of the historical knowledge and cultural context of the biblical authors."[10] We needn't trouble ourselves overmuch about whether Solomon is the author of Song of Songs, as the first verse of that book claims. Nor is there anything deeply troubling, from a Catholic point of view, about seemingly conflicting accounts of who killed Goliath (1 Sam. 17:50 and 2 Sam. 21:19) or how Judas Iscariot died (Matt. 27:5 and Acts 1:18). These minor details may tell us what sort of author was

6. Joseph A. Fitzmyer, SJ, *The Interpretation of Scripture* (New York: Paulist Press, 2008), p. 8.

7. *Dei Verbum*, 6.

8. See R. C. Sproul, *Scripture Alone: The Evangelical Doctrine* (Phillipsburg, PA: P. & R. Publishing, 2005).

9. See Southern Baptist-Catholic Conversation, "Report on Sacred Scripture," *Origins* 29, no. 17 (1999): 266-68, at p. 267.

10. Ronald D. Witherup, *Scripture: Dei Verbum* (New York: Paulist Press, 2006), p. 90.

writing and what he had heard about these events, but their apparent contradiction does not threaten the reality of God's communication of a saving love to us. Often enough these details have a deeper harmony, though. However Judas died, the biblical text seems to agree that in some way he was overcome by the gravity of his sin. Whoever killed Goliath, the history of Israel sees God active in the lives of flawed, outnumbered, and/or outsized people, spurring them on eventually to be God's cultural and religious vessel for salvation to the world. Similarly, Pope Benedict XVI (pope from 2005 to 2013), before he became pope, noted that "the problem of the six days [of creation in the Book of Genesis]" is no longer an "urgent issue" for the relationship between science and religion, because the Bible is merely presenting a "theological framework" through which to glimpse the fact that the "world comes from the power of God and is his creation."[11] Thus, the church, I think, would agree with Orthodox theologian Theodore G. Stylianopoulos when he writes that "the overarching purpose of scripture is not the mere conveyance of religious knowledge but rather the personal self-disclosure of and intimate communion with the mystery of God."[12]

Indeed, there is nothing scary about the suggestion that some more literary portions of the biblical text are inspired fiction. Hundreds of years after Jesus was born, the Jewish scholars of the Talmud debated matters of Jewish law and interpretation of the Bible. They debated about the interpretation of the Hebrew Scriptures or *Tanakh* as it is called by Jews (which is essentially the Protestant Old Testament, though see the discussion of the canon below) precisely because they cared about the Bible, as God's revelation, so very much. God's revelation is precious, and if there is more to be garnered from reflection on it, then so much the better. One of the things these scholars debated was whether certain portions of the Bible were fiction — helpful, inspired fiction, mind you, but fiction nonetheless. Here is a portion of one of their disputes:

> One of the rabbis sat in the presence of R. Samuel b. Nahmani and expounded: Job never existed, it is all a parable. He said to him: For one such as you we have the verse: "There was a man in the land of Uz,

11. Joseph Cardinal Ratzinger, *Salt of the Earth: The Church at the End of the Millennium (An Interview with Peter Seewald)*, trans. Adrian Walker (San Francisco: Ignatius Press, 1997), p. 31.

12. Theodore G. Stylianopoulos, "Scripture and Tradition in the Church," in *The Cambridge Companion to Orthodox Christian Theology*, ed. Mary B. Cunningham and Elizabeth Theokritoff (Cambridge: Cambridge University Press, 2008), pp. 21-34, esp. p. 22.

Job was his name" (Job 1:1). He replied: But according to you, how do we interpret: "The poor man had nothing, save one little lamb which he had bought and raised" (2 Sam. 12:3). [This was part of the prophet Nathan's fictional parable to King David.] Is it anything but a parable? Here, too, it is all no more than a parable. If so, replied the other, why is his name and the name of his town mentioned?[13]

There is no definitive resolution of this debate given. Now, suppose that this unnamed scholar, who claims that the Book of Job is simply a parable, were right. How would this change our view of the Bible? As far as I can tell, it would simply suggest that not every event described in the Bible is a historical fact. Yet that would only be a problem if the Spirit of God regarded it as necessary that we *take* all of these elements to be historical fact. If the Book of Job should turn out to be fiction, this would take nothing away from the lessons that can be learned from such a text of wisdom literature. Why wouldn't the ancient Israelite culture have fictional moralistic stories that inculcate their cultural values? Think of how many cultures do have such things. There's nothing in Catholic doctrine on Scripture that says that Job *is* a parable, but there's no obvious reason why Job could *not* be a parable, either. The parable was a common way for rabbis to teach, which is why Jesus used them often.

The Talmudists engaged in this kind of debate about the Scriptures because they *did* care about the Bible; they did not want to miss its true message. They recognized that the Bible itself is a very unique text, and to be religiously interested in it is to be religiously interested in a very complex text with many rich layers of meaning. From one point of view, the Bible is not one book so much as many, but it does converge on one message.[14] Just think of the different literary genres represented by the story of Jonah (which in Hebrew has the vocabulary and tone of a children's story), as opposed to the legal matters treated in books like Leviticus and Deuteronomy. The Psalms reach beautiful poetic heights, but they give us little raw data. Presenting raw data is not the *job* of the Psalms. This is no more of a *problem* than is the very existence of a Shakespearean play or sonnet. The Psalms were meant to be sung, and Deuteronomy was clearly not meant to be sung.

13. *The Talmud: Selected Writings,* trans. Ben Zion Bokser (New York: Paulist Press, 1989), p. 194.

14. Pope Benedict XVI, *Verbum Domini,* 39.

It is important to understand that the issue of literary genre is more important in Judaism and Christianity than it is in Islam, at least with regard to each religion's sacred texts.[15] The reason for this is that if you read through the Qur'an, you'll find that it has, for the most part, only one genre. It purports to be a divine communication, and the speaker is God. The Christian Bible has many genres, and this means that there are many different things it means to express, and often in many and varied ways. This does not mean that we should not interpret the Bible literally. It means that there is more to the "literal" sense of the Bible than we might have thought. As the Pontifical Biblical Commission once noted, the "literal" meaning of "gird your loins" (Luke 12:35) just is "be ready for action."[16] Even a text's "literal" meaning has everything to do with what the author, and the Holy Spirit, meant to convey.

In order to understand what the Holy Spirit means to convey in Scripture, however, the Catholic Church claims that it is important to have the guidance of the church. After the so-called "apostolic age" ended (traditionally speaking, after the death of the last apostle),[17] there was a fairly long period of some hundreds of years in which the Church Fathers wrote. This group included people like St. Ignatius of Antioch (who died sometime around 107), St. John Chrysostom (d. 407), and St. Augustine (354-430). Their writings are often deeply scriptural, and it was common practice in the early church to produce commentaries and preach homilies, or sermons, on the Scriptures, even as it now is again today in the Catholic Church.

Scripture is not simply for scholarly scavenger hunts, though. As the 2010 apostolic exhortation from Pope Benedict XVI *Verbum Domini* noted, the work of the biblical scholar is not done until she or he explains the meaning of the word of God for today.[18] Nevertheless, it is true that some of the church's philosophers and theologians were engaged in work that was pretty abstract and somewhat distant from the Christian needs of the faithful. The Protestant Reformer Martin Luther (1483-1546) found this deplorable, and railed against it, especially in his "Disputation against

15. See Joseph Cardinal Ratzinger, *God and the World: A Conversation with Peter Seewald,* trans. Henry Taylor (San Francisco: Ignatius Press, 2002), pp. 151-52.

16. Pontifical Biblical Commission, *The Interpretation of the Bible in the Church,* II.B.1, in *The Scripture Documents: An Anthology of Official Catholic Teachings,* ed. and trans. Dean P. Béchard (Collegeville, MN: Liturgical Press, 2002), pp. 244-317, p. 280.

17. O'Collins and Farrugia, *Catholicism: The Story of Catholic Christianity,* p. 101.

18. Pope Benedict XVI, *Verbum Domini,* 33.

Scholastic Theology."[19] Shortly after Luther's Reformation, the Council of Trent (1545-1563) met in the Catholic Church. In contrast to the Protestant dictum of "Sola Scriptura" ("Scripture alone" in the sense of Scripture being the only *unquestioned* authority[20]), the Council of Trent emphasized the dual role of Scripture and tradition in the Catholic Church, without settling the question as to precisely how they related to one another. As important as these two elements are for Catholics, one unfortunate side-effect of this decision was that, in the subsequent years, the church became afraid that individual Catholics might interpret the Scriptures on their own (apart from the tradition of the church), and the church tended to treat the Bible as "the Protestant book," which often meant that it was not intended for individual Catholics in their private lives.[21]

While I think that this represents a deficiency in the way the Catholic Church of that time approached the Scriptures, it is also true that there were excesses to which the Protestant Reformation tended. As historian Jaroslav Pelikan notes, "The Reformation began, so the saying went, when there was a pope on the seven hills of Rome, but now there were seven popes on every dunghill in [Luther's native] Germany."[22] Certainly Luther never intended this, but the rapid multiplication of denominations, all claiming to be the one church of Christ, especially in the United States, is a tragic consequence of the Reformation and the sometimes excessive way that people (often Protestants themselves) read Protestantism's sole reliance on Scripture, since, as most Protestant theologians nowadays will openly admit, the tradition of the church is an important source for discerning the true meaning of Scripture.[23]

Earlier we mentioned Vatican II, which is called an "ecumenical" council by the Catholic Church, since it is supposed to be an assembly that in some sense represents the church as a whole. The Catholic Church generally recognizes twenty-one such councils, of which the Council of

---

19. *LW* 31, pp. 9-16.

20. See James R. Payton, Jr., *Getting the Reformation Wrong* (Downers Grove, IL: InterVarsity Press, 2010), p. 157.

21. See Joseph A. Fitzmyer, SJ, "The Second Vatican Council and the Role of the Bible in Catholic Life," chapter 1 in Fitzmyer, *The Interpretation of Scripture: In Defense of the Historical-Critical Method* (New York: Paulist Press, 2008).

22. Jaroslav Pelikan, *Whose Bible Is It?* (New York: Penguin, 2005), p. 166.

23. See Timothy George, "An Evangelical Reflection on Scripture and Tradition," in *Your Word Is Truth: A Project of Evangelicals and Catholics Together,* ed. Charles Colson and Richard John Neuhaus (Grand Rapids: Eerdmans, 2002), pp. 9-34.

Trent was one. We will discuss what such a council is in the next chapter, but for now, we should mention the document produced by Vatican II, the most recent of these councils, called the *Dogmatic Constitution on Divine Revelation,* or *Dei Verbum,* as it is also known in Latin. One of the things this document did was to return the Catholic Church to an insistence that the Scriptures should be widely available to all Christians.[24] Since, at a certain point in the years after the Council of Trent, one pope had condemned the view that "the reading of Sacred Scripture is for all,"[25] this was an important step. On this point, Catholic theologian Ronald Witherup frankly admits, "The fact is that the Catholic Church had been largely inattentive to the Bible for centuries."[26] At least since *Dei Verbum,* however, the church has openly encouraged the regular private reading of the Bible, as well as encouraged biblical scholars both inside and outside of the church to keep abreast of the latest developments in their field.

Another important emphasis that can be found in *Dei Verbum* is that the human authors of Scripture were "true authors."[27] That is, on the Catholic view, the writers of Scripture did not simply write a transcript of a divine monologue. Instead, the writers of Scripture were genuine authors, and wrote according to their own situation and according to their own historically conditioned way of conceiving of things. Thus *Dei Verbum* explicitly exhorted the faithful to pay attention to biblical genres.[28] In doing this, we need to ask: What is the text really *trying* to say? That is a difficult question to answer when we consider the Old Testament, which includes such different types of writing. Indeed, what is Ezekiel's vision of God trying to say? What are the Psalms trying to say when we read of the violent rage of the psalmist in Psalm 137? What does God mean for us to learn from the texts in which these episodes are included? These are difficult questions, and sometimes the psalmist's rage reaches beyond what Christian love would teach us.

The Movement of Scripture

The Hebrew Scriptures, or Christian Old Testament, clearly have a certain "angle" and even vested interest in certain things. Despite the fact that

24. *Dei Verbum,* 22.
25. DH, 2480.
26. Witherup, *Scripture,* p. 7.
27. *Dei Verbum,* 11.
28. Vatican II, *Dei Verbum,* 12.

the Hebrew writers sometimes give way to outrage and other troubling emotions, fundamentally, the Jewish people had, and in some sense, still have, according to the Catholic Church, a special relationship to God that includes a certain amount of privileged access to God's revelation.[29] For instance, the Old Testament has a vested interest in preserving the Jewish people's sense of God's involvement with their lives, which is why the Old Testament's histories always include God's active, and sometimes miraculous, intervention in their events, when secular histories would have probably left this kind of material out. This does not mean that the events never occurred, but it does mean that the Bible sometimes presents events in a very dramatic way. It is important to note that the dramatic way of presenting these events has certain functions. One of its functions is to make it possible for a people largely dependent upon oral history to retain a sense of their identity.

The Hebrew Scriptures need to preserve the time-honored institutions of the Jewish people and to ensure that those institutions are kept sacred in the future. Thus, the Old Testament tells us that God rested on the seventh day (Gen. 2:2), despite the fact that God is eternal and no more rests on a particular day than plays tennis on a particular day. The Sabbath was a time-honored religious institution of the Jewish people, and it was retained, albeit transformed, by the Christian tradition. The Sabbath was, as Jesus notes, made for human beings (Mark 2:27), but it is important to note that God made human beings, and furthermore made them the sorts of beings, and the world the sort of place, for whom and for which the Sabbath is an important expression of God's relationship with us.

When we move into the New Testament, we find that it begins with a unique literary genre known as the Gospel. Gospels are recollections of Jesus' life and teaching. They have a privileged place in the Catholic liturgy just because they are so fundamental to the church's understanding of Christ. Indeed, part of the point of liturgy in the Mass is to prepare us to receive the words of Scripture in the right way. You can see this whenever you go to a Catholic Mass. A characteristic Sunday Mass has an Old Testament reading, a New Testament reading (often from the letters of Paul or some other epistle), and then a Gospel reading. The Gospel is read by someone with some level of ordination, such as a priest or deacon. The Gospel is shown to the congregation, who stand as it is shown, and those present trace the sign of the cross on their heads, their lips, and their

---

29. Vatican II, *Nostra Aetate*, 4.

hearts, and pray to receive the Gospel with openness to God's will. The Christian claim is that the Old Testament looks forward to the Gospel, and the New Testament epistles look back on the events related by the Gospels. Gospels take us nearer to the Lord's own heart than any other reading does.[30]

The wisdom of Jesus is timeless, and the problems Paul's letters and the other epistles address often have much in common with the issues of our times, to be sure. At the same time, the Bible always has an intended audience. It intends to communicate something to the hearer and the thing that it means to communicate is what is important. When the Gospel writers put down their own understandings of Jesus, their accounts are different. This is not a religious problem at all, any more than it is a problem that when I write a letter I think about the person to whom I am writing the letter. The Catholic Church has various advisory commissions and "congregations" that exist to help with functions that basically are under the purview of the pope, who usually approves major official documents issued by these organizations. One such commission is the Pontifical Biblical Commission, and it is worth quoting the Pontifical Biblical Commission on the Gospels here:

> Out of the material they had received, the sacred authors selected especially those items that were adapted to the varied circumstances of the faithful . . . ; these they recounted in a manner consonant with those circumstances and with that end. . . . For this reason the exegete [interpreter of Scripture] must ask himself what the Evangelist intended by recounting a saying or a fact in a certain way, or by placing it in a certain context. For the truth of the narrative is not affected in the slightest by the fact that the Evangelists report the sayings or the doings of our Lord in a different order, and that they use different words to express what he said, not keeping to the very letter, but nevertheless preserving the sense.[31]

When Matthew writes his Gospel, he has in mind a Jewish community of Christians, so when he goes to give his genealogy of Jesus, he begins with

---

30. Vatican II, *Dei Verbum*, 18.

31. Pontifical Biblical Commission, "Instruction on the Historical Truth of the Gospels" or *Sancta Mater Ecclesia*, 2.9 (April 21, 1964), in *The Scripture Documents*, pp. 227-35, esp. pp. 230-31.

Abraham and shows, along the way, how Jesus is born to the house and line of David, the great king (Matt. 1:1-17). This would have been important to Jewish readers who needed some confirmation of the fact that he was the Messiah they had anticipated.

Luke, however, is writing for a Greek-speaking audience. He explicitly addresses his Gospel to Theophilus, a Greek who would have very little understanding of the concept of a Messiah (which is a Hebrew word), so it would do no good to tell him that Jesus was descended from Abraham and David. So Luke's genealogy goes all the way back to Adam (the first human being), and not just to David or Abraham (Luke 3:23-38). Matthew wanted to emphasize that Jesus shared a Jewish heritage with his audience. Luke wanted people to understand that Jesus shared the common human plight. Both of these are essential things to remember about the Christian message.

The idea that the writers of the Bible did not have a thought in their minds but were simply passive vessels when they were writing is simply not faithful to the text itself. The writers of the Bible are theologians, of a sort, and studying their work should be the "soul of theology."[32] The difference between the Gospel writers' theology and contemporary theology is that their theology consists of the unrepeatable, irreplaceable, and sometimes scraped-together memories of the Lord Jesus Christ himself by those who were near enough in time to his earthly life to be inspired to write a devotional account of it.

When I speak of the biblical text as "scraped-together," I do not mean that the writings themselves needed correction;[33] I mean that they were passionate responses to the crisis that the church might lose the knowledge of Christ. The writers of the New Testament wrote what they wrote because they knew it needed to be written. Unlike the matter of whether or not Jonah *really* spent three days of his life in a great fish, the matters of Jesus' life (though perhaps not the exact timeline), death, and resurrection are of the utmost importance for our salvation. So the apostles and writers of the Bible didn't wait for the most profound and elegant writers to be converted to Christianity. Indeed, the Greek grammar of some of the Gospels is not always that good. Luke's Gospel, which is a well-written exception to the point about grammar, is nonetheless written for a person

---

32. *CCC*, 132.

33. Pontifical Biblical Commission, *Sancta Mater Ecclesia*, 2.11, in *The Scripture Documents*, p. 232.

who would like to know what occurred in the life of Jesus. These texts were not sent to the historical libraries, because no such libraries at the time would have cared. The Gospels were written by devoted followers of Jesus for devoted followers of Jesus, who needed, above all things, to *remember* the Lord.

Another reason why we should not think of the writers of the Bible as passive vessels of commandments from God is that the writers themselves sometimes make it clear that this view is simply false. Paul himself, when he is writing his epistles, sometimes claims that he has no clear teaching from the Lord, but has a piece of advice that he thinks is trustworthy. He writes, "Now, in regard to virgins, I have no commandment from the Lord, but I give my opinion as one who by the Lord's mercy is trustworthy . . ." (1 Cor. 7:25). There are times when apostles and writers self-consciously mean to teach something as given to them by the Lord. There are other times when they are simply trying to figure out how to teach communities and to resolve questions and problems with what guidance they have from the Lord. Paul's considered judgment as an apostle in this matter is an important source for Christian self-understanding, even if he did not feel called at that point to articulate his advice with the same authority he used in other contexts.

The Church and the Bible

This view of the Bible should teach us something about the early Christian church. The early Christian community was struggling with how to understand itself in the light of Jesus' life, death, and resurrection. Specifically, it was trying to understand how it was supposed to take stock of its Jewish heritage and, at the same time, preach the Gospel of Jesus to the entire world. No longer was this a Gospel for Jews only. It is in this environment that we get letters sent by very particular apostles to particular communities who struggle with very particular issues. The intent of these letters is not to settle every possible point, but to settle the ones that are pressing for the community right then and there.

In approaching the Bible, therefore, we need to recognize that sometimes there is a seed within the Bible that later grows, through theological reflection on it, into a full-fledged tree that itself produces fruit. Everything that is definitively settled in and by the Bible is worth believing and should be believed. However, not everything worth believing is definitively settled in and by the Bible. The fact that something cannot be found explicitly in the Bible does not mean that it is false, nor does it mean that God has left us with no trustworthy means for discovering whether it is true or false. The Bible itself tells us that, when faced with a difficult decision of whether Gentile converts should be obligated to obey the Jewish law, the apostles got together in Jerusalem and, after much debate (Acts 15:7), they issued the following decision, which was sent to the Gentile communities through Judas and Silas:

> The apostles and the presbyters, your brothers, to the brothers in Antioch, Syria, and Cilicia of Gentile origin: greetings. Since we have heard that some of our number [who went out] without any mandate from us have upset and disturbed your peace of mind, we have with one accord decided to choose representatives and to send them to you along with our beloved Barnabas and Paul, who have dedicated their lives to the name of the Lord Jesus Christ. So we are sending Judas and Silas who will also convey this same message by word of mouth: "It is the decision of the holy Spirit and of us not to place on you any burden beyond these necessities, namely, to abstain from meat sacrificed to idols, from blood, from meats of strangled animals, and from unlawful marriage. If you keep free of these, you will be doing what is right. Farewell." (Acts 15:23-29)

Now, everyone knows that there is more involved in a good Christian life than just doing these things, and so when the decision says that it will not "place on you any burden beyond these necessities," it does not mean to do away with the Ten Commandments, as if the church didn't care whether its members were or were not violent criminals. It's referring especially to the Jewish dietary laws and laws about the circumcision of males. How many of these laws should Gentiles have to follow? This is the question the council met to answer.

Imagine yourself as a first-century Gentile Christian when this decision was made. As the text goes on to say, Christians were delighted (Acts 15:31). You, as a first-century Gentile Christian, are delighted that the Spirit of God and the apostles who are God's messengers came to this decision. Now you have your answer. When someone asks you whether Gentiles must follow, for instance, all the dietary laws of the Jewish religion, you respond by saying, "Oh no, we needn't follow all the Jewish laws. Didn't you hear of the decision made by the council of the apostles in Jerusalem?" This is a good response when faced with such a question. You, a first-century Gentile Christian, can hardly point your finger at Acts 15 in the Bible, as that book was certainly not in wide circulation as of yet, and definitely not yet understood as part of the Bible, as Christians now claim it is. But the decisions of the apostles are authoritative for you.

Similar things occur in later centuries. Consider the doctrine of the Trinity. Anglican theologian Alister McGrath, in his *Introduction to Christian Theology,* notes that the Bible simply does not directly teach the Trinity. The word, after all, was basically invented by Tertullian, an early Church Father, when he was trying to emphasize at once the unity and tri-personal nature of God without compromising either. However, McGrath adds that "Scripture bears witness to a God who demands to be understood in a Trinitarian manner."[34] While we will save the discussion of God's nature for later portions of this text, the Catholic and broadly orthodox Christian doctrine of the Trinity is that God is three persons (Father, Son, and Holy Spirit) in one undivided substance. There was a great deal of theological haggling that had to be done to come up with this definition, and there were clear terms that one was and was not allowed to use in talking about the Trinity. The Bible does not use the theological terms that became necessary to resolve these disputes. But what it does offer us is a monotheistic God who must be understood as tri-personal, as Father, Son, and Holy Spirit.

Clearly, we should engage people with reason and begin by discussing what we both find authoritative. But Christians have long since agreed on some basic parameters for how to talk about the Trinity, even if some points, such as whether the Spirit proceeds from the Father and the Son or simply the Father, remain matters of dispute between Western (Protestant and Roman Catholic) and Eastern Orthodox churches.[35] These parameters were arrived at in a similar way to the way in which the apostles at the Council of Jerusalem arrived at their decision, and the Bible records that incident precisely because that was how things were settled. They were not settled by looking at Luke's version of the Gospel. At that time, Luke's voice would have been at most one party to the debate, a debate that the Bible itself tells us occurred. This is the very biblical reason why Catholics

---

34. Alister McGrath, *Introduction to Christian Theology,* 4th edition (Oxford: Blackwell, 2007), p. 249.

35. Timothy (Kallistos) Ware, *The Orthodox Church,* new edition (London: Penguin, 1997), pp. 210-18.

do not *need* to justify every element of their faith by pointing to incontrovertible biblical testimony.

So the apostles themselves are allowed to make decisions for the whole church, but why should we extend this privilege beyond their time period? After all, one might say, the real authority in the church is Jesus, and it was the apostles who knew him best. It is certainly true that the apostles knew him best, especially Peter, James, and John, who were often called to join him where others were not invited. The trouble with this objection is that the apostles together decided that, after Judas Iscariot's departure from their ranks, they would need a successor for Judas. So they chose one, with the assistance of the Holy Spirit. His name was Matthias (Acts 1:26), "and he was counted with the eleven apostles." Perhaps you can imagine Matthias at the Council of Jerusalem. Maybe he shifted in his seat a bit, thinking that these eleven folks were chosen by the Lord Jesus in person, and he was the new guy in town. But gradually, we can imagine him finding his place among the apostles. Maybe the first few times he spoke up he felt a bit inadequate, but, after a while, he began to understand the experience of Jesus that the apostles had, as well as his own. He also, no doubt, began to understand why they should make the decisions they made. These were the authority figures in the early church, and they were responsible for how the Gospel message should be interpreted. The original apostles had successors, and Catholicism believes that they have in one form or another always had them. The successors to the apostles in the modern church are called bishops.[36]

Before discussing the way that tradition relates to the Scriptures, as well as the teaching office of the bishops of the church (which we'll discuss in the next chapter), we should briefly discuss the canon of Scripture. Every sacred text has some historical account to be given about why it came together between two covers (or more) the way it did. It can only be in light of its experience with Jesus that the Christian community would decide which books would form part of the Bible we know. The New Testament books were actually decided upon much earlier than the canon of the Old Testament, with influential decisions made on the current list in the year 382, and with the same list being finally adopted for East and West in 692.[37] Indeed, nearly all Christian communities (certainly the Orthodox, Catholic, and mainline Protestant communities) agree on the contents of

36. *CCC,* 861-62.
37. See Pelikan, *Whose Bible Is It?,* p. 117.

the New Testament. We should find this unsurprising. The New Testament is the sacred record of the early Christians' experience with Jesus. There were many other texts that were to vie for inclusion in the canon, but the church needed to decide what an authentic representation of its experience with Jesus was. Christ is the lens through which the contents of Scripture needed to be discerned.

The trouble is that exactly *which* scriptures Judaism considered authoritative, at which points, and for which reasons, is not always entirely clear. There are two competing canons that we should mention here. First, let us consider the tradition of the Septuagint. The Septuagint was a translation of the writings of the Hebrew Scriptures into Greek. There is a popular account of how King Ptolemy Philadelphus of Egypt, sometime in the third century BCE, commissioned seventy-two Jewish scholars to translate their scriptures to Greek for the sake of the Alexandrian library (the term "Septuagint" originates from the Greek word for "seventy"). The legend continues that these scholars produced identical translations and this was taken to be confirmation of the scriptures' status as inspired texts. As Jaroslav Pelikan notes, the more likely explanation seems to be that Jews who were dispersed throughout the world needed to be provided with their Scriptures despite the fact that many could no longer read Hebrew. In any case, the Septuagint seems to have been in fairly wide circulation in the Jewish community sometime prior to the Advent of Christ, to the extent that the New Testament writers, who wrote in Greek, often quoted this version directly. Another account of the canon of Jewish Scriptures is of the meeting of rabbis at the city of Jamnia sometime in the late first century CE. Pelikan writes, "After the fall of Jerusalem in 70 CE and the rise of the Christian movement, the Jewish community felt obliged, in closing ranks, to fix the limits of its Bible more precisely."[38]

The decision about which books to include in the Christian Old Testament would not have been an easy one to make. Although the Septuagint was in use during the time of Jesus and the apostles, and the writers of the New Testament appear to have been familiar with it, it cannot be said with certainty whether each book of the Septuagint was, simply by its inclusion in the Septuagint, regarded as inspired Scripture for Jews at that time. The process of translation moved slowly, and it's not clear whether it may or may not have moved in stages of more and less authoritative books. At the same time, the canon evidently adopted at Jamnia, or at any rate, by con-

38. Pelikan, *Whose Bible Is It?*, p. 47.

temporary Judaism as its *Tanakh,* was chosen at a time when the growth of the Christian movement, and its use of Hebrew Scriptures, appears to have alarmed some leading Jewish scholars.

Catholics have some books in their Old Testament canon not found in the Old Testament canon for Protestants. Catholics call these "deuterocanonical," which means that they were included in the canon after a lengthier process of debate. The deuterocanonical or, as many Protestant Christians call them, "apocryphal" texts, which were included in the Septuagint and were not included in the Jamnian canon, reflected a more Hellenized Judaism, and some of these texts appear to have been originally written in Greek.[39] These texts, with the exception of 3 and 4 Maccabees, are included in the Catholic Old Testament canon. Some of these texts are included as portions of other books, such as the story of Susanna or Bel and the Dragon, as chapters 13 and 14 in the book of Daniel. Protestants will find a common Catholic translation, such as the New American Bible, to include seven more books in its Old Testament than Protestants will find in theirs, namely, Tobit, Judith, 1 and 2 Maccabees, Wisdom, Sirach, and Baruch. As the New Testament is also written in Greek, the decision of first-century Judaism not to include these texts may have been partly motivated by a desire to check the growing influence of the movement away from traditionally Hebrew sources toward Gentile and Christian patterns of thought. If this is the case, it's not clear what sort of status we should award the decisions of the rabbis at Jamnia for the Christian church.

The point here is that it is impossible to argue about the canon as if its table of contents was bestowed from on high without any human intermediary. Although the Septuagint is, in many ways, the basis for the Catholic and Orthodox canons, neither of those traditions grants final canonical status to 4 Maccabees (and the Catholic Church does not grant it to 3 Maccabees), which is included in the Septuagint. Although the Protestant traditions follow the Jewish *Tanakh* in excluding the deuterocanonical books, the restriction of the canon in this way is not beyond question. From a Catholic point of view, the matter essentially rests on the question of whether there is a church that is guided by the Spirit to make decisions about such matters. This is a strong reason why the church finds the need to put confidence in tradition, whose relationship to Scripture we must now briefly discuss.

39. See DH, 1502-5.

Tradition's Relationship to Scripture

We've just discussed how there needed to be a decision made by the church as to the limits of the canon of Scripture. The Bible "transmits past revelation and completes that revelation,"[40] but it does so with the aid of the believing church and her tradition. This does not mean that the Bible has authority *because* it is the church's book. Rather, as *Verbum Domini* has it, "the Church is built upon the word of God."[41] The Bible has authority because it is the unrepeatable testimony of the heritage, person, and apostolic community of Jesus Christ, who is God's supreme revelation. The church's tradition is also a resource for this testimony, and that is why it has authority. It is through the church's tradition that, according to Vatican II's *Dei Verbum,* "the Church's full canon of the sacred books is known, and the sacred writings themselves are more profoundly understood."[42] There would be no canon if there were no church to decide upon it, through the guidance of the Holy Spirit. Equally, there would be no church if her members did not witness the living Christ and his message of salvation and set down their testimony as a rule of faith. Consequently, Christians must trust the church at some point; the only real question is how far into history one does so.

Even in *Dei Verbum,* the issue of how to understand tradition in relation to Scripture is a very difficult matter. The important thing to recognize, however, is that both flow "from the same divine wellspring" and both together "form one sacred deposit of the word of God."[43] The Council of Trent, in response to the Reformation's reliance on Scripture alone as a final authority, decreed that the saving truth of the Christian message was "contained in the written books and unwritten traditions, that have come down to us, having been received by the apostles from the mouth of Christ himself or from the apostles by the dictation of the Holy Spirit." Trent also declared that both Scripture and tradition were to be given the "same sense of loyalty and reverence."[44]

These statements suggested to many at the time that there were two sources of revelation itself, Scripture and tradition. In this context, it is

40. See Avery Cardinal Dulles, SJ, "Revelation, Scripture, Tradition," in *Your Word Is Truth,* pp. 35-58, esp. p. 49.

41. Pope Benedict XVI, *Verbum Domini,* 3.

42. Vatican II, *Dei Verbum,* 8.

43. Vatican II, *Dei Verbum,* 9, 10.

44. DH, 1501.

important to remember that, according to the Catholic Church, the church is the custodian, not only of revelation, but also of her doctrinal statements on it. It is not for the casual observer to tell just what a doctrinal statement entails, since the language is always carefully chosen, and reflects debates that are not immediately obvious. In fact, the "two-source" question was debated at Vatican II and was not solved in the church until Vatican II declared that there was just one deeper source of revelation, namely, God's communication of his saving love, that gives rise to both Scripture and tradition.[45]

But just what is tradition supposed to be and how does it relate to Scripture? Tradition means to "hand on" something that one has been given, and in this case, *Dei Verbum* notes that the apostles "by their oral preaching, by example, and by observances handed on what they had received from the lips of Christ, from living with Him, and from what He did, or what they had learned through the prompting of the Holy Spirit."[46] In this sense, Scripture and tradition are clearly interdependent, and that is how *Dei Verbum* presents their relationship. Scripture, as written down and bound within two covers, transmits a permanent inheritance for the Christian tradition. In the early centuries of Christianity, the Scriptures were often referred to as a "rule" of faith. Once a text is written down, it must be appealed to and abided by for those who claim it as an authority. The Scriptures can never be outdone for guidance in the Christian life because we latecomers only know Christ as communicated to us in and by the Scriptures. As *Dei Verbum* points out, quoting St. Jerome, "ignorance of the Scriptures is ignorance of Christ."[47] Tradition, therefore, needs Scripture to keep it housed within the meaning of the Lord Jesus Christ, who is himself "the fullness of all revelation."[48]

At the same time, a reliance on Scripture itself, as we saw in the introduction, makes it clear that Scripture is never really *alone.* St. Paul, in 1 Thessalonians 2:15, writes, "Therefore, brothers, stand firm and hold fast to the traditions that you were taught, either by an oral statement or by a letter of ours." The impression one receives from this is that it is perfectly possible that some information has been communicated by the apostles that may not have been written in letter form, and holding

---

45. Vatican II, *Dei Verbum,* 10.
46. Vatican II, *Dei Verbum,* 7
47. Vatican II, *Dei Verbum,* 25.
48. Vatican II, *Dei Verbum,* 2.

fast to this oral statement (or unwritten tradition) is exactly what the Bible itself would have us do. Now, it's also possible that this other information found its way into a different biblical book than 1 Thessalonians, but that's really an insignificant point when one considers the Gospel of John's statement that if everything Jesus did were to be "described individually" there would be no end of books authentically relating Jesus' life and times (John 21:25). We are always discerning more about the love of God in Jesus, and this is why Christians continually read the Bible. It is also why there is "growth in the understanding of the realities and the words which have been handed down" in the church's tradition.[49] But the process of learning more and more from the Scriptures in the church's teaching tradition need not be restricted to individuals. The church itself can discern more and more from Scripture as it returns, again and again, to the revelation entrusted to her.

So far we've seen reasons to think that Scripture and tradition are mutually reinforcing. The teaching tradition of the church was a rule for deciding upon the canon of Scripture that then became a rule of faith in the future. But Scripture itself, as in the verse from 1 Thessalonians above, appears to give legitimacy to the teaching tradition of the apostles. From this point of view, Baptist theologian Timothy George's willingness to talk about the "coinherence" of Scripture and tradition for Protestants seems apt.[50] The Bible is the church's book, and Christians should always find it unsurprising if, untutored by the church's discipline of reading of the Scriptures, someone reads the Bible on her own, and comes to very different conclusions than the church has reached. This is also why many Catholics feel strange when challenged with the question of where some article of their faith appears in the Bible. As the late Catholic biblical scholar Raymond Brown said in a similar connection,

> I received my knowledge of Catholic doctrine from my parents and from catechism, not from reading the Scriptures. Scriptural study came later in my life and has served to clarify and make precise doctrine that I already knew — much in the same way it has served the Catholic Church in the 20th century. That sequence has meant that personally I have never found critical interpretation of the Bible a threat to my faith. I know full well that some regard this admission as a sign that my

---

49. Vatican II, *Dei Verbum,* 8.
50. See George, "An Evangelical Reflection on Scripture and Tradition," p. 21.

interpretation of Scripture must necessarily be blinded or prejudiced or skewed. However, I do not think it irrational or dishonest to have a greater confidence in the guidance of God experienced in the church, the community of God's Son, than in my abilities as a scholar, which might theoretically lead me to other conclusions.[51]

What Brown means to tell us here is that he is more inclined to trust the "community of God's Son" than he is inclined to trust his individual abilities to interpret the Scriptures. Indeed, to try to justify some doctrine using *one's own* interpretation of the Bible is not the typically Catholic way. The Catholic way is to think carefully and prayerfully through the Scriptures in communion with the church's long history and teaching. To try to justify (or for that matter refute) some particular doctrine using only Scripture presupposes that we ourselves have the ability to supplant a long line of interpretation that in some way goes back to Christ and the apostles themselves.

But are there some things that are in tradition that have nothing to do with Scripture? On the one hand, everything in the message of Jesus will resonate with the authentic tradition of his message. On the other hand, Cardinal Augustin Bea, a leader at Vatican II, wrote that *Dei Verbum* did not intend to resolve every aspect of this question.[52] He noted that one could hold either that "all revealed truths" are implicitly in the Bible, or one could hold that some "revealed truths" came to the church through the oral traditions of the apostles alone. In my view, not very much will be gained by deciding this question. Scripture and tradition are interdependent and revelation forms an integrated whole. If the church, in reading the Scriptures, owed an idea to the apostolic tradition that had been passed down, then that idea would in some way be suggested or foreshadowed by the Bible itself. Whether that would amount to being "implicit" in the Scriptures would simply be to haggle over words. In any case, we know from the Gospel of John that there is more to know about Jesus' life than could be explicitly written down in any book, and we must trust God and his church that we will be given all that we need to know in this life from Scripture and tradition. On this point, Orthodox theologian John Meyendorff writes that "Scripture, while complete in itself, presup-

51. See Raymond E. Brown, "Scripture and Dogma Today," in *The Catholic Faith: A Reader*, ed. Lawrence S. Cunningham (New York: Paulist Press, 1988), pp. 7-15, at p. 15.

52. Witherup, *Scripture*, p. 97.

poses Tradition, not as an addition, but as a *milieu* in which it becomes understandable and meaningful."[53]

There is, however, a way in which the teaching tradition of the church moves through the centuries, and teaches both how to understand the Scriptures and how to grasp tradition's continuing role. That teaching tradition is often called the magisterium, and its job is to discern the word of God, whether through Scripture or tradition, for the people of God in the church. It is important to note that the magisterium "is not above the word of God, but serves it, teaching only what has been handed on."[54] Its teachings come from bishops, popes, and councils, but these track the whole church's abiding sense of faith as well. The Catholic Church claims that, when the magisterium intends to be teaching a truth of faith in a way that is permanent, it cannot err.

Of course, not everything uttered by a bishop or even a pope is infallible. Perhaps the best way to describe the magisterium is that some of its past decisions, in being taken by the church to form permanent elements of her inheritance of faith (sometimes called the "deposit of faith"),[55] are incorporated into the church's understanding of the word of God, either as Scripture or as tradition. But the present decisions of the church, in regard to how to live a Christian life and how to understand Scripture and tradition, are part of the church's ongoing discernment of revelation. So, the magisterium is not a third entity alongside Scripture and tradition, so much as it is the teaching of the church, born from Scripture and tradition, constantly and with the help of the Holy Spirit, discerning what is, and what is not, its inheritance from Christ and the apostles. This is why it is called the "living, teaching office of the Church."[56] On this point, Timothy George notes that "Evangelicals and Catholics differ on the scope and locus of the magisterium but not on whether it exists as a necessary component in the ongoing life of the church."[57] Very few Christians really believe that the church does not discern the word of God through the centuries. The real difference is in *how* the church discerns the word of God (and with what materials at her disposal), not in *whether* she discerns the word of God.

---

53. John Meyendorff, *Living Tradition: Orthodox Witness in the Contemporary World* (Crestwood, NY: St. Vladimir's Seminary Press), p. 16.

54. Vatican II, *Dei Verbum*, 10.

55. *CCC*, 84.

56. *CCC*, 85.

57. George, "An Evangelical Reflection on Scripture and Tradition," p. 33.

It is important to emphasize that the magisterium is not revealing new truths in proclaiming that some doctrine is a part of the deposit of faith handed down in Scripture or tradition. Rather, the understanding that develops within the church over the years depends entirely upon the foundational revelation of Jesus Christ in Scripture and tradition. The information in what is called the deposit of faith is not what grows; what grows is the church's *understanding* of what is included in the deposit of faith. The way it does this is through the work of leaders, whom the Holy Spirit guides in the teaching of the Christian faith. In the next chapter we will discuss who these leaders are and in what ways they determine the teaching of the church.

Chapter 2

The Church and Her Magisterium

When I was a senior in college, I took a class in which I was presented with a sheet that surveyed the way we as students identified ourselves with regard to religious affiliation. There were many options, but the list reflected the fact that I was living in a predominantly Christian area. The options were categories like: atheist, agnostic, Jewish, Muslim, Buddhist, Catholic, Lutheran, Reformed, Christian Reformed, Baptist, Methodist, Episcopalian, Orthodox, nondenominational Christian, Christian, and so on. Now of course, there are many divisions within non-Christian communities too, so the fact that the Christian community is divided is certainly neither unique nor new. But what did I pick? I picked "Christian." I was raised in a denomination called the Reformed Church in America, and while I did identify with the Reformed tradition in certain ways, I felt more comfortable identifying as a Christian because I wanted to follow Jesus (which is not to say that I did it particularly well) and I had a bit of an independent streak going. Besides, I was sure I wanted to follow Jesus, but I was not totally sure about any one way of doing that besides the way I thought was outlined in the Bible.

I think this is the way many Christians feel. In my area, communities that used to proudly identify as the "Reformed Baptist Church" or "Calvin Christian Reformed Church" now post signs identifying to the general public as "Harbor Church" or "Calvin Church." I don't blame them. One of the characteristics of our times, it seems, is a kind of malaise when we're presented with too many options. For a time, Protestant communities were very good at presenting people with options, but now, perhaps because the options are so extensive, many people are searching for a Christian community that offers them what they perceive to be the authentic Gospel, rooted in the Scriptures, without trying to "sell" them an overly exclusive theological story. That's what I was thinking when I circled "Christian" over "Reformed."

Yet here's the trouble. Wanting to separate the Gospel from "human traditions" (see Col. 2:8) is laudable, but who will separate the Gospel wheat from the human chaff? It can't be just any old pastor who *says* he or she is teaching from the Bible. We'll need to verify that the teaching really does come from the Bible. But then, who is in a position to do that? Is it a task left to me? Is it my job to figure out what the "Gospel essentials" are? Surely everyone is aware of denominations breaking from one another by the thousands based on *their* own understandings of what is and what is not essential. Then again you might think the whole doctrinal approach seems a little ridiculous, since of course no one can tailor a church doctrine according to one's own preferences and interpretations. There are bound to be some surprises in Jesus' message. So it might seem better to try to find a "church home" where a good community of people are trying to live a certain sort of Christian life. But what is the selection procedure here? Surely I shouldn't just pick a pastor I like. That won't get me any further from self-indulgent religiosity, and in any case, pastors change. Nor, of course, will simply picking a community of people do the trick because the people change, and in any case, this approach flirts with treating one's faith like a social club. What is the solution?

If picking a church is this difficult (and I never have trouble finding people who think it is), why would Catholicism be any better off? I think there is a reason. As the Anglican writer C. S. Lewis's (1898-1963) fictional demon Screwtape once quipped, "The search for a 'suitable' church makes the man a critic where the Enemy [i.e., God] wants him to be a pupil."[1] We cannot engineer our religion based on what we want, but at a certain point religious people have to believe that if a need is dire enough, then God in his mercy will have a plan for meeting it. That is why, according to the Catholic Church, the faith, while recorded in a definitive way in the Scriptures, was nevertheless originally transmitted to the apostles, and they themselves transmitted it to others.[2] As the late Avery Cardinal Dulles writes, "In establishing the Magisterium, Christ responded to a real human need."[3]

---

1. C. S. Lewis, *The Screwtape Letters,* revised edition (New York: Macmillan, 1982), letter XVI, p. 73.

2. *CCC,* 77-79.

3. See Avery Cardinal Dulles, SJ, *Magisterium: Teacher and Guardian of the Faith* (Naples, FL: Ave Maria University Press, 2007), p. 4.

The Catholic Church claims continuity with this early apostolic teaching. That is why apostolic succession is so vital to the Catholic vision of the faith. The apostles were the ones entrusted by the Lord with the task of teaching Christians to observe all that he had commanded them (Matt. 28:20). No doubt they saw one of their charges as writing down some of what they had been commanded along the way, but they also had the job of helping others to understand what they had written, and what in it was essential to the message of the Lord. Modern-day Catholics see the bishops (along with the pope as the bishop of Rome) to be successors to the apostles in this task. The Orthodox Church can also claim continuity through apostolic succession, and the Catholic Church feels especially close to these churches because of this link. To illustrate, I was once at a seminar of some scholars who were discussing the very nerdy thing of their "philosophical family tree." One's dissertation advisor, it was said, might have studied under so-and-so, who studied under so-and-so, and so on until one got to a final person who studied under *Kant!* (For philosophers, tracing your lineage back to Kant would be rather like finding out that you're a distant cousin of the royal family in England or the Kennedys in America.) An Orthodox priest in the room just chuckled and said, "I don't like to drop names, but as a priest my lineage goes back to *Jesus.*"

Our job in this chapter is to treat the issue of the teaching office of the church, or the "magisterium." In doing so, we will pay special attention to the papacy, and we'll also discuss a bit about how the Catholic Church understands bishops and councils and their role in the church. Most Christians in the broadly orthodox traditions (Catholic, Orthodox, and most Protestant traditions) accept the testimony of the first seven councils. So the fact that Catholics think that something important happened at such councils is not distinctively Catholic. However, the Catholic Church recognizes more of these councils than any other Christian community, and the teachings from these councils are quite distinctive. In fact, some of the distinctive teaching has to do with how councils themselves are run, and the way the "college" of bishops is structured. The major source of distinction here is the pope, the bishop of Rome. The reason the bishop of Rome attains this status is because of the importance of his "see" in Rome for early Christians. This is why the Vatican is called the "Holy See." It is also important because Peter, the leader of the apostles, was, according to tradition, martyred in Rome. For this reason, we need to begin by discussing, at some length, the role of the pope in the Catholic Church.

The Role of the Papacy

One important form of communication from a pope is the letter. Particularly significant letters that the pope means to circulate to the whole church and all people of good will are sometimes called "encyclicals." These are major documents, though there are other classifications of letters from the pope, and some are more and some less authoritative. Pope St. John Paul II, in his encyclical letter on Christian ecumenism, *Ut Unum Sint*, discussed the responsibilities of the pope. He wrote,

> It is the responsibility of the Successor of Peter to recall the requirements of the common good of the Church, should anyone be tempted to overlook it in the pursuit of personal interests. He has the duty to admonish, to caution and to declare at times that this or that opinion being circulated is irreconcilable with the unity of faith. When circumstances require it, he speaks in the name of all the Pastors in communion with him. He can also — under very specific conditions clearly laid down by the First Vatican Council — declare *ex cathedra* that a certain doctrine belongs to the deposit of faith. By thus bearing witness to the truth, he serves unity.[4]

Let's notice a few things about this statement. First, note that the point of the ministry of the pope is to safeguard the unity of the church. That is likely to sound strange, since nowadays the church's doctrine on papal primacy is a point of division. In thinking about this, however, consider Catholic theologian Hans Urs von Balthasar's (1905-1988) story of a conversation he had with another famous thinker, Swiss Reformed theologian Karl Barth (1886-1968). According to Balthasar, Barth told him, "You Catholics have it good; at least you know what you have to keep to in matters of faith. We others have to get along with people whose supposed faith is miles away from what we consider evangelical truth."[5] This recalls our earlier discussion of the difficulty of finding a Christian community with which one can agree.

In our day, it is easy to find people who claim to be Christian and disagree with others who claim the same title over matters that each per-

---

4. St. John Paul, *Ut Unum Sint*, 94.
5. See Hans Urs von Balthasar, *A Short Primer for Unsettled Laymen*, trans. Sister Mary Theresilde Skerry (San Francisco: Ignatius Press, 1985), p. 40.

son might consider fundamental to his or her faith. While the Catholic Church knows that, for example, Protestants are rightly called Christians,[6] it also knows that the unity of Christ's faithful was wounded by the crises of the Protestant Reformation. Even though both sides of such battles were at times to blame,[7] the Catholic Church continues to believe that it has preserved the legacy of Christ's church in its essence, even though other churches and communities contain elements of truth and salvation. The unity the Catholic Church prizes is the unity of its Lord, its faith, and its baptism (Eph. 4:5). In order to bring about the unity of the faith, sometimes one needs an indication of what its boundaries are. When the essence of the church and its faith is at stake, it has always been the role of the church to say that certain errors violate that unity, and the pope plays a role in doing that.

The second point to notice about what St. John Paul has said here is that the pope can speak infallibly, under certain very precise conditions. This means that the doctrine enunciated is "irreformable" but not that it is "unrefinable" and can never be analyzed for how it applies to new conditions.[8] What are the conditions under which a pope can teach doctrine that is "irreformable"? The most important restriction on the pope's power is evident in the documents of the First Vatican Council (1869-70), an ecumenical council that defined the doctrine of papal infallibility as a dogma for Catholics. This restriction is simply that popes must not, in defining a matter of faith, "disclose a new doctrine," but must "reverently guard and faithfully explain the revelation or deposit of faith that was handed down through the apostles."[9] It is important to remember that the pope does not *make* truth; the pope, like the church, *discerns* truth. The object of the pope's discernment in this regard is the deposit of faith, theological issues suitably connected with it, and the moral life that is worthy of a Christian.[10] Where infallible pronouncements on matters of doctrine are concerned, the truth declared by a pope had always been true, but through the discernment of the church the pope is finally in a position to *say* that it is true.

The case of a pope speaking *ex cathedra* is very rare, but it should be noted that this does not mean it is as rare for the Catholic Church to

6. Vatican II, *Lumen Gentium*, 15.
7. *CCC*, 817.
8. Dulles, *Magisterium*, p. 66.
9. DH, 3070.
10. See Dulles, *Magisterium*, pp. 63-64.

speak infallibly through other means, as we will discuss below. Usually cited in the litany of *ex cathedra* pronouncements are the definition of Mary's Immaculate Conception in 1854 by Pius IX, and the definition of Mary's Assumption into Heaven in 1950 by Pius XII. These are generally regarded as cases of a pope defining a dogma infallibly through an *ex cathedra* statement. When the pope does this, though again this is very rare, it is called an exercise of the extraordinary magisterium. It is important to keep several things in mind when considering an infallible statement by the church. The first is that "even while true in the technical sense, a dogmatic statement may be ambiguous, untimely, overbearing, offensive, or otherwise deficient."[11] It is not always easy to trust in the guidance of the Holy Spirit when the church suffers some of her worst treatment from her members, but the authority of such dogmatic statements must be appropriated by the church. To be sure, in the list of popes, there are certainly those whom few would expect to see in heaven. Yet even saintly people (and of course many popes were not at all saintly) are not always at their best. Of this, the great Catholic thinker Blessed John Henry Cardinal Newman (1801-1890) once wrote that "Cyril, I know, is a Saint; but it does not follow that he was a Saint in the year 412."[12] A pope's authority can never outstrip the authority that Christ meant for Peter to have, but we know that Peter himself was at times in the wrong and was corrected by his fellow apostle Paul (Gal. 2:11-14). It may also be worth remarking that St. John Paul says that in confronting Peter about his denial, Jesus was "very strict" with Peter to prepare him for the office he would hold. St. John Paul goes on to indicate that the office of the papacy is thus born from Christ's mercy for Peter and must always serve that mercy.[13]

The pope also speaks often in ways that are intended for the guidance of the church, though these pronouncements carry varying degrees of authority. They do not, of themselves, carry what is sometimes called the "charism" of infallibility, but they are important sources for the faithful, and they reflect the current teaching of the church on some particular issue. Catholics are to adhere to these decisions with "religious submission

11. See the Roman Catholic Reflections in "Teaching Authority and Infallibility in the Church," in *Teaching Authority and Infallibility in the Church: Lutherans and Catholics in Dialogue VI,* ed. Paul C. Empie, T. Austin Murphy, and Joseph A. Burgess (Minneapolis: Augsburg Press, 1980), p. 45.

12. Newman, *Historical Sketches,* new edition, vol. 2 (Westminster, MD: Christian Classics, 1970), p. 341.

13. St. John Paul, *Ut Unum Sint,* 91 and 93.

of mind and will,"[14] which certainly presumes that the Catholic faithful must give the pope's decisions a serious hearing and the benefit of any doubt they might have. This is not the same thing as believing something irreformable that belongs to the deposit of faith, but it should be understood as motivated by belief in the truth of the Christian faith and trust in the church's role as teacher.[15]

Catholics have a serious duty to form their consciences through the teaching of the church, whether that teaching is held to be infallible or not. Even if they cannot agree on some matter that is not held to be a part of the essence of Catholic faith itself, they should not actively work to oppose the church in its teaching. In a well-known case, John Courtney Murray (1904-1967), a famous priest and Jesuit theologian, could not agree with the then current teachings of the church on religious freedom. Murray, however, accepted the judgment that he should not publish in the area for a certain period, and in fact his own views helped the church come to a deeper understanding at Vatican II. Although the deposit of faith does not fundamentally change, the disciplines and norms of the church through the ages have undergone development and refinement, as when the church began authorizing parts of the Mass in the vernacular at Vatican II, in a shift of a longstanding practice of using only Latin within the Mass in the Latin rites. Papal pronouncements can pertain to doctrine and also to the discipline of the church. By far the majority of statements by popes are not considered infallible (at least not of themselves), and important aspects of some statements by popes have even been revised in the history of the church.

Any given pope has a tight schedule, to be sure, and plenty of personal responsibilities, so it should not be surprising that the pope has an entourage of advisors who help him craft the documents and speeches issued from his office. In fact, there are so many ways in which the pope's attention in governing the church is called for that there are arms of the papacy that exist for various purposes. These are somewhat broadly referred to as the "Roman Curia." The Congregation for the Doctrine of Faith issues many documents on the church's doctrine, and is probably the most visible of these, especially since the former head (or "prefect") of this congregation under St. John Paul was Joseph Cardinal Ratzinger, now emeritus Pope Benedict XVI. In the past, this body could and did condemn various

---

14. Vatican II, *Lumen Gentium*, 25.
15. See Dulles, *Magisterium*, pp. 93-94.

teachings and even suspended theologians and their teaching privileges in the pope's name and through his authority. Nowadays the latter is less common, and the documents issued by this Congregation are usually more invested in giving a rationale for the doctrine the church esteems as true. This office (in times past often called the "Holy Office") will probably always be controversial due to its function and history as the "descendant" of the Roman Inquisition.[16] Since Vatican II's reform (and renaming) of this Congregation, however, it has functioned more as "an institution for the promotion of good doctrine" than as a weapon against false doctrine, though it has undertaken some disciplinary action.[17] Other entities such as Pontifical Commissions and Councils exist primarily as advisory bodies to the papacy, but they draw essentially on the authority of the pope, and some of the major documents produced by them are approved for publication by the pope.

These bodies (Congregations, Councils, Commissions, etc.) are often headed up by cardinals, who are, broadly speaking, advisors to the pope. Cardinals are usually required to be bishops. An exception to this was Avery Cardinal Dulles, mentioned earlier in this chapter, a Jesuit priest who was a theologian and was honored by being "created" a cardinal as the saying goes. Being a cardinal is a special recognition directly from the pope that carries with it, under ordinary circumstances, the responsibility of becoming a cardinal elector, or a voter in the election of the next pope (the cardinal electors also constitute the pool from which the next pope will almost certainly be selected). However, when cardinals reach the age of eighty, they are no longer allowed to vote in the election.

St. John Paul decreed that there is a maximum of 120 cardinal electors and also forbade any jockeying for position or promising of votes (or denials of votes) in a conclave prior to the election.[18] When the conclave has begun upon the recent death of a pope, all are to maintain the "strictest secrecy, with regard to everything that directly or indirectly concerns the election process itself."[19] The reason for this is fairly obvious. Political maneuvering should be eliminated (or, more realistically, minimized) in the election of a spiritual leader such as the pope. Our modern phenomena of

16. John W. O'Malley, *What Happened at Vatican II* (Cambridge, MA: Harvard University Press, 2008), p. 56.

17. O'Malley, *What Happened at Vatican II,* p. 287.

18. St. John Paul, *Universi Dominici Gregis;* see introduction and chapter 6, paragraph 79.

19. St. John Paul, *Universi Dominici Gregis,* introduction.

polling and campaigning are out of place in relation to this vote. Electors are also not to promise courses of action in the event of being elected pope prior to actually being elected, which is presumably supposed to eliminate "platforms" on which people might be elected. The task of the papacy is to guard the revelation given from God and to respond to crises that require the pope's attention, not to resort to rhetorical strategies to achieve power.

We should say something at this point about the election of the most recent pope, Pope Francis, and the resignation of Pope Benedict XVI that led up to it. It is true that the resignation of a pope is very rare and had not occurred for hundreds of years. The way in which Pope Benedict resigned is, in some way, new as well. He cited the fact that he did not have the strength to continue his papacy because of his advanced age.[20] In the 1995 movie *The American President,* the fictional U.S. president is talking to his closest advisor, who is remarking on the demands of the presidency. He reminds the president that if every house in the United States had a television when Franklin Delano Roosevelt ran, it would never have elected a man in a wheelchair. Certainly, the U.S. presidency is quite different from the papacy, but it is reasonable to think that things have decisively changed for both with the advent of modern media. St. John Paul famously had the charisma of an actor. His very presence was theatrical, and he could teach without opening his mouth or writing a word. Pope Benedict XVI, by most accounts of his papacy, had a much more serene and humble presence. St. John Paul decided, not without some noted trepidation, to remain as pope until his death. During his final years it was clear to all that he was suffering greatly, but he sought to teach Christian discipline through his own sufferings. This was a precious gift to the church. At the same time, it was a gift that matched his personal vocation and charism (a gift from God to a person for the benefit of the community). Pope Benedict XVI watched St. John Paul closely in these final years as Cardinal Ratzinger and admired him greatly.

Pope Francis recently lauded Pope Benedict's courageous decision to lay aside his papacy as a "marvelous example" of another kind.[21] Through prayer and discernment, Pope Benedict learned of his own vocation. He felt the Lord calling him to resign so that the office of the papacy could be run as effectively as the church deserves. No doubt he felt St. John Paul had come to the right conclusion to teach in a precious and difficult manner

---

20. See Pope Benedict's speech *Declaratio* dated 10 February 2013.
21. See Pope Francis's audience dated 30 June 2013.

through suffering, but Pope Benedict seemed to know that doing so in his own declining health was not his charism. St. Peter died a martyr-pope in Rome, and there should probably be a certain presumption that, if one is able to minister in an effective way, one should hold the papacy until one's death. But Pope Benedict concluded, in prayer and humility, that his own role was to die in Christ out of the papal spotlight, and to me that seems a faithful and courageous decision.

Origins of the Papacy

We've briefly covered some of the contours of how the papacy functions, but perhaps a more urgent and interesting question is how the papacy ever originated. The question is full of historical twists and turns, and can only be discussed here in a very brief way. Nonetheless, the papacy has been, and continues to be a stumbling block for many other Christian churches, especially the Orthodox Church. A reunion between the Orthodox and Catholic churches would be much more feasible were it not for Vatican I's definition of papal infallibility. Once papal infallibility was defined as a dogma for Catholics, many theologians began to wonder whether there would ever be another ecumenical council. But for many Christian traditions, such councils were the model for how Christ's church would make momentous decisions in the past. Why would the Catholic Church define a doctrine that is so divisive?

The place to start in considering this issue is of course, Scripture, and the New Testament in particular. Matthew 16:17-19 is an important biblical text here. Peter has just given a confession that Jesus is "the Messiah, the Son of the living God." In response, Jesus says,

> Blessed are you, Simon, son of Jonah. For flesh and blood has not revealed this to you, but my heavenly Father. And so I say to you, you are Peter, and upon this rock I will build my church, and the gates of the netherworld shall not prevail against it. I will give you the keys to the kingdom of heaven. Whatever you bind on earth shall be bound in heaven; and whatever you loose on earth shall be loosed in heaven.

This passage seems to give a great deal of unique authority and gravity to Peter's role. What precisely does it involve? In this connection it is interesting to consider the Old Testament figure Eliakim, called the "master of the palace" of Hezekiah, the king of Judah (Isa. 36:3). Earlier in Isaiah, God notes that he will "place the key of the House of David on his shoulder; what he opens, no one shall shut, what he shuts, no one shall open" (Isa. 22:22). Eliakim seems to be a kind of representative, or vicar, of the king, and he is given the keys to the house of David. These keys are important because they belong to the king, but are being entrusted to Eliakim. Similarly, in the New Testament, Christ holds the key of David (Rev. 3:7), but this key, refigured as the "keys to the kingdom of heaven," is being entrusted to Simon Peter in the Gospel narrative above.[22]

Several Church Fathers and many non-Catholic scholars in our day have suggested that the rock on which Christ intends to build his church is actually Peter's confession, rather than Peter himself.[23] From the point of view of the other biblical parallels, however, this seems a surprising interpretation to me. It is Peter who is being entrusted with authority in this episode. It is also strange, if the rock is merely Peter's confession, that Peter himself is given a new *name* by Jesus, a name that means "rock."[24] It is also worth noting that many other passages exist in the New Testament where there seems to be some dignity of leadership that Peter has among the disciples and apostles.[25] Even St. Paul seems conscious of having to oppose even Peter "to his face" in Galatians 2. Indeed, a collaborative project on Peter's role in the New Testament and beyond between Protestant and Catholic scholars agreed that in the context of the infant church, "Peter was the most important of the Twelve [apostles] in Jerusalem and its environs."[26] It seems unlikely that Peter just emerged with a privileged role; rather, it seems that Jesus gave him a privileged role.

In the early centuries after the deaths of the apostles, the see of Rome assumed a particularly prominent place in the consciousness of the church. It is simplistic to call this prominent place merely a "primacy of honor." Due to the martyrdom of Peter and Paul in Rome, there was a tendency to treat Rome as a center for the faithful transmission of the faith, and even

22. See St. John Paul's General Audience from November 25, 1992, especially paragraph 7.

23. See Olivier Clément, *You Are Peter: An Orthodox Theologian's Reflection on the Exercise of Papal Primacy* (New York: New City Press, 2003), pp. 25-26.

24. See Joseph Cardinal Ratzinger, *Called to Communion,* trans. Adrian Walker (San Francisco: Ignatius Press, 1996), p. 60.

25. See Acts 1:15; 2:14; 2:37-38; 3:12; 4:8; 5:3; 5:15; 5:29; and 15:7, for instance.

26. See *Peter in the New Testament,* ed. Raymond E. Brown et al. (Minneapolis: Augsburg Press, 1973), p. 161.

as "the final court of appeal for disputes among bishops."[27] By the end of
the fifth century, the bishop of Rome was referred to, by prominent figures from the East and the West, as the "successor of Peter," and turned
to for jurisdictional help as well as certain forms of guidance in matters of
doctrine.[28] While there is a limit to how much one can infer from the fact
that historically, the church in Rome had this kind of status, it is important
to recognize. On this point, even Orthodox theologian Olivier Clément
notes that there has been some "amnesia" within the Orthodox tradition
about the primacy of Rome in the early church.[29] It would be fair to note
this of some Protestant traditions as well, though Catholic dialogue with
Protestant traditions on the papacy has perhaps farther to go than with the
Orthodox Church. In an interesting passage, Lutheran theologian Robert W. Jenson notes the prominence of Rome in a particularly vivid way.
He writes:

> If all the great dreams came true and the unity of western Christendom
> could be reconstituted and in such a fashion that all of the protestant
> objections to the medieval system were reckoned with, you would still
> have to have some kind of institution of this unity. And it would be silly
> to propose locating it anywhere but in Rome. What argument could
> you bring for Kansas City?[30]

Nevertheless, noting a widespread amnesia does not lift the burden
of discussing the rationale for this office. Now it's certainly true that the
papacy as we know it today developed only over time as the church came
to recognize more and more the responsibilities and privileges of the successor of Peter. Pope St. Boniface I (pope from 418 to 422), in 422, wrote
that "it has never been allowed that that be discussed again which has once
been decided by the Apostolic See [Rome]."[31] Clearly, he is appealing to a
fairly wide consensus, and there are plenty of similar affirmations before
and after this period. A good deal earlier, in the third-century writings

27. See Brian Daley, SJ, "The Ministry of Primacy and the Communion of Churches,"
in *Church Unity and the Papal Office,* ed. Carl E. Braaten and Robert W. Jenson (Grand
Rapids: Eerdmans, 2001), pp. 27-58, esp. p. 42.

28. See, for example, DH 235.

29. Clément, *You Are Peter,* p. 72.

30. Quoted in David S. Yeago, "The Papal Office and the Burdens of History: A Lutheran View," in *Church Unity and the Papal Office,* pp. 98-123, esp. p. 106.

31. DH, 232.

of St. Cyprian, there is a famous text whose first version indicates that a "primacy" was given to Peter among the other apostles, and the "chair" that he represents is a signal of the unity of the church.[32] Cyprian seems to have removed some of these words later when he was in a dispute with Pope St. Stephen of Rome (pope from 254 to 257). The more interesting question, however, is why Cyprian ever had to revise his text in the first place. It is generally agreed that this is because Pope Stephen was already making more exalted claims for the papacy than Cyprian liked. Indeed, already in the first century, Pope St. Clement, the bishop of Rome (reckoned the fourth pope, who reigned until the year 97), wrote to the Corinthians to settle a dispute, thus using a kind of universal authority over the whole church to do so.[33]

Now the college of apostles is the source for unity of the church for Catholics, provided the college is understood with the pope at its head.[34] How shall we understand this "headship" of the pope? From a Catholic point of view, it is true that, in one sense all bishops are equal (no bishop is any more or less a bishop than any other, and there is no new ordination for the pope), but it is also true that the pope has jurisdiction over the universal church. The early church had a strong sense of the preeminence of the Church of Rome and the very early sense (as in St. Ignatius of Antioch, who was a student of the apostle John and is thought to have been appointed to his post at Antioch by the apostle Peter) that bishops are points of unity for their own churches. All bishops are supposed to have due regard not just for their own church, but for the whole church.[35] But surely this has special significance for the bishop of Rome, the holder of the Roman primacy.

Let's discuss the role of the Roman primacy a bit more. The idea that all bishops are equal in authority and that none exercises a presidency over the others is not a very good fit for St. Peter. But even the Orthodox Patriarch of Constantinople Athenagoras I acknowledged Pope Paul VI to be the successor of Peter in a historic meeting of 1964.[36] A better fit is for there to be successors to the apostles, and for one person to be the visible head of that group, even though each member is a full member. In my role as a faculty member at a college I have served on several committees. One

---

32. See Cyprian, *The Unity of the Catholic Church*, 4, in *The Unity of the Catholic Church/The Lapsed*, trans. Maurice Bévenot, SJ (New York: Newman Press, 1956), pp. 46-47.

33. DH, 102.

34. *Lumen Gentium*, 22.

35. *Christus Dominus*, 6.

36. Clément, *You Are Peter*, p. 83.

such committee was the Human Subjects Review Board, which reviews proposals for research having to do with human subjects. Academics being what they are, it's more difficult to get them together over the summer to meet (when classes are generally not in session). So when people are away, sometimes the chair of the board reviews proposals and gives them "expedited review." Now this is inadequate to understand the role of the pope, but I want to use it to make a point. It would no doubt be marvelous to be able to get all the bishops of the world together (or represented) any time an issue sprang up that called for a response by the church, but it's unrealistic. It's also unrealistic to expect that all the bishops, even if they were gathered together, would be able to respond with one voice to each emerging crisis in the church. Christ knew what he was doing when he gave Peter the keys to the kingdom, and the early church knew that it should turn to Rome as a source and guarantor of unity. After Peter's death in Rome, the bishops of Rome began to assume more of the burden of leading the church in a way that was modeled on Peter's role as visible head of the apostles.

Many of the questions that called for the pope's resolution were cases in which one party needed to be forbidden to censure another, or when a bishop or prominent leader was advocating an idea that needed to be checked before heresy began infecting too many Christians. When such judgments are called for, many of them must carry permanence by their very nature (otherwise, the next generation will feel free to take up the same theological error). While there have been cases of theologians being forbidden to publish on a particular topic while the issue continues to be investigated, one needs to imagine what happens when a bishop (as in the case of the Nestorian heresy), priest, or someone with a wide scope of influence has been publicly active in promoting an opinion that is judged dangerous to the faith. In these cases, there must be a judgment, and the decision must carry universality and finality. Otherwise, those who have been following this person will raise up their movement again later or simply transfer it to another area. The further the church spread, the more important the centrality of Rome would become. Thus, the church's understanding of the role of the papacy grew until it was understood to possess the ability to speak on matters of urgent importance with the same infallible authority that a council could exercise. Recall, though, that the fact that the Catholic Church's understanding of doctrine develops is no objection to church teaching, any more than one could object to a seed sown in revelation blossoming forth into a full-flowered tree.

Now when a pope in the Chair of Peter is called upon to respond to a crisis, one can expect that he will consult with other experts and bishops, which in fact is quite common. You might well expect that when the bishops are gathered together in an ecumenical council, the pope finds it difficult to judge how much he should intervene in the discussion. His position as head of the assembly carries weight that should neither be inflated nor deflated by what he says in the context of the meeting. Consequently, you would expect there to be controversy surrounding the interventions of the pope at ecumenical councils, but that he does from time to time contribute to the discussion, which is in fact what happened at Vatican II. You would also expect that, to preserve the integrity of the meeting itself, the pope, when he contributes as a member of the assembly, does not find that all of his proposals are accepted by the assembly, which is again what happened at Vatican II.[37] This is not to say that it is always easy to understand where the pope's authority starts and stops at a council. There were many questions about this at Vatican II. Indeed, in many earlier councils popes simply did not attend, though then the absence of a pope (or the presence of his representatives) is as significant a factor as his presence. The question of authority cannot be avoided, thorny as it is. The thing to recognize here is that the inevitable questions of governance arise not because the mode of governance is erroneous, but because the participants in it are human.

In our time there have been many encouraging signs that the papacy is no longer the scandal it has sometimes been. While Vatican I defined the infallibility of the pope, Vatican II emphasized the college of bishops and made it clear that bishops are "not heads of a branch office of the Vatican."[38] Individual bishops have their own authority over their churches, though they must be in communion with the whole college of bishops and with the pope as the head of that college. St. John Paul's encyclical *Ut Unum Sint* noted that the papacy, "while in no way renouncing what is essential to its mission, is nonetheless open to a new situation."[39] In that same encyclical, he also echoed Pope St. Gregory the Great's (pope from 590 to 604) famous understanding of the office of the papacy, "*servus servorum Dei* ['servant of the servants of God']." In doing this, he indicated that power in the papacy must always be connected with service.[40]

---

37. O'Malley, *What Happened at Vatican II*, p. 202.
38. O'Malley, *What Happened at Vatican II*, p. 176.
39. St. John Paul, *Ut Unum Sint*, 95.
40. St. John Paul, *Ut Unum Sint*, 88.

It is not difficult to find examples of bad popes throughout history. As is well known, Pope Leo X (pope from 1513 to 1521) is alleged to have said, "Since God has given us the papacy, let us enjoy it!" If this allegation is true, it is a clear instance of separating power from ministry. By contrast, we might think of the widely publicized recent decision of Pope Francis (who began as pope in 2013) to wash the feet of the incarcerated during his first Holy Thursday Mass. While it's difficult to tell what kind of harvest dialogue will reap at this point, efforts are clearly underway to bring more unity to Christ's church. In recent years, the humble service of devoted and holy popes has given us fitting examples of how popes can lead through service.

Councils and Bishops

We noted in the last chapter that the council was a fairly natural way for the early church to organize itself in making decisions. We even have a record of the Council of Jerusalem in Acts 15, a sort of first council of the church. At such meetings, one would expect that the voices of the apostles would carry the most weight (if indeed anyone else was invited), but nothing would prevent the apostles from discussing how their particular communities were responding to various challenges to the faith. In a similar vein, bishops, as successors to the apostles, have every reason to be especially zealous that the faith of the people they represent is given its unique voice. At the same time, the bishop is not simply a representative (as if the church were a democracy) but is himself Christ's representative and not the pope's. Thus, Ignatius of Antioch, not talking about any particular bishop, but of the office of the bishop in general, writes, "[W]e must regard a bishop as the Lord Himself."[41] It's clear enough in context that Ignatius does not mean that we should *worship* the bishop the way we worship Christ, but he does appear to mean that we should harken to the teaching of those charged with teaching in a faithful way. After all, Jesus himself told those who had been commissioned to proclaim the kingdom of God that "[w]hoever listens to you listens to me. Whoever rejects you rejects me" (Luke 10:16). All bishops are responsible to Scripture and tra-

41. See Ignatius's epistle to the Ephesians, 6, in *Early Christian Writings*, trans. Maxwell Staniforth, revised and edited by Andrew Louth (London: Penguin, 1987), pp. 59-68, at p. 63.

dition and are the servants of revelation. This is as true of the pope as it is of any other bishop.[42] Thus, if someone in a teaching position were to contradict the deposit of faith, clearly he would no longer be listening to Jesus and Christians must listen to Christ. Nevertheless, Christ himself had it in view that some should carry on his message, and when they do so faithfully, we listen as to Christ.

Bishops have charge over a diocese, and dioceses are usually organized into clusters themselves. The bishop has full administrative and jurisdictional power over his diocese, though of course each diocese is also in communion with the pope, and the pope has jurisdictional authority over the entire church. Nevertheless, there is a general presumption, called subsidiarity, that things should be handled at the local level unless for some reason they need to be taken to a higher level. Thus, several dioceses are organized into a province. My diocese is the diocese of Grand Rapids, Michigan, but the province is that of Detroit, and the bishop there is the archbishop. Sometimes archbishops may also be cardinals who may be serving in especially prominent provinces, like that of New York, for instance. Bishops of large countries also have large conferences, such as the United States Conference of Catholic Bishops. While they do not override or besmirch the authority of individual bishops, nevertheless they provide guidance for Catholics of a particular country. Sometimes, throughout the history of the church, bishops have called local councils, or provincial councils. We still have records of some of these in the early church. The importance of these councils tended to vary based on the crisis they were assembling to handle, the prominence of the city or province in which they took place, the bishop presiding over them, and so on. Sometimes they were so important that they led to major decisions by ecumenical councils or popes. However, since Vatican II, this influence has largely been assumed by bishops' conferences.[43]

It's important to note that there are three ways in which the church can speak infallibly, but in order to glimpse these we will use the terms "the magisterium of the bishops" and "the magisterium of the pope." The bishops have both an ordinary and an extraordinary magisterium. The extraordinary magisterium is used when the bishops, with the pope as their head, gather in an ecumenical council and intend to teach something defin-

---

42. See the Congregation for the Doctrine of Faith's 1998 document, *The Primacy of the Successor of Peter in the Mystery of the Church*, 7.

43. Dulles, *Magisterium*, pp. 55-56.

itively. This is how the articles of faith such as the nature of the Trinity and the nature of Christ's divinity in fact became incorporated into Christian doctrine. As we noted in the last chapter, the Catholic Church recognizes twenty-one such councils. Not every word of a council document is infallible teaching, but when a council uses clear language to teach something, that doctrine is usually understood to be irreformable. Examples are when a council uses language like "This Holy Council believes and confesses" or when the council definitively rejects some doctrinal or moral heresy by saying "If anyone does not confess . . . let him be anathema."[44] An example would be when the Council of Trent rejected any view that denied that, in the Eucharist, the whole substance of the bread changed into the Lord's body, and the whole substance of the wine changed into the Lord's blood.[45]

The bishops also have an ordinary magisterium, however. In the exercise of their "ordinary and universal" magisterium, the bishops, with the pope as their head, can also teach infallibly. This happens when, all throughout the world, the bishops are "morally unanimous" in teaching some doctrine through the evidence of their teaching, faith, and liturgical practice. Pope Benedict XVI, in an interview prior to his election to the papacy, noted that "[w]hat bishops teach and do in unison over a very long time is infallible; it is the expression of a bond that they themselves did not create."[46] Dulles gives the example of the Roman Mass which calls Mary "ever-virgin," a title that belongs to Mary irrevocably, but has never been defined in an extraordinary way.[47] No one could retract this title of Mary; it is too securely received by the church's faithful and the deposit of faith.

The pope, too, has both an extraordinary and an ordinary magisterium. The extraordinary magisterium of the pope is used when he defines some matter of faith *ex cathedra,* which we have already discussed. The ordinary magisterium of the pope is exercised when the pope issues some teaching that does not claim to be infallible. Most cases of an encyclical would probably work this way, though an encyclical usually does give an important and authoritative teaching to which the faithful should listen carefully. The pope can also confirm when the "ordinary and universal" magisterium" of the bishops has already been definitive in regard to some

44. Dulles, *Magisterium*, p. 68.

45. DH, 1652.

46. Joseph Cardinal Ratzinger, *Salt of the Earth: The Church at the End of the Millennium (An Interview with Peter Seewald),* trans. Adrian Walker (San Francisco: Ignatius Press, 1997), p. 209.

47. Dulles, *Magisterium*, p. 67.

doctrine, as St. John Paul did in the case of the teaching that abortion is a grave evil.[48] It is also the ordinary universal magisterium of the bishops that was invoked when, in 1994, St. John Paul appealed to the fact that the priesthood is reserved to men, which we will discuss in chapter 6.

It will seem presumptuous to many non-Catholic Christians that the Catholic Church believes it can teach doctrines infallibly. I can recall having conversations with some of my family about articles of Christian faith that we share (such as the Trinity, the nature of Christ, and so on), and I can recall some of them bristling at words like "infallible" or "irreformable" about even such foundational doctrines. While it is true that the church should always be reforming, as the Protestant reformers claimed, it is not difficult to find elements of Christian faith that seem beyond reforming. "Reformation" can always mean calling oneself back to a renewed life in Christ, and in that sense the church should always be reforming.[49] But what serious Christian can imagine entering a fourth Person in the Trinity? Would we still be Christians if it were claimed that Jesus were not really divine? There are certainly groups who contest these doctrines, but when they do, they often look at the historic Christian traditions as committing a kind of apostasy from how they saw the faith of Jesus. We would do the same if we were to "reform" the essence of the Christian faith.

At the same time, there is both unity and diversity in the way that the church approaches her doctrine and life. There is one fundamental faith of Christ's church, but there are particular cultural circumstances in which Christians experience that faith. For example, Catholics understand that the Virgin Mary has appeared to people of faith through the years to show mercy. The example of the apparition of Our Lady of Guadalupe in Mexico in 1531 to St. Juan Diego is part of the faith of the church. But it is also inescapably cultural. Not only did Mary's apparition give hope to a population that was experiencing widespread oppression, but she used miraculous signs that were culturally significant to do so. The facts surrounding Mary's apparition became so deeply entrenched in the faith of the Americas that eventually it became part of the church's calendar and liturgy the world over. Even now, the fact that it is part of the universal church's faith does not mean that the feasts (December 12 for Our Lady of Guadalupe and December 9 for St. Juan Diego) are equally important for all Catholics. Each individual Catholic bears the marks not just of the universal church,

48. St. John Paul, *Evangelium Vitae*, 62.
49. See Vatican II, *Unitatis Redintegratio*, 6.

but of the particular church and culture in which her faith matured and is still maturing. Catholicism thus bears a symbiotic relationship to the cultures in which it finds itself. The church can help to give certain features of a culture's identity to itself, but the culture's experience of the faith can ultimately help to shape the faith itself.

Finally, it is worth emphasizing that religious freedom is a vital component of how the church, in the years since Vatican II especially, has come to view the world. Christ's church is one, and its teaching office is the shepherd of the truth of the Gospel. Tolerance, where possible, is good not because error is good for people, but because coercion is bad for people. The right to religious freedom, said Vatican II, is based on the dignity of the human person.[50] Human beings have an obligation to form their consciences in the best way available to them, and to teach their children in the best way that they know how. Forcing people to conform to a way of thinking, even if the message is true, often does violence to their ability to follow their consciences. What the Catholic Church has recognized is that religious freedom is required as the context in which people can make up their minds in a truly genuine and voluntary way. Since the church, in her office as teacher, is also a caring mother, she must desire the loving obedience that can only be fostered in freedom.

Certainly, one can deny the faith, or do something that can incur the penalty of excommunication. But the church is neither interested in restricting people's reasonable freedom of conscience even to go against the faith, nor is she interested in restricting the scope of God's infinite mercy.[51] She is simply holding fast to her confession of one Lord, one faith, and one baptism (Eph. 4:5). Nevertheless, God's mercy extends in ways and places that we are not yet able to understand, and we earnestly hope, with God, and with the church, that each person will be saved and come to knowledge of the truth (1 Tim. 2:4). Meanwhile, Catholics pray for the courage to speak the truth, the humility to know when words are not called for, and the grace to love in all situations.

.

50. Vatican II, *Dignitatis Humanae*, 2.
51. *CCC*, 2272.

Chapter 3

God and Humanity

Recently, my young daughter was trying to get her pajamas on. She has a bit of a strong will, and as I tried to explain to her that she had her night-shirt on backwards she insisted that she did not. Of course, multiple witnesses sometimes help. So when my wife confirmed that, yes, she did have her shirt on backwards she relented. She might have been persuaded in another way, though. She might have actually slept a night in the shirt put on backwards, and slept a night in the shirt put on properly. This would have shown her that wearing a shirt the way it was sewn to be worn is more comfortable than going against the design of the fabric. Indeed, once the seamstress or tailor sewed up the shirt so that one side was front and one side was back, even the seamstress or tailor would not be in a position to just *say* that one side was front or back, because the garment itself would provide that information. Even if a fashion designer attempted to defy convention and claim that a shirt obviously fitted for front and back in a particular way was *really* just the opposite, it would be a short-lived fad at best, just as wearing one's baseball cap backwards or sideways may be fashionable from time to time but we still know perfectly well that the cap is *sideways* or *backwards* with respect to how it was made to be worn.

Now consider the possibility that God created the world in a way similar to how the seamstress or tailor knitted the shirt. Once the shirt is sewn up, even the seamstress or tailor cannot just say that the shirt is backward when it is not. Similarly, while there are very few things that God could not change about the world, there are some that God could not change without changing the nature of creation itself. For instance, God cannot make a human being's ultimate good consist in something other than God. Also, plunging knives into people for no good reason at all is

54

evil. While it's helpful to have a divine command confirming our duty not to kill, human beings simply cannot flourish if people are going about and killing for no good reason (though see below on Genesis 22). Of course, in many respects God could have created different sorts of creatures with different conditions for survival and happiness, but that's just the point: these would have been *different* creatures. The idea that many moral truths come from God through God's ordering of the creation rather than through God's direct command is what the church means by natural law.

What natural law claims is that some features of our lives as human beings are part of the nature of the creation God already brought about. Scripture can confirm much that we can already know, but we are capable of understanding certain basic moral truths through the reason that God has given us, even without revelation. This also means that, according to the church, all of us can know them to some extent even if we don't believe in God or Christianity. Of course, due to the effects of sin in our lives, this is more difficult, and we are prone to rebellion and error, but even apart from a special initiative of grace in our lives, it is possible to know certain basic moral truths.[1] The natural law is also, by its very nature, subordinated to God. Thus, when St. Thomas Aquinas explains the near-sacrifice of Isaac in Genesis 22, he notes that the power to withdraw life from anyone belongs to God as a matter of both eternal and natural law, so a divine command constitutes a good reason to withdraw someone's life, even though this means that it is not murder at all.[2]

None of this is to say that we are capable of knowing about God and about God's world all by ourselves, because there is no such thing as "all by ourselves." The Swiss Reformed theologian Karl Barth once protested that people could not know God *of themselves*.[3] To this objection, a Catholic should call for a distinction. We do need revelation to know the Christian God as Trinity, as incarnate in Jesus Christ, and so on. This is the living faith that comes from God and that saves. But when it comes to an understanding of God's basic attributes, the source of that knowledge is not only revelation, but also reason. That reason is something that Christians can turn to even in conversations with non-Christians. These non-Christians are not puffing away purely on their own steam, either, because there sim-

---

1. *CCC*, 1959-60.

2. *ST*, I-II.94.5, reply to objection 2.

3. Karl Barth, "No!: Answer to Emil Brunner," in *Natural Theology*, trans. Peter Fraenkel (London: Geoffrey Bles, 1946), p. 117.

ply is no such thing. We can turn aside from God, but God is always preparing us for himself, and "the *preparation of man* for the reception of grace is already a work of grace."[4] We always bear the mark of our Creator, and our lives are already saturated with God's presence whether we experience them this way or not. Our reason is always aided by God because everything is. Even what we can know through natural reason is, according to St. Thomas Aquinas, "a participation in the divine light."[5]

But why think that we should be able to know anything at all about God without special revelation? Well, for one thing, the religious life for a human being is an all-absorbing way of life. We should justly be disappointed if there were absolutely no reason to begin it. Instead, says the church, "God, the first principle and last end of all things, can be known with certainty from the created world by the natural light of human reason." Indeed, "Without this capacity, man would not be able to welcome God's revelation."[6] There is no such thing as a pure leap of faith. God is always at work in our lives and preparing us for faith. To be sure, human beings, like everything else, are nothing without God. But God *chose* to create us in such a way that his light reaches us when we know any truth (since God is truth) just because of what we were created to be. God's light also reaches us in an extraordinary way when we welcome his revelation in Jesus through the Scriptures, and this is a revelation that goes beyond our natural knowledge. But sometimes that revelation itself confirms that God is already at work in our natural reason, as when Romans 1:20 says "[e]ver since the creation of the world, his invisible attributes of eternal power and divinity have been able to be understood and perceived in what he has made."

There are things that we can know about how to live flourishing human lives that do not require us to read Scripture. When I say that, I don't mean that this is the best way to know them; I only mean that those who have *never* read the Scriptures are not left without some divine guidance. Every human culture has had some understanding that it is wrong to kill without good reason or sufficient provocation. When we get to the finer points, sure, some cultures have different ideas about what constitutes killing, and what a good reason for doing it might be. That is to be expected. The fact that the church thinks that human beings can come to

---

4. *CCC*, 2001, italics original.
5. *ST*, I.12.11, reply to objection 3.
6. *CCC*, 36.

know some things about God and morality without the assistance of her own Scriptures or a special revelation from God does not mean that everything the church thinks could be known in this way is *obvious*. 2+2=4 is obvious enough to any adult of sound mind, but the wrongness of euthanasia, which, according to Catholic teaching, belongs under the heading of natural law, may be less obvious, and revelation helps to supply what, through sin, we can no longer know very easily. Some things that are true are not always obvious, and sometimes their truth is something finally discerned over a long period of time, through the work of more than one person, and a generous helping of grace. Other truths, such as the Trinity, can be known *only* through revelation.[7]

We will be discussing the natural moral law more in the final chapter, where we will raise it in the context of the Catholic Church's understanding of the human person. In the next section we will shift the focus to God, since there are many things concerning God that the church claims can be known through natural reason without a special revelation, though they may be confirmed by Scripture or tradition. To see what this distinction is all about, in the next section we will consider some things that we can know about God through natural reason (this is called "natural theology") and, in the following section, some that we cannot.[8] I will finish this long chapter with a brief discussion of how God exercises providence over the world despite human sin.

God and Reason

Let us first consider some things that can be known about God through "natural reason." The first, interestingly enough, is that there is a God. As a teacher of philosophy, I constantly read papers that discuss the matter of God's existence. Almost none of my students seem to take seriously the idea that reason could show that there is a God. What these students typically mean is that God's existence cannot be "proven." The trouble is that only a handful of them seem to have a clear idea of what a "proof" for *anything* would be. If you're nervous about the notion of a "proof" because you're still twitching from the last time you saw the 1999 film *The Matrix* and wondered whether you were *really* plugged in to a huge harvester of

7. *CCC*, 237.
8. See St. John Paul, *Fides et Ratio*, 9.

human energy and all of your day-to-day experience was an illusion, then you're probably not going to be comfortable with the idea that we can "prove" God's existence. On the other hand, carrying that kind of suspicion with you everywhere you go, if you *really* meant it, would be deeply unhealthy. You couldn't believe that your friends or parents were who they said they were (in fact, you couldn't believe that you had friends or parents at all), and every time you ate your lunch you'd feel like you were taking your life into your hands. Most of us who are adults have reckoned with such outlandish possibilities and have a fairly stable barometer for what we're best positioned to know in our daily lives. Extreme skepticism is not the place to start when considering what we can know about God.

Every time you execute a proof in mathematics or anywhere else, you have to start with something. It is no different in philosophy, where any interesting conclusion is derived from premises, usually ones we know from day-to-day experience. *The Catechism of the Catholic Church* notes, of "proofs for the existence of God," that we should not fixate too much on the term "proof." Rather, we should recognize that there are "converging and convincing" arguments that open us to God's revelation.[9] When we look at the world, there are several pieces of data in our experience that seem inadequately explained by the hypothesis that there is no God. One is that the world appears very well ordered. An argument that begins with this insight is called the Design Argument.

Philosopher Robin Collins notes that life in our universe appears to vitally depend on some very "lucky" coincidences. For example, he notes that if a neutron were not almost exactly the size it is, then life would not be possible. If the Big Bang did not have almost exactly the strength it had, then life could not have resulted from it. Likewise, if gravity had been stronger or weaker by one part in 10^{40} then stars like our sun could not exist.[10] This gives us something to think about when we encounter claims like those made by famous physicists Stephen Hawking and Leonard Mlodinow to the effect that "because there is a law like gravity, the universe can and will create itself from nothing."[11] For one thing, those who believe in God are not usually prepared to let gravity go without ex-

9. *CCC*, 31.

10. See Robin Collins, "The Fine-Tuning Argument," in Kelly James Clark, ed., *Readings in the Philosophy of Religion*, 2nd edition (Buffalo, NY: Broadview Press, 2008), pp. 84-95, at p. 85.

11. Stephen Hawking and Leonard Mlodinow, *The Grand Design* (New York: Bantam, 2010), p. 180.

planation. Gravity itself is not nothing but calls for an explanation. For another thing, in Collins's example above, it is not merely gravity but the *strength* of gravity that is peculiar and needs an explanation, and it seems difficult to explain it through mere chance. The Design Argument just says that the order we find in the universe is surprising and implausible if there is no designer. Therefore the view that there is a God is seen to be much more likely. But what if, as some physicists now argue, there are many universes and this world is just one of the possibilities that are really out there? If so, one may not need a God to explain the existence of just one world among many. I think there are three main things to say in response. First, the uniqueness and peculiarity of human experience that is not reducible to physical material is itself one of the reasons the church points to as evidence for God's existence.[12] There is still something about my consciousness, life, and unique set of choices that suggests a designer. Second, the more complex the set of universes gets, the more the *set* of universes needs a designer. Sure, this universe might not be the only one, but then how did the vastly more complex set of universes arise? As Collins suggests, doesn't a universe generator need an explanation as much as a universe? Third, even if the Design Argument doesn't work, the fact that there is *anything at all* still needs explaining.

This last point is why I think there is another more powerful reason to think that God exists. When we watch any one of the innumerable crime dramas on TV, we often witness detectives arriving at the scene of a crime and trying to discern why it happened and who the perpetrator was. They look for information about the victim to discern motive, information about the weapon and surrounding environment in the hopes of learning about the perpetrator (perhaps through fingerprints and other evidence). In doing this, the investigators assume that, whether or not they can eventually prove the reason for the crime, there *is* a reason. No detective ever stops looking at the clues and suggests that perhaps the murderous bullet just "popped" into existence without any explanation at all. Our minds resist the idea that events occur without any cause or explanation at all. Indeed, if it were really possible for things to just "pop" into existence, then it seems that it would be more common for things to do so than it appears to be.

Everything around us needs some kind of explanation for the way it is. If you look for an explanation for my entering the world, a good place to start would be with my parents. If you're interested in inquiring into the

12. *CCC*, 33.

formation of the earth, a good place to start would be with the formation of our solar system, and so on. Every time we look for an explanation for something in this world, we're always reaching back to something earlier. That is to say, everything around us is dependent on something else. Now the Greek philosopher Aristotle (384-322 BCE), who was not an atheist, had no problem with the idea that matter had always existed. He thought there was a God; he just didn't think God was a *Creator,* even though nowadays we tend to associate God very closely with being the Creator. So suppose, merely for the sake of the argument, that we grant the atheist the claim that it is *possible* for matter to have always existed (though Christians do not think it actually so), so that each thing could have been preceded by some other set of things that contributed to its existence the way my parents contributed to my existence. Even if this circle can go back in time infinitely, we are right to want an explanation for *why* there is anything at all, even if we were to grant that there had always been something. Sooner or later, we'll either reach a point where everything that is has no explanation whatsoever or we'll reach a point where there is an explanation for why there is something rather than nothing that does not need any further explanation. That is, sooner or later, we'll reach a point where there is no Ultimate Reality or we'll reach a point where there is one. It seems to me that the idea that there is no Ultimate Reality is very strange. It is tantamount to claiming that everything there is, down to tadpoles and neurons, and up to galaxies and dark matter, has absolutely no ultimate explanation. It's not that we can't discover it; it's that, on this view, there *is* none. But closing a murder case because the weapon could have popped into existence without any explanation is absurd. Failing to inquire into an ultimate explanation for existence itself seems at least as strange.

The Catholic Church has a great deal of respect for philosophy. Pope St. John Paul II called it "one of the noblest of human tasks,"[13] so please forgive me if I dwell on philosophical theology for a couple more paragraphs. What follows in this section concerns the Catholic Church's doctrine of God, and some of it can be difficult to explain. If God is anything at all, God is Ultimate Reality, the ultimate explanation for anything else that exists. But what would something have to be in order to be Ultimate Reality? Clearly an ordinary human body won't be Ultimate Reality, since those are easily overcome by sickness, death, and even decomposition. Many of us enjoy watching bullets bounce off of superheroes but the reality is

13. St. John Paul, *Fides et Ratio,* 3.

that organic human bodies don't work that way. Could Ultimate Reality be something more like a soul? As Plato (427-347 BCE) once suggested, the invisible might be more permanent than the visible, so perhaps a soul is closer to what we're after.[14] This won't do either. Suppose that when we think about abstract concepts or when we make a free decision we are using our soul. That kind of soul is reflecting on and making decisions based on things that already motivate it. Thus, when someone asks me whether I'd like mushrooms on my pizza I say no. This isn't because I freely chose to dislike mushrooms. I just don't like them. As far as I'm concerned, my dislike of mushrooms is just part of who I am, and it's not a part I chose. This point, of course, means that I am not Ultimate Reality. This is obvious, but the reason this obvious truth is so is more interesting. For one thing, I am not Ultimate Reality because much of who I am is simply not anything I chose. In that way, who I am is a result of a cause, or set of causes, that preceded me and is responsible for me. But Ultimate Reality is never the result of some other cause; if anything it is the cause for some other result.

So whatever Ultimate Reality is, it will have to be independent. But if Ultimate Reality is really independent then it can't be the case that it is like me in being motivated to do things by other factors to which it appeals for its decisions. Ultimate Reality cannot receive its being from something else; it cannot be idiosyncratic and just *prefer,* say, brown eyes to blue. The *Catechism* says, "All creatures receive all that they are and have from him [i.e., God]; but he alone *is* his very being, and he is of himself everything that he is."[15] You and I distinguish between who we are and other things that are true about us. We tend to think that *who* we are is, to a certain extent, up to us, and *what* we are is, to a certain extent, not up to us. Consider these facts about me: I am from Dutch ancestry, I have very little hair (as my daughter frequently reminds me), and I cannot dunk a basketball on a regulation hoop. The first one is true regardless of what I choose. Many advertisements tell me that the second one could be altered, but in any case that would involve a decision by *who* I am to change *what* I am. Perhaps with a great deal of difficult muscle training that I will never undertake the third could still be changed, but the point is that who I am is different from what I am. All things that are not Ultimate Reality have a distinction within them between the kind of thing that they are (such as a tiger) and the particular thing that they are (such as Tony). God, however, does not.

14. Plato, *Phaedo,* 79a-80e.
15. *CCC,* 213.

We read earlier that God is "of himself everything that he is." What that means is that the kind of thing God is, is also the particular thing that God is. This is why there can be only one God; God is not a kind of thing that anything else could be (such as a tiger).[16] An example might help. To say that "Melissa is good" is to say that she is good and her goodness is something that she does possess, but could have failed to possess. In fact, with humans, it's sometimes a credit to a person to say that she possesses something she could have failed to possess. To say that Melissa is a morally good person is to say that, when confronted with a range of options, she chose wisely and made herself a morally good person. With God it is different. Everything that is "in" God as an attribute is the same thing as God. One implication of this is that when we say "God is good" what we mean more precisely is that "God is perfect goodness." God is also wise, and so God is also wisdom. You might think that this means that God has parts, but in reality it does not. It is simply a recognition that when *we* think of goodness, wisdom, justice, and so on, we are still only imperfectly groping toward the divine nature, which is the source of all of these concepts and transcends them.[17]

This view that whatever is in God is God is known as the doctrine of divine simplicity, and it was taught as a doctrine of the church at the First Vatican Council (1869-70), though it was widely held in Christianity until fairly recently, and is affirmed in documents such as the Reformed tradition's *Belgic Confession*.[18] This doctrine seems strange to many people, but the Catholic Church sees it as the result of a commitment to God's Ultimate Reality. With us, we undergo changes through time, but this means that we come to possess attributes that we did not have in the past. From whom or what are we given them? If God changes throughout time, then God's reality seems to be affected by other things. Created things are just that: created. They began to exist when their parts came together. But if this were true of God then God would be the *result* of some process or thing and would not be Ultimate Reality. This is also a reason for why the church sees God as eternal, meaning that God is not subject to time but rather exists outside of it and knows everything that occurs in the order of time all in one eternal glance.[19] For me, tomorrow is another day, but for

16. *ST*, I.11.3.

17. *ST*, I.13.4.

18. DH, 3001. See also article 1 of the *Belgic Confession*, in *Ecumenical Creeds and Reformed Confessions* (Grand Rapids: CRC Publications, 1988), pp. 78-120, at p. 78.

19. DH, 3001-3.

God tomorrow, together with all times and places, is "right now." However, God is not static, as if God were an impotent immaterial blob powerless to do anything but exist. Rather, God is supremely active because God is not anything other than God's eternal activity. Let me explain.

Aquinas distinguished between potentiality and actuality. When I am playing baseball and actually at bat, I am not yet but only potentially running toward first base. In baseball, some event needs to happen to "trigger" my *actually* running to first base, which could be the bat hitting the ball, the pitcher hitting me with it, or my receiving a "walk." The point is that I am awaiting an event to *change* something about me. Because everything waits on God and God waits on nothing, Aquinas objected to the idea that God would have anything "potential" about him that awaited a trigger to raise it to actuality.[20] There is actuality and potentiality involved in my existence even when I sleep. This is why God is so different from you or me, and part of why God is ultimately incomprehensible to us in this life. God neither slumbers nor sleeps (Ps. 121:4). God is not a combination of potentiality and actuality, as we are. Right now I am sitting, but I am potentially walking. When I am walking, I will be potentially sitting, and some event will occur to trigger all of these changes. Since nothing can "trigger" God to move, God has no potentiality. Rather, God is pure actuality, but God remains eternal because the act that God is does not "take place" in time. The "act" that is God is never begun, finished, or exhausted. Thus, God's providence over creation is not exercised by God entering into time to do each thing at each time. Rather, everything that has occurred and will occur in creation is a temporal result of the one single eternal act that is God.[21]

While we will visit the topic of human freedom a bit later in this chapter, for now it is important to say a few things briefly about the way the Christian God relates to human beings and the created order. One thing you might do in this context is worry about whether a God like the one I've described could possibly be free. The first thing to say in response is that if creation were not a real choice, then the cause for it would not itself be Ultimate Reality, since something else would be causing it. While God could not create a morally bad world, because the world would always be a reflection of the order and goodness of the Creator,[22] God's

---

20. *ST*, I.3.6.

21. See, for example, Eleonore Stump and Norman Kretzmann, "Absolute Simplicity," *Faith and Philosophy* 2 (1985): 353-82, at p. 356.

22. Ludwig Ott, *Fundamentals of Catholic Dogma*, ed. James Canon Batible, trans. Patrick Lynch, 4th edition (1955; reprint Rockford, IL: Tan Books, 1960), p. 84.

choice of a morally excellent world springs from himself and not from anything else. While this does require a belief that the world itself is good, and that whatever evils are found in it cannot be traced back to its good Creator, that is a burden any Christian will need to bear. Remember that everything in God as an attribute is God, so God is perfect goodness. This is why God's choice of the world is not like my being of Dutch ancestry. I do not choose to have Dutch ancestry; I just do have it. But God is goodness itself, and so any choice God makes will be authored both by moral goodness and by God.

Although God cannot choose evil, the reason God cannot choose evil is because God cannot be mastered by desires to do something out of keeping with who he is. God's blessed happiness is perfect all by itself.[23] God cannot be made happier by creating things than God would have been without creating anything at all, since again, if this were the case, God would be dependent on creatures for his happiness.[24] Thus, God could have created nothing at all, and God could also have created a different world. The reason God could have created a different world is that each world could be bettered in certain ways, by creating more creatures or higher ones (like more angels instead of slugs). Given the number and variety of creatures this world holds, God has given it an order consistent with the goals he has for the world and with justice for its creatures. In this sense, the world is morally perfect, with regard to God's endgame in it, even if many moments in it seem less than perfect. If God had made more creatures or different ones, then there would be a different kind of created world. Nevertheless, as long as the order befits God's moral perfection and goodness to his creatures, God could create different worlds.[25] God could always give a world more beauty than justice would require, or more creatures of higher dignity than he chose to create. God's creation is gratuitous because the majesty of God's very nature is already infinite. No finite world can ever fully express his infinite goodness. This is one reason why the Catholic Church rejects the view that this is the "best possible world," since there is no such thing. God is free from necessity in the act of creation.[26]

23. DH, 3001.
24. Ott, *Fundamentals of Catholic Dogma*, p. 83.
25. *ST,* I.25.6, reply to objection 3.
26. *CCC,* 310, and DH, 3025.

The God of Trinitarian Faith

What we can know about God through reason involves us learning about God through contemplating our world and ourselves, both of which "attest that they contain within themselves neither their first principle nor their final end."[27] Natural knowledge of God is helpful and important, but it is not the kind of knowledge that signals friendship and intimacy. We might compare the general knowledge we have of someone through a basic description with the knowledge we have of a close personal friend. It is friendship with God that we seek and for which we were created. Natural reason can supply us with helpful information regarding what sort of being to be on the watch for, but it is only by a relationship with this person that we can come to know and love God. We cannot initiate this relationship, because for each of us it has already been initiated.

To illustrate this, remember that earlier we mentioned the Reformed theologian Karl Barth. He claimed, quite rightly, that "man is of himself unable to find access to the revelation of God."[28] If what you think is going on in natural theology is the attempt to actually start up a relationship with God all by yourself, then of course you will be suspicious of this. If you were to approach a person you hadn't met but with whom you wished to initiate a relationship and started relaying how well you knew her already, instantly you would be rebuffed as a "stalker." But this is the wrong way to look at natural theology. God has already initiated the relationship by creating us with an inner compass towards himself, since he is our highest good. Natural theology is, to be sure, not the saving relationship with God that we urgently desire. But it is a good deal more like running after someone who has consciously left signs (or "breadcrumbs") of where to look for him or her than it is like stalking someone else as if he or she were prey. The footprints have not been rubbed out; God *wants* to be found. While our vision is blurry due to sin, there are signs that, when thought upon with care, will prepare us for God's revelation.

But what might happen when God does reveal himself, not simply by our "locating" him (we could never know enough of God to really do that) but by God's loving revelation of himself? What do we find out about God? This is the realm of Christian theology, where we know God through his revelation in Jesus Christ recorded in Scripture and presented in the

27. *CCC*, 34.
28. Barth, "No!," p. 116.

apostolic faith. These are the mysteries of Christian faith, which only revelation can disclose. A brief word here about "mysteries" is appropriate.
The mystery of the Trinity, which we will discuss here only briefly, is the
paramount mystery of Christian faith.[29] To say that this is a mystery is
not to say that we should not seek to know it better. It is rather to say the
opposite. Our search into the mysteries of God, if done prayerfully and
humbly, is a way of loving God with our mind (Mark 12:30). How could
we claim to love God if we were not captivated by him? By the way, don't
let that remark discourage you if you don't happen to find God "captivat-
ing." As I try to argue in the chapter on the afterlife, God is at the source
of everything that ultimately captivates us.

"Mystery" is not a card one throws to shut down discussion. It is a
promise that the delight of contemplating God will never end. Nonsense
never makes sense simply because the person uttering it calls it a mystery,
and Christians have a responsibility not to proclaim nonsense. We can
and should use reason, even in thinking about the mysteries of faith, to
do several things. We should answer those who object to Christian faith
and claim that it is nonsense, by showing that it is not. We should develop
arguments using other claims of faith to show how the faith is knit together
as a whole. Finally, we should use reason to prepare our minds and those
of others for the revelation that Christians welcome. As the apostle Peter
says, we should "always be ready to give an explanation to anyone who
asks you for a reason for your hope" (1 Pet. 3:15). Even when dealing with
mysteries, our intellects should be wide awake.

At this point, let us consider the preeminent Christian mystery,
namely, the Holy Trinity. This book is not a systematic treatise on Catholicism. If it were, the Trinity would have, at minimum, its own chapter,
and it would be necessary to weave a discussion of the Trinity into many
areas of Catholic life and thought in a different way than I can do here. This
book concerns the way Catholics tend to approach the world, and what
facets of that approach are distinctive with regard to Catholicism. Most of
Christianity agrees about the basic parameters of how to understand the
Holy Trinity, even though one aspect of that doctrine aggravated some
earlier tensions between the Christian East and West. Still, the Trinity is
fundamental to any Catholic worldview even if portions of it are not distinctive, and so we will discuss the doctrine at some length here.

The early Christian church understood itself as a new covenant in

29. *CCC*, 234.

Jesus that fulfilled earlier covenants God had made with the Jewish people. Jesus claimed that he did not come to abolish but to fulfill the law and the prophets (Matt. 5:17) and the covenant that the one God had made with Israel. While it would be possible to believe him if the new covenant were a little different, it would not be possible for faithful Jews to believe Jesus if he ushered in an entirely new system with new gods. The Jewish faith stood, and stands, on the belief in one God. The Christian faith must do so as well if it is to be a fulfillment and not an abolition of the Jewish faith.

At the same time, there was something new in Jesus' message. As Pope Benedict XVI points out, in his discussion of a book by Rabbi Jacob Neusner, what was new in Jesus' message was "himself."[30] In the Gospel of John, Jesus claims, "I came from God, and am here; I did not come on my own, but he sent me" (John 8:42). In the same discussion with some of the Pharisees, Jesus noted that "Abraham your father rejoiced to see my day; he saw it and was glad." At that point the Pharisees were indignant and wondered how he could know Abraham. Jesus responded with the astonishing claim that "before Abraham came to be, I AM" (vv. 56-58). Now there are a number of things to point out here. First, the fact that Jesus claims that before Abraham was "I AM," although strange in English, harkens back to the time of Moses, when God revealed his name to Moses, upon being asked what it was. God replied, "I am who I am." God added, "This is what you will tell the Israelites: I AM has sent me to you" (Exod. 3:14). It's no wonder that the Pharisees were outraged. A man had just claimed to be God. It's also worth pointing out that, in our discussion of God as Ultimate Reality, God is the only being whose existence is not derivative upon anything else. It makes sense that God, the one eternal and truly independent being, would distinguish himself by his unique reality.

Also, while many claim that the Gospel of John, the latest Gospel that was written, presents a different message than the Synoptic Gospels of Matthew, Mark, and Luke, Pope Benedict points out that it is precisely through reflecting on Matthew's Gospel that it becomes clear that "Jesus understands himself as the Torah" and this echoes the Gospel of John's claim that Jesus is the Word of God (John 1:1).[31] Thus, rather than insist on each dictate of the Torah, such as each minute observance of the Jew-

---

30. Pope Benedict XVI (Joseph Ratzinger), *Jesus of Nazareth: From the Baptism in the Jordan to the Transfiguration,* trans. Adrian J. Walker (New York: Doubleday, 2007), p. 105.

31. Pope Benedict XVI, *Jesus of Nazareth: From the Baptism in the Jordan to the Transfiguration,* p. 110.

ish Sabbath (Saturday), Jesus himself, as the fulfillment of the Torah, can interpret the Jewish covenant anew. Significantly, Sunday, the Lord's Day, is the first day of the new creation in Christ's resurrection, which is, for Christians, the fulfillment of the Jewish Sabbath.[32] Pope Benedict writes, "If Jesus is God, then he is entitled and able to handle the Torah as he does. Only on that condition alone does he have the right to interpret the Mosaic order of divine commands as only the Lawgiver — God himself — can do."[33]

We will discuss the person and work of Christ in the next chapter, but for now it is important to note that the church developed the doctrine of the Trinity in part by reflecting on God's revelation in Jesus. Jesus often referred to himself as the Son of God, and claimed that he was sent by the Father, as we have already seen. The church understood Jesus' person as fundamental to his message. At the same time, we also learn from the Gospels that Jesus is unique. It is not simply a possibility for all of us that Jesus is teaching us, as if merely his *example* were the message and not *him*. Rather, Jesus' relationship to the Father is one that we can only participate in and not repeat. Our resurrection is *in* Jesus (1 Cor. 15:22).

Now Jesus commanded his disciples to baptize "in the name of the Father, and of the Son, and of the holy Spirit" (Matt. 28:19). This formula is important, because it puts the Spirit on the same plane as the Father and the Son. The Holy Spirit is called the Advocate by Jesus, and what he has to say about the Holy Spirit is not easy to understand. Much of what Jesus himself says is in the Gospel of John, where we read, "I will ask the Father, and he will give you another Advocate to be with you always" (John 14:16). Jesus continues: "When the Advocate comes whom I will send you from the Father, the Spirit of truth that proceeds from the Father, he will testify to me" (John 15:26). Finally, Jesus notes, "He will not speak on his own, but he will speak what he hears, and will declare to you the things that are coming. He will glorify me, because he will take from what is mine and declare it to you. Everything that the Father has is mine; for this reason I told you that he will take from what is mine and declare it to you" (John 16:13-15). The reason I am quoting these passages at such length is that they have to do with a contentious doctrine in Trinitarian theology. The doctrine is known as the filioque, and it is Latin for "and the Son." The Nicene-Constantinopolitan Creed, which Catholics recite during Mass,

---

32. *CCC*, 2174.

33. Pope Benedict XVI, *Jesus of Nazareth: From the Baptism in the Jordan to the Transfiguration*, p. 115.

reads, "I believe in the Holy Spirit, the Lord, the giver of life, who proceeds from the Father *and the Son,* who with the Father and the Son is adored and glorified."

The debate behind this doctrine is long and complicated. The divide concerns whether to accept the clause "and the Son" into the creed or not. The Catholic Church accepts it, and the Orthodox Church does not. Yet the reality is a good deal more complicated than that. Before saying anything else, it is important to note that the sentence that follows the filioque is not in dispute. Both the Catholic and the Orthodox churches believe in the central Trinitarian claim that the Father, the Son, and the Holy Spirit are to be adored and glorified. It is also important to note that the Trinity is not a society that just happens to have only three persons. As St. Ignatius of Antioch claims, to the Father, Jesus is "word of His own from silence proceeding."[34] This is because the Father is the original source for the Son, and the Spirit likewise proceeds from the Father; the question is simply how. The clause "and the Son" was added at a later date, and the creed without it remains an authentic expression of the Christian faith.[35] In fact St. John Paul himself celebrated Mass without the filioque in 1995 as an ecumenical gesture.[36]

Both sides can cite scriptural sources. As we saw, Jesus claims that the Spirit "proceeds from the Father," but he also notes that he will send the Spirit (John 15:26). There are also several places in the New Testament where the Spirit is called the Spirit of the Son, as for instance, in Galatians 4:6. When considering the Son's role, we might listen to Catholic theologian Gerald O'Collins, who notes that even the original creed without the filioque did not claim that the Spirit proceeded from the Father *alone.*[37] We need to remember that the Son and the Spirit are not creatures, and so they were always and have always originated from the Father. To say that the Spirit proceeds from the Father is always to say that the Father *of the*

34. See Ignatius's epistle to the Magnesians, 8, in *Early Christian Writings,* trans. Maxwell Staniforth, revised and edited by Andrew Louth (London: Penguin, 1987), pp. 69-75, at p. 73.

35. See the Pontifical Council for Promoting Christian Unity, "The Greek and Latin Traditions Regarding the Procession of the Holy Spirit," pp. 36-37. An English translation may be found in *Catholic International* 7 (1996): 36-43.

36. A. Edward Siecienski, *The Filioque: History of a Doctrinal Controversy* (Oxford: Oxford University Press, 2010), p. 4.

37. Gerald O'Collins, SJ, *The Tripersonal God: Understanding and Interpreting the Trinity* (New York: Paulist Press, 1999), p. 140.

Son is the source of the Spirit. What rightly worries Orthodox Christians is the idea that the Spirit will be subordinated to the Son when each of the three persons must be equal in dignity.[38] To understand this worry, let us briefly consider some of the Trinitarian convictions that must be respected in this dialogue.

Christian philosophers Jeffrey E. Brower and Michael C. Rea use the fifth-century creed sometimes called the Athanasian Creed (though its proper name is the *Quicumque*)[39] to derive what function as three rules of Trinitarian faith:

1. There is exactly one God.
2. The Father is God, the Son is God, and the Holy Spirit is God, and
3. The Father is not the Son, and the Holy Spirit is not the Father or the Son.[40]

As Brower and Rea point out, the first claim is intended to rule out the heresy of polytheism. Christians must believe in only one God, just as their Jewish forebears did and do. At a very early stage, polytheism was a real threat for the Christian community, as when the second-century heretic Marcion was "expelled" from the Christian community in 144.[41] He believed that the creator in the Old Testament was an evil god who was unrelated to the Father proclaimed by Jesus. He also rejected the entire Old Testament and kept only portions of the Gospel of Luke and letters of Paul. Also the first claim is intended to rule out tritheism, or the claim that each person is a separate God. The second claim rules out what we might call subordinationism, or the idea that any one of the persons is less in dignity than any other. Remember, if God has no parts, then each person must be entirely God. This is why the heresy known as Arianism, which takes its name from Arius (c. 250-c. 336), and was very widespread at certain points in the early years of Christianity, was ultimately rejected at the Council of Nicea in 325. Arius claimed that the Son was a special sort of creature, but still a creature, and not divine. The third claim rules out the heresy sometimes known as modalism, or Sabellianism, after the third-century heretic

38. Timothy (Kallistos) Ware, *The Orthodox Church,* new edition (London: Penguin, 1997), p. 215.

39. DH, 75-76.

40. Jeffrey E. Brower and Michael C. Rea, "Understanding the Trinity," *Logos* 8 (2005): 145-57, p. 147.

41. O'Collins, *The Tripersonal God,* p. 96.

Sabellius, whose view was essentially that the three divine persons were "merely three self-manifestations of the one God, three different relationships that the one God assumed successively in creating, redeeming, and sanctifying."[42] When I was just old enough to know something was not quite right, I distinctly recall a woman from my childhood faith community asserting that "I've never understood why people have trouble understanding the Trinity. I am a wife, a mother, and a daughter." Unfortunately, this is a version of the heresy of modalism. Here there is one reality (one woman) *behind* each of these roles (wife, mother, and daughter), and the roles are not distinct persons. Biblically speaking, there is every reason to worry about this heresy. As O'Collins points out, Jesus is not praying to himself when he invokes the Father.[43] The Trinitarian persons are not facets of a reality that lies *behind* them; rather each is really God. Still, there are not three gods, but one God. There are three persons, and one divine substance. This is the Trinitarian mystery.

As we said, however, the fact that something is a mystery does not preclude prayerful contemplation of it. Nor would it be adequate for Christians to stand idly by while the mysteries of their faith are attacked, ridiculed, and misunderstood. The doctrine of the Trinity is not nonsense, but it behooves the Christian to *show* that it is not nonsense. To a certain extent, analogies can be helpful as long as they are not relied upon to deliver the whole truth. Some are less helpful than others, though. A Muslim student of mine once asked about the analogy of water's being a vapor, a liquid, and a solid. This is not terribly helpful for the Trinity because it is modalist. The "economy" of God's work as Creator, Redeemer, and Sanctifier can be seen as principal actions of the various persons, but as with water, the three states are not even true at the same time. There is also the problem that this one molecular structure *behind* the ice expresses itself through different manifestations. Another analogy one might consider is the analogy of the egg, with its yolk, albumen, and shell. But this suggests that God is made up of three parts, and that these parts *comprise* God instead of the Father *being* God, and the Son *being* God, and the Spirit *being* God, even though they are inseparable.[44]

The so-called Social Trinity or the social model of the Trinity is another common analogy. A family is a sort of society, and it is often invoked

---

42. O'Collins, *The Tripersonal God*, p. 104.
43. O'Collins, *The Tripersonal God*, p. 86.
44. DH, 532.

to explain the Trinity. This option has to be taken more seriously than the others if only because it echoes some of the traditional language of Father, Son, and Holy Spirit to some extent. But there remain some questions. According to the Council of Florence's "Decree for the Copts" (1442), the three persons are "one substance of the three, one essence, one nature, one Godhead, one immensity, one eternity, and everything [in them] is one where there is no opposition of relationship."[45] That is, except when it comes to the Son's being the Son and not the Father, and when it comes to the Spirit's being the Spirit and neither the Father nor the Son, everything in the Godhead is one. Social Trinitarians often suggest that the Godhead is an essence in the way that "lion" is a general species and, to recall Disney's *The Lion King,* say, Mufasa, Simba, and Nala (particular lions) are all instances of this general category. But if you have a doctrine of God as explicit about the oneness and simplicity of God as the Catholic Church's official doctrine, which I find persuasive, then it will be difficult to see how the social model is not a form of polytheism. But even more than that, I personally find the social model problematic because it is *not mysterious enough.* Centuries of Christian thinkers have claimed this to be the pre-eminent mystery of Christian faith, one we can never fully understand. What is difficult to understand about the social model, for me, is how such a God could ever really be one, or how that God could be Ultimate Reality. I have no difficulty at all understanding how such a God could be three persons, but that seems to me to be the thing that, as a Christian, I *should* find mysterious.

A perfect family, however, would have some of the harmony of mind and will that we presumably want to see in a model of the Trinity. In fact, the great mystical theologian Richard of St. Victor (d. 1173) argued that the Trinity was the only way to have perfect love in the Godhead since real love is "never found anywhere in an isolated individual" and that perfect love must also go on to share itself with a third, since "shared love is properly said to exist when a third person is loved by two persons harmoniously and in community, and the affection of the two persons is fused into one affection by the flame of love for the third."[46] Richard may have been a bit more confident in his ability to prove this than we might be, but there is wisdom here. In his encyclical *Dominum et Vivificantem,* St. John Paul said:

---

45. DH, 1330.
46. Richard of St. Victor, *The Trinity,* 3.20 and 3.19 respectively, in *Richard of St. Victor,* trans. Grover A. Zinn (New York: Paulist Press, 1979), pp. 393 and 392.

It can be said that in the Holy Spirit the intimate life of the Triune God becomes totally gift, an exchange of mutual love between the divine Persons, and that through the Holy Spirit God exists in the mode of gift. It is the Holy Spirit who is the personal expression of this self-giving, of this being-love. He is Person-Love. He is Person-Gift. Here we have an inexhaustible treasure of the reality and an inexpressible deepening of the concept of person in God, which only divine Revelation makes known to us.[47]

Christianity preaches a God who is so supremely one that nothing can comprise him as if he had parts. Yet Christianity also preaches a God so harmonious in the love it shares as a family of persons that we cannot even say that they are different in substance.

But how do these persons originate? Here we must remember the filioque controversy. In 1995, at St. John Paul's request, the Vatican's Pontifical Council for Promoting Christian Unity published "The Greek and Latin Traditions Regarding the Procession of the Holy Spirit," which made it clear that the Spirit proceeds *from* the Father *through* the Son, and that while "the Spirit does not precede the Son,"[48] nevertheless, the "Father alone is the principle without principle . . . of the two other persons of the Trinity."[49] We should try to explain this a bit. The Son is "born of the Father before all ages," as the Nicene-Constantinopolitan creed says. It is the Father that begets the Son. The divine nature does not do this; the person of the Father does. While all the persons are eternal, the Father is the person from whom the other persons ultimately take their origin. Nothing prevents this from occurring in eternity, just as we could imagine a rock always having been in a particular spot in the ground and always making and having made the indentation it makes (though of course this is an imperfect analogy). The love of the Father and the Son plays a role in the procession and identity of the Spirit. Since the Father is acknowledged to be the ultimate source of the Son and the Spirit, and there seems some agreement on the fact that the love the Father has for the Son is important when it comes to the procession of the Spirit, there is some promise in this ecumenical dialogue.

47. St. John Paul, *Dominum et Vivificantem,* 10.
48. Pontifical Council for Promoting Christian Unity, "Greek and Latin Traditions Regarding the Procession of the Holy Spirit," p. 42.
49. Pontifical Council for Promoting Christian Unity, "Greek and Latin Traditions Regarding the Procession of the Holy Spirit," p. 37.

The specifics will be continue to be debated, but at the present time, there is much more charity in the discussions than there had ever been in the past. Both traditions can recognize that the Spirit "*comes from* the Father *through* the Son."[50] For St. Augustine, this meant that the Father is the ultimate source for both the Son and the Spirit, but that the procession of the Spirit by the Son is a gift from the Father to the Son. Orthodox theologian and Metropolitan Timothy (Kallistos) Ware invokes Augustine here as someone with whom the East could be in fruitful dialogue.[51] Both traditions also seem capable of recognizing that there have been extremes toward which they have each tended in the long history of this dispute. The purpose of the filioque in the West was to "stress the fact that the Holy Spirit is of the same divine nature as the Son."[52] This is a way of combating Arianism, but if the unity is emphasized too much the persons will dissolve into one another, and we will have modalism. Similarly, many Orthodox theologians are concerned that in the filioque the full divinity of the Spirit is downplayed or subordinated to the Father and the Son. This is a worthy concern to have, but if the persons are separated too intently out of concern for their dignity we will simply have tritheism. Ware notes this when he says, "If pushed to extremes, the western approach leads to modalism and Sabellianism, just as the eastern approach leads to tritheism. . . . Yet the great and representative thinkers, in both east and west, did not push their standpoint to extremes."[53] Both traditions should now recognize that the "monarchy" of the Father in being the ultimate origin of the Son and the Spirit should not be compromised and that it is too simplistic to suggest that the Spirit proceeds from the Father *alone*. We certainly pray for Christ's church on the long journey to unity, but small steps toward reconciliation, such as we can see even now, are encouraging.

It is a challenge for any Trinitarian doctrine to understand what we can mean by three persons in a God that is so closely united. But again, we must preserve the unity of God to safeguard both his Ultimate Reality and the Christian continuity with the God of Judaism. We do need to be wary of a "committee" of persons in the Godhead with three wholly separate and distinct consciousnesses. O'Collins argues that it is better to

50. Pontifical Council for Promoting Christian Unity, "Greek and Latin Traditions Regarding the Procession of the Holy Spirit," p. 41, italics original.

51. Ware, *The Orthodox Church*, pp. 216-17.

52. Pontifical Council for Promoting Christian Unity, "Greek and Latin Traditions Regarding the Procession of the Holy Spirit," p. 38.

53. Ware, *The Orthodox Church*, p. 217.

think that "one consciousness exists in a threefold way and is shared by all three persons, albeit by each of them distinctively."[54] We also need to be open to the idea that what "person" means in relation to God is different (though ultimately more accurate) than what we mean in talking about a finite human "person." What keeps the Trinity from being nonsense is that there are not three substances, but one substance, and there is not one person but three persons. Yet, the Father is God, and the Son is God, and the Spirit is God, not by being loosely connected to some fourth "divine essence" (as if they were merely three "arms" or "tentacles" of God), but by themselves being God. Thus, the only way the Catholic can say the persons really differ in themselves is just by being Father (the begetter), and by being Son (the begotten), and by being Spirit (being spirated or "breathed"). This indeed is a mystery, and we shall never comprehend it fully, even in heaven. But we owe the Holy Trinity our worship and honor and in doing so we do well to correct misunderstandings.

I will raise a final worry about the Trinity before proceeding to a few remarks about the mystery of divine and human cooperation. Why use "Father" and "Son" instead of "mother" and "daughter"? Although the word for "Spirit" in its New Testament Greek is gender neutral ("neuter") and in Hebrew is feminine, "Father" and "Son" are clearly masculine. Some have attempted to replace this language with less gender-exclusive language such as "Creator, Redeemer, and Sanctifier." If this language were to replace the traditional language in every case, or even in the more important cases, that might indeed spell trouble. One difficulty with replacing the traditional language is that it attempts to correlate the transcendent persons in the inner life of God too exactly to concrete functions in the world. But earthly functions take their meaning from God, not the other way around. The Trinity would still be the Trinity if God had created nothing at all. Another problem is that this formula assigns "roles" to the persons despite the fact that such operations are the common work of the Trinity and not only the work of one divine person.[55] Nevertheless, it is of course the case that God is beyond gender, and that "Father," if we intend it in its bare, straightforwardly human sense, can be misleading even of the first person of the Trinity.

Theologians attempt to give reasons for why Jesus might have chosen the language of "Father, Son, and Holy Spirit," and this is not the place to

---

54. O'Collins, *The Tripersonal God*, p. 178.
55. See Pope Leo XIII's encyclical *Divinum Illud Munus*, 3.

enter into the dispute. Still, we cannot say that Jesus was simply a prisoner to the prevalent view of women in his culture, since he defied that culture at several points regarding the place of women, as St. John Paul himself points out.[56] St. John Paul also notes that human fatherhood and motherhood *both* bear a likeness to the eternal generating of the Son that we call God's divine Fatherhood which is "totally different" from human fatherhood.[57] Whatever the reason Jesus chose this language, however, the Catholic Church believes that it is important to obey his command to baptize with this Trinitarian invocation. In fact, the Vatican's Congregation for the Doctrine of Faith insisted on this language for valid baptisms because the church is not at liberty to substitute other formulas in the sacraments.[58] None of this, however, suggests that we must constrain our imaginations to merely human categories that of course cannot encompass God. We baptize in obedience to the Lord's command, and we experience the world as members of Christ (1 Cor. 6:15), but Jesus himself had a many-faceted relationship with God. Our life with and in Christ is also many-faceted. Indeed, with Julian of Norwich (1342-1423?), we are at liberty to experience God's personal revelation in ways that, for us, answer also to the care of a mother. Although Julian has never been formally declared a saint, she is lauded in the Catholic Church for her mystical vision, and she saw fit to call even Jesus "mother."[59]

Providence and Sin

In this final section I will discuss how the Catholic Church sees the nature of divine providence and human rebellion. Only a brief treatment of enormously controversial issues can be attempted, but again, the aim is not to answer every question but to give the resources for a more fruitful

56. See St. John Paul, "Letter to Women," 3.

57. See St. John Paul, *Mulieris Dignitatem*, 8.

58. See the Congregation for the Doctrine of Faith, *Responses to Questions Proposed on the Validity of Baptism Conferred with the Formulas "I baptize you in the name of the Creator, and of the Redeemer, and of the Sanctifier" and "I baptize you in the name of the Creator, and of the Liberator, and of the Sustainer"* (dated 1 February 2008) and the accompanying commentary.

59. See Julian of Norwich, *Showings*, long text, 58th and 59th chapter, in *Julian of Norwich, Showings* (Mahwah, NJ: Paulist Press, 1978), pp. 293-97. See also Pope Benedict XVI's audience dated 1 December 2010.

conversation about what is distinctively Catholic here. Let us recall the doctrine of God we discussed earlier. We noticed that God is pure actuality, and that everything in God is God. God, as we said, is one single eternal act. Thus, my very existence is an effect in time of God's eternal activity, since everything owes its existence to Ultimate Reality. As the great Lutheran philosopher and theologian Søren Kierkegaard (1813-1855) put it, "one single moment without him and then the world is nothing."[60] If I were to pick up my son and lift him in the air, we could distinguish between me and my act of lifting him. My hands are the things that make contact with him, and they might reach under his arms and raise him up, but this activity is something that is distinct from me, and this one activity is not responsible for his existence; it is merely partially responsible for this *change* in his existence. With God it is different. Everything about me, down to my physical body and every aspect thereof, as well as my spiritual being relies at every moment for its existence on God's sustaining power. Certainly things have natures that endure, but even the life-cycle of a tree owes its endurance to the power of God.

But, as we know from our discussion of divine simplicity, the power of God is not anything separate from God himself. God's power is God, just as God's goodness is God. When I lift my son in the air, I need to make contact with him in order to bring this about. God also makes contact with everything that exists, including me, in order to sustain it. Should God withdraw being from anything, it would immediately cease to exist. The deepest answer to why any one thing exists is that God wills it to exist. But that just means that God must be making contact with that thing at the deepest level of its being. However, since God is God's eternal action, it is not an *extension* of God that is making contact with me at the deepest level of my being, but God himself. That is, my being is finally anchored in Ultimate Reality, in God. God is thus in everything by his active presence "innermostly," says Aquinas, who notes that, since God is eternal activity, God is in me as a fire is in that which it burns.[61] It is no wonder that one of the early Christian Desert Fathers, in response to a request by a monk for what more he could do than observe a moderate Christian life with a bit of fasting and prayer, claimed that "if you will, you can become all flame."[62]

---

60. Søren Kierkegaard, *Practice in Christianity,* ed. and trans. Howard V. Hong and Edna H. Hong (Princeton: Princeton University Press, 1991), p. 155.

61. *ST,* I.8.1.

62. *The Desert Fathers: Sayings of the Early Christian Monks,* trans. Benedicta Ward (London: Penguin, 2003), p. 133.

In one sense, God is in everything, though, as we will discuss below, we can depart from God's will even as he sustains us. Even the demons in hell, because they still exist, have God within them, sustaining their existence.[63] Still, God is not in us as if God were a part of us, nor are we a part of God, just as my son is not a physical part of me when I lift him, nor am I a physical part of him.

Another dimension of this is worth emphasizing. Since God is eternal, and God's knowledge is not different from God himself, God does not know the world *after* he created it, as if his knowledge were like ours in needing the thing to exist first in order to know it. God knows everything, according to the way it exists, from his eternal vantage point. This is why Aquinas argued that, while we humans know things because they exist, for God, things exist because he knows them.[64] I like to throw chalk during class, mostly to help wake up the occasional student who was up too late the night before. Sometimes I throw a piece of chalk at the board and ask "Who did that? Was it God or me?" If I'm talking about Aquinas, there's usually enough ambiguity in the context that I get both answers, but usually not from the same person. Actually "both" is the right answer, though. God is always the primary cause of my existence and even of my actions, in relation to which I am what is called a "secondary cause."[65]

An obvious question to raise at this point is how there can be evil in a world that God sustains. Here again, I cannot hope to provide a final answer to this deeply troubling question, but it would not be consistent with the focus of this book to dwell overlong on this issue, because every Christian, and even everyone who believes in God, will need to believe that somehow God's existence is compatible with the existence of *some* evil. This, of course, is a mystery, but it is important to emphasize that God does not directly intend evil. This raises an important principle in Catholic theology, namely, the principle of double effect. The basic idea here is that we can directly intend something good even while there may be a bad effect that we can even foresee, even though we do not intend that. At a very basic level, we use this principle in our lives every day. My young son hates it when I comb his hair, and, while I do it as gently as I can, he squirms and whimpers when I do. His hair is very curly and it needs to be managed. I certainly don't intend to make him uncomfortable,

63. *ST,* I.8.1, reply to objection 4.
64. *ST,* I.14.8.
65. *CCC,* 308.

but I do intend that his hair be healthy and clean, and that can't happen without some mild discomfort. Similarly, I might have a wound that needs cleaning, and so I put some rubbing alcohol or peroxide on it. This results in a sting (I knew it would) but the good of cleaning the wound is what I intended. Now, obviously, there's a certain proportion that needs to be observed here. I could certainly disinfect a wound with fire as well as with rubbing alcohol or peroxide, but it would be foolish to clean a wound with a blowtorch because the "cure" would be worse than the "disease."

God intends some great goods, such as a loving relationship with his creatures that simply cannot be secured without allowing those creatures the ability to steer away from what he would have them do. To force people to love you is not to have their love at all. Although God sustains our being in allowing us to turn away from his will, he doesn't directly intend the evil we do. Now of course part of the mystery of the problem of evil is that it's not always easy to see how God is observing the proper proportion. At times we question whether the good of free creatures is really "worth" the extreme evil that they clearly bring about, as well as the unfortunate accidents that we can't necessarily put down to someone's evil intention. This is especially troublesome when we consider that God does intervene with miracles from time to time, and so why doesn't God do so when we want him to? There is no easy solution to this problem. One thing to consider, though, is that at the most difficult times in our lives, it's not clear that what we really want is an "answer." It seems to me that, in the face of evil, what we really want is comfort. God can provide that through his grace (which is not to say that the path is an easy one) and through our loved ones in times of crisis. But if we try to arrogantly storm the heavens, insisting that God answer for his crimes, we may very well find our impudence rewarded with silence. As many philosophers of religion have argued, it is reasonable to expect that a finite intelligence would have about as much ability to comprehend an infinite intelligence as my young son would have to comprehend why I need to comb his hair. Christians ultimately believe that God is good and just and that we, apart from his grace, are not. God intends a great good for the universe, and it is good to pray and petition, so long as we can be humble enough to understand that we *cannot* perfectly understand how God will reconcile all to himself, even though he will (Col. 1:20).

While on the topic of divine and human freedom, it is well to mention the Catholic Church's perspective on predestination. In my experience, it's not uncommon to hear Catholics proclaiming that "predestination" is a "Calvinist" or "Protestant" thing, and that the Catholic Church eschews this entirely. The reality, while complicated, is that this is false. "Predestination" is as misleading in Catholicism as it is in Protestantism. Few Christians seriously believe that God's predestination tramples our human freedom. God is eternal, and so God's eternal will is not executed "before" our free actions, but is rather in eternity consistent with their freely occurring in time. Thus, the *Catechism* claims, "When therefore he establishes his eternal plan of 'predestination,' he includes in it each person's free response to his grace."[66] In the Reformed tradition of Protestant Christianity, a synod met in the Netherlands in 1618-19 to discuss the nature of God's predestination or "election." It produced a text now called *The Canons of Dort*. This text, which is accorded a positive role in many Reformed denominations, rejected "Arminianism," which essentially claims that God elected people for heaven based on whether he knew they *would* make good use of the grace he *could* give them and respond in faith. *The Canons of Dort* rejected this claim because it appeared to suggest that humans could do something of their own, thus ultimately "meriting" their election. The predominantly Calvinistic strain thus insisted that no cause other than God's good pleasure could be assigned for God's selection of some,[67] though nowadays many Reformed communities are not nearly as vigorous against Arminianism as they once were.

In the Catholic tradition, this debate could be recast as the debate between the Thomists and the Molinists. Following Thomas Aquinas, Thomists insist that God does not predestine according to such foreseen "merit" (and remember that there is no merit in the Catholic tradition without grace). The Molinists, following Luis de Molina (1535-1600), claim that God did in fact predestine according to what he knew human beings would do if given certain graces.[68] Both sides claim that one can only be sentenced to hell (reprobated) on account of sins, and not by the direct decree of God. Now there are endless controversies here, and the philosophical and theological debate over this even today is hotly contested. What is interesting about this dispute in the Catholic Church, though, is that neither option is seen as heretical.[69] In fact, each opinion has its primary following in a particular order of the church; the Thomistic opinion

66. *CCC*, 600.

67. See *The Canons of Dort*, article 9, in *Ecumenical Creeds and Reformed Confessions*, pp. 122-45, at pp. 124-25.

68. Ott, *Fundamentals of Catholic Dogma*, p. 243.

69. DH, 2565.

is usually followed by the Dominicans (Aquinas's order) and the Molinist opinion is usually followed by the Jesuits (Molina's order). I was taught in my childhood Reformed tradition to reject Arminianism in favor of Calvinism, but my Catholic faith leaves this question open for me. What the Catholic Church does teach, however, is that God exercises providence over the world and knows all, including the free actions of human beings that have not yet taken place in time.[70]

While the action of God in "predestination" is a mystery, so too is the fact that we as human beings can defy God's will for us and even what is ultimately in our best interest (because God is our highest good). The *Catechism* calls this a "radical" possibility.[71] Adam and Eve, as the biblical story goes, committed sin against God in choosing their own will over God's. The Scriptures often attest to a pervasive condition of sin that was passed down in some manner. In Psalm 51:7 the psalmist claims, "I was born guilty, a sinner, even as my mother conceived me." Romans 5:18 notes that "just as through transgression condemnation came upon all, so through one righteous act [of Jesus] acquittal and life came to all." This first human transgression was not the first sin. Rather the Catholic Church teaches that spiritual beings known as angels existed prior to the human fall into sin, and that some of them had their own fall into sin.[72] While this voice of temptation can play a role in seducing us into sin, it cannot obviate our own responsibility. The first human beings were constituted in such a way that they were in harmony with God, each other, and creation itself, and this is called "original justice."[73] While short of heaven, this was a very great grace for humanity.

Yet human beings fell, and in "original sin" the harmony of original justice was lost. Through this sin death entered the world, as well as a weakening of the powers of human reason, an inclination toward sin, and exclusion from paradise and heaven. The Catholic Church also teaches that these consequences are passed down through "propagation" and not by "imitation."[74] Christians of many stripes differ on some of these details. Eastern Orthodox Christians have a lighter view of the fall than the Catholic Church takes, but the Orthodox nonetheless usually agree that

70. DH, 3003.
71. *CCC*, 1861.
72. *CCC*, 391.
73. *CCC*, 374-76.
74. *CCC*, 419.

human beings "automatically inherit Adam's corruption and mortality" even though they disagree about inheriting the guilt of Adam's sin.[75]

It's worth briefly reflecting on this idea that we could inherit the deprivation of original justice in such a way that, apart from God's redemption, we could never attain salvation. It is important to note that the Catholic view does not hold that we inherit "original sin" as a personal fault;[76] only that we acquire the consequences of the first sin through hereditary descent. But even then, why inherit anything spiritual at all? Well, for one thing, it is a mistake to think the physical and spiritual planes do not affect one another. If you struggle with depression because of a chemical imbalance, this will shape (though not destroy) your spiritual life. Similarly, children's prospects for happiness are hindered if they are raised in terrible environments, such as impoverished and/or abusive homes. Nor does this merely come about through imitation of bad habits, since we know that some genetic predispositions are inherited at least to some degree. But these examples still seem quite different from original sin. Why would God not allow human beings into heaven (without their redemption) just because of the sins of their first parents?

To this difficult question a few things should be said. First, it is revealing that no one claims angels transfer to one another a bad condition. Angels are pure spirits, but human beings are bodily. Our bodily frames, but also our perspectives on the world, are shaped in profound ways by our heritage. If one of our ancestors were to have moved from Chicago to New York, generations later this would have affected our family. In a similar way, when Adam and Eve turn away from God in the hope of metaphorically greener pastures, it is not unthinkable that God would see them as choosing for them and their "house" a spiritual destiny. We are punished for personal sins, not inherited consequences. This is true, but God's offer of spiritual friendship is gratuitous and unmerited. No one "deserves" heaven, even before their personal sins occur. Why then does God punish those who never committed a personal sin with hell? To be honest, we have reason to believe God doesn't. In the seventh chapter, we will treat heaven, hell, and purgatory, and discuss why the doctrine of "limbo" is no longer taught in the Catholic Church. But even if limbo were still taught (and it is not), consider what older theologians said it was. As we will see, Aquinas claimed that unbaptized infants who went to "limbo" were not

75. Ware, *The Orthodox Church*, p. 224.
76. *CCC*, 405.

in a position to know the spiritual happiness they were missing by being excluded from heaven, and they were even given some natural happiness. Thus, being deprived of original justice is more like God recognizing the human race's interconnectedness, even spiritually, than it is like God unmercifully punishing people for the sins of their parents. Once human beings are in a position to respond to God's offer of salvation, then it is because of that rejection that they can ultimately experience the spiritual pain of that rejection.

But isn't original sin just an artifact of bad biological anthropology? Isn't the biological record just inconsistent with the idea that human beings ever descended from a single pair? In response, let's start by noting that there is a worthwhile reason to want to claim that we are all descended from a common ancestor in some sense, and that is the danger of racism.[77] All human beings are not fundamentally different, and the very idea of "race" is itself a controversial category, since biology simply does not track with our modern notions of "race." Moreover, the truth of original sin is the "reverse side" of the Gospel truth that Jesus is the Savior of humanity.[78] Yet, God could create sons of Abraham out of stones (Luke 3:8). Something important was achieved by Jesus entering into our human heritage in a real way, not just by appearing in human flesh but by being *born* as a human being. There may be reasons to want biological descent to play a role, not just in the redemption of human beings, but in the predicament from which they are redeemed.

Certainly nowadays many people argue that the evolutionary data are not consistent with a historical Adam and Eve. Currently the best genetic evidence suggests that the biological human population never really came to a "bottleneck" in which all of humanity was concentrated in a tiny fraction of the population. Monogenism is the idea that all human beings are descended from a single human person or pair, and polygenism is the view that the current human population is descended originally from more than a single pair.[79] Pope Pius XII (pope from 1939 to 1958) affirmed monogenism and rejected polygenism in his 1950 encyclical *Humani Generis*. More recent church documents have not changed this teaching, but they have been more circumspect in talking about the biological descent

---

77. See Monika K. Hellwig, *Understanding Catholicism*, 2nd edition (New York: Paulist Press, 2002), p. 41.

78. *CCC*, 389.

79. Pius XII, *Humani Generis*, 37.

of human beings.[80] Recently church leaders have been briefed regarding evidence against the "first parents" proposal or monogenism.[81] This signals that church leaders are listening to competent scientific authorities, and that is important. However, there is reason to believe that it may not be wise to give up on monogenism just yet.

Kenneth Kemp grants the evolutionary data but argues that we can distinguish the biological species from the philosophical and theological species of human beings. Kemp suggests that perhaps human beings had subhuman ancestors that looked like human beings, but did not yet possess a rational soul or a spiritual destiny and so could not be called philosophically or theologically human. Then perhaps a pair with both of these arrives on the scene. This pair might then commit a first sin, and pass down its consequences to their biological and theological descendants (which could replace the remaining population of merely biological humans within a few centuries). While this view is different from the classical story, we need to remember two things. First, as we have said in the first chapter, the Bible is not intended as a history book. It uses literary forms to communicate spiritual truths. If monogenism is one of the truths that frames the reality of Christian salvation, then it is important to preserve. Second, this theory may be thought strange because it concedes so much to scientific inquiry. But that is not an objection to the Catholic way of proceeding. Faith and science are ultimately in harmony, for Catholics, and although the truths of faith may sometimes surprise us with their mystery and wonder, they may not and will not conflict with what God's gift of reason within us can show. If the wisdom of the church judges that the truth of monogenism needs to be preserved, that would be neither theologically surprising nor scientifically troublesome.

In this chapter we have traveled a considerable theological distance to communicate some Catholic ways of looking at the relation between God and humanity. Our discussion has ranged from natural law to natural theology, reason to revelation, divine unity to divine Trinity, and divine-human cooperation to human sinfulness. The Catholic Church tends to see cooperation with God as the model for a life well lived, while departure from God's plan, while a mystery in its own right, has far-reaching consequences. To address these far-reaching consequences, the eternal

---

80. See Kenneth Kemp, "Science, Theology, and Monogenesis," *American Catholic Philosophical Quarterly* 85 (2011): 217-36, p. 220 n. 12.

81. Kemp, "Science, Theology, and Monogenesis," p. 224 n. 25.

God entered time and our human reality. He was born a lowly infant to his mother, a young but incomparably courageous woman, and to his Father, the Lord of the universe. In the next chapter we will discuss the person and work of Jesus Christ.

Chapter 4

The Person and Work of Christ

In 2009, the movie *Avatar* opened to great fanfare. In it, a futuristic military operation from earth is mining a precious mineral on a distant moon called Pandora. The moon is inhabited by an indigenous people known as the Na'vi. The Na'vi consider themselves custodians of their peculiar moon, and their spirituality is strongly tied to it. The Na'vi are also formidable creatures (ten feet tall), and naturally it is in the best interests of the military to get to know the Na'vi culture. However, they find the best way to do this is through inhabiting the bodies and minds of specially constructed avatars, or creatures that look like Na'vi but whose conscious lives are the lives of the human persons operating them. As the movie progresses, the military shows itself to be an evil, destructive power. The lead character, Jake Sully, a military man, joins a Na'vi rebellion against the military force. At the end of the movie, it is suggested that Jake finally becomes a Na'vi himself through a religious ritual.

When I first saw this movie, I was left with one question: What would this really involve? What would it be to become a Na'vi if you were human before? To be quite honest, I have real doubts that the movie's storyline could survive a philosopher's scrutiny. But while *Avatar* — for me, at any rate — was just a fun movie, Christians believe that a related question must be asked about the incarnation of Jesus Christ: What would it really involve? In this chapter, we'll begin by reflecting on the mystery of Christ and his person and then consider his atoning work. Finally, we will discuss how we as humans appropriate that in our redemption.

The Person of Christ

Some two thousand years ago a man was born in Judea. He went about do-ing good (Acts 10:38), healing people, and teaching them to love God and one another. He not only offended the sensibilities of the Jewish religion in which he was raised, but was executed in a brutal manner by the Ro-mans using a method they favored for political criminals. Shortly after his execution, his disciples were proclaiming that he had risen from the dead and appeared among them. Soon they began to make exalted claims about him, expounding upon claims he seems to have made about himself. They seemed to craft an entire cosmology with him at its center. They claimed that in Christ all things were summed up (Eph. 1:10), that he was the "first and the last" (Rev. 1:17), that "in him all things hold together" (Col. 1:17), and, indeed, that he was and is the eternal God (John 1:1). What could have been so special about this one human life?

The short answer is that it is in this person that God reveals himself to us. God's revelation certainly was in the teaching of Jesus. Fundamentally, however, God's revelation to us *is Jesus.* Many of us need to recover a bit of how shocking all of this is. Islam is a beautiful religion that is devoted to one God. Indeed, as Pope St. John Paul II claimed,[1] Christians and Muslims worship the same God, the God of Abraham, Isaac, and Jacob. Yet, Mus-lims reject any depiction of God because such a thing would be idolatry, giving to a creature the worship due only to God. Many Jews refuse to use the name of God at all. Christians who think this is strange are suffering from a kind of amnesia. For Christians, the iconoclastic controversy over the use of images in worship was addressed at the Second Council of Nicea in the year 787 and it was decided that sacred images of Christ and others could be made and venerated, but it was a bitter controversy.[2] The reason icons are permitted and approved is that they are principally of Christ or because of Christ and they are legitimate because of his incarnation.[3] Similarly, when I studied Biblical Hebrew, my professor taught me never to vocalize the proper name of the God of Israel (sometimes rendered "Yahweh"). It is a practice I have tried to continue since then. In 2008, the Vatican's Congregation for Divine Worship and the Discipline of the Sacraments issued a letter to bishops' conferences forbidding the use of

1. St. John Paul's General Audience dated 5 May 1999.
2. DH, 600-603.
3. *CCC,* 1159.

the God of Israel's proper name in liturgical contexts.[4] Yet Paul notes that God bestowed on Jesus "the name that is above every name" (Phil. 2:9). It is not because Muslims and Jews are too persnickety about representations or invocations of God but because of the surpassing uniqueness of the incarnation that we dare to represent Christ and invoke him by name as God in worship. By the life of this one humble man everything is changed. Why is he so unique?

To see why this is so, let us consider a number of early ideas about Jesus that were condemned by the church. We have already discussed a reason in the last chapter for why the early Christians needed to see Jesus as the incarnation of God himself. But they needed to understand the way in which that Incarnation took place as well. Some answers were not going to be faithful to their experience of Jesus. One multifaceted threat the early church faced has been known through the ages as Gnosticism. Gnostics tended to see things in a very dualistic manner. That is, they thought of matter as evil but spirit as good, light as good and darkness as evil. They sought spiritual knowledge but shunned the body and regarded it as worthless. While this does help to explain their largely dismissive attitudes toward sexuality, it also explains why they might think a God would never really tolerate becoming incarnate in the way Christians confess that Jesus did. To take a particularly vivid example, consider one of the Gnostic writings, the pseudonymous Gnostic *Apocalypse of Peter,* which may have been written in the third century. In this text, Jesus is portrayed as conversing with Peter and claiming that the "fleshly part" or the "substitute" is the one being seized, sentenced, and crucified while the *real* Jesus is supposedly elsewhere, laughing at all of this.[5] This is a clear instance of the Gnostic error known as Docetism, a term that comes from the Greek word for "seeming" because in the view of the Docetists, Jesus only *seemed* to suffer.

It is not surprising that the church would have rejected a view like this. Those who followed Jesus knew him as a *real* human being who was emotionally and physically connected to this world. He joined himself, in the mold of the Hebrew prophets, to the cause of the poor and the

4. See Congregation for Divine Worship and Discipline of the Sacraments, *Letter to the Bishops Conferences on the Name of God,* dated 29 June 2008. A copy is available at http://www.adoremus.org/CDW_NameofGod.html. Accessed 11 July 2014.

5. See *Apocalypse of Peter* (VII, 3), trans. James Brashler and Roger A. Bullard, in *The Nag Hammadi Library in English,* ed. James M. Robinson, 3rd ed. (New York: Harper, 1988), pp. 372-78, at p. 377.

oppressed, was tempted by the devil (Luke 4:1-13), was moved with pity (Matt. 15:32), lamented over Jerusalem (Matt. 23:37-39), and struggled mightily with his impending death (Matt. 26:36-46). The Jesus they knew was not an impostor, and his death, especially for those who grieved over it, was real.

The Jesus the apostles knew was so connected to this world that ultimately the church resisted anything other than the doctrine that he was fully human. But to suggest that his divinity was simply tacked on at some point in his life and was lacking at others would mean that certain parts of his life, no doubt those prior to his active ministry, were less worthy of God's divine presence than others. This would suggest, again, that Jesus' message was somehow more important than he himself. But, as we have often had occasion to note, Jesus' life is itself God's revelation, not just what he did, though of course his actions and teachings could only issue from the right sort of person. There was not first a merely human person answering to Jesus of Nazareth who was then "scooped up" by God to be his vessel for salvation to the world, much as if he were a sports team's draft pick. To claim otherwise is to fall into the error known as Adoptionism, the idea that God "adopted" an already-complete, but merely human, person to become a kind of "super-Jesus."

The discussion of the movie *Avatar* earlier on should have also suggested another Christological alternative that is not going to work. Jake Sully and his collaborators in that movie are the only consciousnesses and the only intellects within their avatars. Thus, at the end of the movie it is suggested that Jake finally *becomes* a Na'vi, precisely because he was *not* one before. Just as Adoptionism claims that there was a historical person, Jesus of Nazareth, that, perhaps at his baptism by John, was selected by God to later become the human being to somehow "house" the divine presence within him, so another heresy claims that there was merely an *animal* nature that the second person of the Trinity inhabited and thereby "upgraded" to live the duration of Jesus' life. This is the heresy known as Apollinarianism, after Apollinarius (or Apollinaris, c. 310-c. 390), the fourth-century bishop of Laodicea. In the 1998 film *Fallen* with Denzel Washington, a particularly vivid scene suggests that a demon named Azazel moves down a busy street from subject to subject through touch, effectively replacing the personalities of its subjects with its own. By contrast, Apollinarians suggest that the human-looking body (with its "sensitive soul") is inhabited, not by a human soul, but by a divine person. The advantage of Apollinarianism is that it doesn't have to explain what might have happened to Jesus of Nazareth prior to his supposed "adoption." For Apollinarians, that entity was never there in the first place. But there are several other problems.

The first problem appeals to the well-known principle that if Jesus is supposed to save our entire humanity, he must *assume* our entire humanity.[6] But he cannot do this if he does not assume a human soul. A humanoid person concocted out of the meeting of a divine person with an animal body simply cannot be said to be a real human being. That kind of being would belong to its own species. There is no reason why this sort of being would need to be born of Mary, or of any woman, nor is there a reason why that being would have the kind of solidarity with human beings that Hebrews 2:17 insists on, when we read "therefore, he had to become like his brothers in every way, that he might be a merciful and faithful high priest before God to expiate the sins of the people." The second problem with Apollinarianism is that it cannot be consistent with the understanding of God that we have discussed in the third chapter. For suppose that God is Ultimate Reality and eternal, as we discussed there, and further suppose, as Apollinarianism holds, that the only real nature Jesus has is his divine nature, clothed, somehow, in the flesh of a human-looking animal. If this is true and Jesus' only nature is his divine nature, then he must experience the world and act through his divine nature, but he could only do that if he were experiencing and acting in time, thus compromising God's eternity.

So far, we have discussed reasons for why Docetism, Adoptionism, and Apollinarianism were rejected. Arianism, which we discussed in the previous chapter, was also rejected by the church at the Council of Nicea in 325. Recall that Arianism taught that there was a time when Christ did not exist, and that, however exalted his status, he was a creature and therefore infinitely subordinate to the one God, whom Arius understood as the Father. The first Christian councils were primarily concerned with Christological heresies, and the second ecumenical council, held at Constantinople in 381, rejected Apollinarianism, as did several papal documents and synods around that time. In 382, the so-called "Tome of Damasus," that is, of Pope Damasus I (pope from 366 to 384), noted: "We condemn those who say that the Word of God dwelling in human flesh took the place of the rational and spiritual soul, since the Son and the Word of God did not replace the rational and spiritual soul in his body but rather assumed

6. DH, 146.

our soul (i.e., a rational and spiritual one) without sin and saved it."[7] This again is an instance of the principle that if Christ is to redeem our nature, he must be united with all of it.

Yet, it is not just a question of being united with all of our human nature, but rather of the human nature's being united with the divine nature in the right way. We might have a real human nature in Christ, and there might even be a real divine nature, too, but how are they related? Can we say that the "Son of God died upon the cross," as Christians have always said?[8] To say otherwise conjures up images of the Gnostic portrayal of Jesus as not having really suffered. Nestorianism would not go to this Docetic extreme, but it is another heresy, so named because of Nestorius (d. c. 451), who had become patriarch of Constantinople. Nestorius appears to have held that not only were there two natures in Christ, but that there were two *persons*. Thus, Nestorius would not admit that Mary was the "Mother of God," but only that she was the "Mother of Christ." Nestorius would not affirm the doctrine of the "communication of idioms" which is part of the faith of the church and affirms that what can be said of Jesus must be said of God, because Jesus is God incarnate. In response, the Council of Ephesus, in 431, affirmed that Mary must not be denied the title "Mother of God," precisely because her son is Jesus Christ, the Son of God and second person of the Trinity.[9] Thus, the Council of Ephesus wanted to insist that the natures of Christ, divine and human, not be separated, which is what would result if there were two persons.

After each council, some crack in the armor of the church's then-current Christology seemed to show itself by one or another heresy coming into the picture to take up a position that had not yet been fully rejected. Thus, after Arianism is rejected at Nicea for its failure to respect the divinity of Christ, Apollinarianism enters the scene and is rejected for its failure to respect Christ's humanity. Then Nestorianism is rejected at Ephesus for failing to respect Jesus' divinity. If you're following the pattern so far, you'd expect the Council of Chalcedon, the next ecumenical council, which was held in the year 451, to deal at least partially with some heresy that failed to respect Jesus' humanity, and you'd be right. Eutyches (c. 378-454) apparently took up the position that the human nature of Jesus was absorbed,

---

7. DH, 159.

8. See Gerald O'Collins, SJ, *Christology* (Oxford: Oxford University Press, 1995), pp. 186-87.

9. DH, 251.

and ultimately erased, by the divine nature so that Christ ultimately would have only one nature, the divine, even though he came "from" two natures. In response the council decided that Christ had two natures "without confusion or change, without division or separation,"[10] that neither nature was erased by the other, and that there was only one person, namely, the person of Jesus Christ, the second person of the Trinity. This means, as Gerald O'Collins and Mario Farrugia put it, that in Christ we are dealing with two natures and one person, or two "whats" and one "who."[11] The idea that in Christ the two natures are united in one "hypostasis," or person, is called the "hypostatic union." We have two natures together that are not blended but distinct and one person, or subject, for both. Since the two natures must be complete, the church also decided against the idea that Jesus did not have a human will, noting that Jesus needed two, a human and a divine will. To claim that Jesus had only one will is a heresy known as monothelitism, though there remain interesting questions regarding Jesus' freedom which we will consider shortly. The basic idea here is that the mission of Jesus Christ takes place on a divine and a human front, and what is done in the human sphere derives from the human nature and what is done in the divine sphere derives from the divine nature. This is why the Council of Constantinople (the sixth ecumenical council in 681) explained that there were "two natural actions" in Jesus.[12]

At this point, we should ask about Jesus' (human) knowledge and his will, since both of those are relevant to action. Now the Catholic view has it that God cannot be other than perfectly good and omniscient. So the divine person, the second of the Trinity, who is the same *person* as Jesus of Nazareth must himself be perfectly good and omniscient, at least with regard to his divinity. Many Christian theologians in recent years have been defending a Christology called "kenotic Christology." This word comes from the Greek word *kenosis,* which means "emptying," and appears in Philippians 2:7, which tells us that Christ "emptied" himself to become a human being and redeem us. Every Christian must find a way to admit Christ's humility in taking on human flesh, but kenotic theologians and philosophers often insist that, in the Incarnation, the second person of the Trinity emptied himself of at least some of his divine attributes, such

10. DH, 302.

11. Gerald O'Collins, SJ, and Mario Farrugia, SJ, *Catholicism: The Story of Catholic Christianity* (Oxford: Oxford University Press, 2003), pp. 153-54.

12. DH, 557.

as omniscience and omnipotence. For my part, as a Catholic, the trouble I have with kenotic theories is that they seem to imply a version of Social Trinitarianism and the view that God exists in time.[13] The kenotic view of God rests on the idea that God the Son empties *himself* of some properties that God the Father and God the Spirit retain, which seems strange if each of them possesses the divine essence. Also, since this self-emptying is a change that does not just occur on the level of the human nature of Christ but is a change within the person of Christ himself, this means that there was a time before Jesus emptied himself of his omniscience and omnipotence and a time during which he lacked these properties. This means that God cannot be eternal in the sense the Catholic Church has accepted and for which I argued in the previous chapter. Kenotic theologians sometimes say that they are defending the Council of Chalcedon's claim that Jesus possessed two natures (human and divine) in one person, but in order to finally reconcile those two natures we need some knowledge of what human nature and divine nature are, and it seems that kenotic Christology is willing to accept a concept of God that I, as a Catholic, simply cannot. It is also worth noting that Pope Pius XII, in a 1951 encyclical, rejected this theory.[14]

So if Jesus retains his divine omniscience, it is worth asking about his knowledge as a human being. The only real problem with talking about Jesus' knowledge is that, understood as a divine person, Jesus has all knowledge, and yet, understood as a human being, there are some things that Jesus did not seem to know. Hebrews 5:8 claims that Jesus *learned* obedience from his sufferings, and Mark 13:32 has Jesus claiming that he did not know the day or the hour of his own return. Saintly theologians through the ages have taken a lively interest in this question. St. Bernard of Clairvaux (1090 or 1091-1153) argued that Jesus was able to learn in a certain sense because, although he knew all things by his divine nature and in his divine person, he did not yet know "by experience."[15] Thus, Jesus could come to "learn" obedience in the sense of experiencing it as a human being, and he could also truthfully claim that he did not "know," because as a human being he

13. This is recognized and accepted by C. Stephen Evans, "The Self-Emptying of Love," in *The Incarnation: An Interdisciplinary Symposium on the Incarnation of the Son of God,* ed. Stephen T. Davis, Daniel Kendall, SJ, and Gerald O'Collins, SJ (Oxford: Oxford University Press, 2002), pp. 246-72, at p. 248.

14. See Pope Pius XII, *Sempiternus Rex Christus,* 29.

15. See Bernard of Clairvaux, *On the Steps of Humility and Pride,* in *Bernard of Clairvaux: Selected Works,* trans. G. R. Evans (New York: Paulist Press, 1987), esp. pp. 107-11.

had not experienced through his senses, the day of his second coming. It's also important to note that the divine knowledge a divine person has and the knowledge a human being through her human nature has, are different. As we said in the last chapter, God knows everything by being in everything, but a human being knows what she knows by experience. The knowledge that a divine essence would have would be very different from the knowledge that a human soul would have, and since the Christology of the Council of Chalcedon does not allow us to blend or confuse the natures, we cannot simply transfer the knowledge of a divine essence to a human soul.[16] We can say, however, that, because of the miraculous union of Christ's soul with his divine nature, Christ "enjoyed in his human knowledge the fullness of understanding of the eternal plans he had come to reveal."[17]

Jesus' human nature likely did not have the omniscience that his divine nature retained, and the *Catechism* does not rule this view out,[18] but it is one thing to be omniscient and another thing to commit a positive error. We need have no worries about claiming that Jesus was the greatest quarterback, midfielder, physician, or painter. These are purely human qualities, and nothing important for God's self-revelation hangs on whether Jesus could have dropped a football or not. In fact, given that Jesus did struggle emotionally, and given his identifying with the meek and lowly, the idea that Jesus was some kind of muscular athletic giant rings oddly with his message for us. Yet we should expect that Jesus was and is a moral example, in that God's self-revelation in Jesus would not showcase someone making poor moral decisions. Some time ago, I was discussing Christianity and veganism with a colleague at another institution who is a vegan Christian. He pointed out that our twenty-first-century overuse of meat and even fish as food could have serious environmental consequences. This seems like a good reason for all of us to consider how to eliminate some (or perhaps all) animal products from our diet, given the worries raised by global climate change in our time. However, he also suggested, arguing from his claim that Jesus' human nature lacked omniscience, that Jesus would not have known all the moral statuses of his actions, perhaps because he was subject to the cultural limitations of his time. In response, I was reluctant to insist that eating fish was wrong at all times in the world's history because the resurrected Christ did it in Luke 24:41-43.

16. *ST,* III.9.1, reply to objection 1.
17. *CCC,* 474.
18. *CCC,* 474.

In this light, I want to urge that Jesus' moral example would not be positively in error. Jesus would not be using the wrong moral theory or be unable to see his way clear to the appropriate progress we sometimes congratulate ourselves on in social issues. Jesus may have had a very "progressive" message for first-century Palestine, and it's also possible that Jesus may have given his full message only to a select few while teaching other radical themes to the throngs of followers the Gospels claim he had. But we should not hold the view that Jesus himself, who suffered and died for us as the culmination of God's dealings with the Jewish people throughout history, made positive mistakes in his life. Jesus' truly human knowledge must "express the divine life of his person,"[19] and that cannot happen if Jesus' moral behavior needs to be positively excused by the fact that he was overcome by the wayward norms of the culture in which he was incarnated. In 1985, the Vatican's International Theological Commission issued a document titled "The Consciousness of Christ Concerning Himself and His Mission," which argued that the biblical evidence gives us reason to believe that Jesus knew, in his human nature, that he was the only Son of God, that he knew the purpose of his mission, and that this mission included dying to save the world from sin.[20]

Jesus clearly had a consciousness of his unique dignity and his salvific role. Whether he could have proven the Pythagorean Theorem as an infant ultimately strikes me as an idle question. What does not strike me as an idle question is whether Jesus would have, if a question were put to him, stepped forward and claimed to know something that he did not know *from his human nature.* We do this when our confidence outstrips our knowledge, and, in many cases, this seems to me to be a form of pride, however rudimentary. We need to find a balance between removing Jesus from real human experience and likening Jesus' human experience too much to ours, which is run through with sin and pride. Pope Benedict XVI writes about Jesus, "As a human being, he does not live in some abstract omniscience, but he is rooted in a concrete history, a place and a time, in the different phases of human life, and this is what gives concrete shape to his knowledge."[21] Indeed, Christians need to find some way to take into account the fact that Jesus grew in "wisdom" (Luke 2:52), and yet, however that oc-

19. *CCC,* 473.
20. See the International Theological Commission, "The Consciousness of Christ Concerning Himself and His Mission."
21. See Joseph Ratzinger/Pope Benedict XVI, *Jesus of Nazareth: The Infancy Narratives,* trans. Philip J. Whitmore (New York: Image, 2012), p. 127.

curred, I submit that it would need to have been, in some ways, an extraordinary process, since it would have lacked the stubbornness, brashness, and willfulness of the young child who screams "I know" to things he clearly doesn't know. To this extent at least, I think Jesus was free from *error*.

The baseline conviction I have been working with when it comes to Jesus' knowledge is that, whatever else we preserve, it is very important to preserve Jesus' human knowledge, especially as it impacted his life as a moral example. But this raises an important question: If Jesus must be a moral example, to what extent was he free to act? After all, I have been urging that Jesus would not be the incarnation of God at all if he had made a positive moral error (and I suggested that all or most positive error has a moral dimension to it). We tend to think of freedom as something that makes one a person as opposed to a robot, and we surely don't want to think of Jesus as a robot. Indeed, part of the Christology that the ecumenical councils maintained included the idea that Jesus had a "human will." But St. Augustine argued that a will that is not free is no will at all.[22] It seems clear that we must believe that Jesus was free in some sense. But if Jesus could not really sin, was he really free?

Although we affirmed that Christ had two "natural actions" and that particular actions spring from an individual's nature, we need to avoid the idea that the two natures in Christ were just bundled together and had nothing really to do with one another. While we do not want to "confuse" the natures, we do want to insist that they were *joined*. God remains eternal, but Christ's human nature was deeply and uniquely joined to the divine nature, and the act of the human nature remains an act for which the divine person is morally responsible. Since there is no human *person* here, it is inappropriate to use only human standards of freedom to evaluate Christ's actions. We must also use divine standards for freedom. Yet, in the previous chapter, we noted that God is incapable of moral evil precisely because the goodness that God is cannot be bested by temptation. We do need to insist that Jesus was really tempted, as in the Garden of Gethsemane, but we cannot claim that this is a mark of anything more than of how united he was to the human condition. It is *human* to want to avoid a gruesome death, but it is *cowardly* to run away from one's duty and mission. Jesus struggled because he was human but not because he seriously considered the way of the coward. After all, it is in this very

---

22. See Augustine, *On Free Choice of the Will*, 3.3, trans. Thomas Williams (Indianapolis: Hackett, 1993), p. 77.

context that we hear Jesus say, "not my will but yours be done" (Luke 22:42). Jesus' will was free, but we have seen that the Catholic tradition holds that human freedom and divine providence are compatible. Later, in chapter 7, we will discuss how true human freedom is freedom for the good, not merely freedom to be able to do evil. Jesus was not able to do evil, but he was able to freely choose the good.[23]

Redemption: Some Preliminaries

I began the last section with a question: What would have made a man who lived two thousand years ago as important and unique as Christians claim that he was? What we did in the last section is explain why he is so important and unique *in himself.* What we haven't yet done is try to explain why he is so important and unique *for us.* This second question is, I think, what many people really want answered. Strangely, it seems to me, few people openly disrespect Jesus. They might in a manner of speaking do what Thomas Jefferson (1743-1826) famously did quite literally, namely, tear out pages of his Bible to arrive at a Jesus that makes more "sense" as a great moral teacher. But few people direct their attacks at Jesus or his message. I suspect that is often because, while the moral teachings of Jesus seem admirable, the uniqueness that mainstream Christianity and the Catholic Church claim for Jesus is, in all honesty, rather difficult to understand. In 1991, a rock band named Live released an album featuring the song "Operation Spirit," which was subtitled "The Tyranny of Tradition." The song admits that Jesus' life may indeed have been a "beautiful" example, but as for Jesus somehow doing something to heal the pain one or another of us (or perhaps each of us) might feel today, a two-thousand-year-old existence seems ill-equipped for that task, the song claims.[24]

This is an important objection, and we should frankly admit that, however well-meaning many Christians are, it is not difficult to poke holes in simplistic theories of Christ's atoning work. Catholic philosopher and theologian Eleonore Stump gives us a version of Christ's atonement that she goes on to criticize, which runs thus:

---

23. See Ludwig Ott, *Fundamentals of Catholic Dogma*, ed. James Canon Batible, trans. Patrick Lynch, 4th edition (1955; reprint Rockford, IL: Tan Books, 1960), pp. 148 and 169.

24. "Operation Spirit" in Live's album *Mental Jewelry* (Radioactive, 1991).

Human beings by their evil actions have offended God. This offense against God generates a kind of debt, a debt so enormous that human beings by themselves can never repay it. God could, of course, cancel this debt, but God is perfectly just, and it would be a violation of perfect justice simply to cancel a debt without extracting the payment owed. Therefore, God cannot just forgive a person's sin; as a just judge he must sentence all people to everlasting torment for their sin. God is also infinitely merciful, however; and so he brings it about that he himself pays their debt in full, by assuming human nature as the incarnate Christ and in that nature enduring the penalty which otherwise would have been imposed on human beings. In consequence, the sins of ordinary human beings are forgiven, and by God's mercy exercised through Christ's passion, they are saved from sin and hell and brought to heaven.[25]

I suspect some Christians could read this and find little to criticize. I have certainly heard many preachers describe the nature of Christ's work in similar terms. But if we are really to make prayerful progress in the mysteries of faith, we can and must seek deeper explanations both so that we can anticipate the difficulties of those who might disagree and so that we can ever more deeply love God with our minds. With that in mind, let us consider several problems with this description.

First, as Stump points out, is the problem that this picture attempts to describe a God who is merciful and just, but it will have difficulty maintaining that. We speak of forgiving people's debts and when we do so we mean that, because of her mercy or generosity, I am no longer required to pay my creditor because *no one* is required to do so; she has *forgiven* the debt. But if that is the action God is taking, why must God (in the person of Jesus) pay for it at all? Why must anyone? If the defender of our first account argues that the first person (the Father) and the second person (the Son) of the Trinity are one in being and so God is himself paying the debt and thus forgiving it, then either the debt really isn't being paid (it's just somehow absorbed by God) or it is really paid and an innocent victim (God the Son) is punished by God the Father for something he had no hand in. The first option makes the cross trivial and the second is a form of divine child abuse. Obviously, some work needs to be done.

25. Eleonore Stump, "Atonement According to Aquinas," in *Philosophy and the Christian Faith,* ed. Thomas V. Morris (Notre Dame: University of Notre Dame Press, 1988), pp. 61-91, at p. 61.

A second difficulty suggests that Christ pays the penalty so that human beings don't have to do so, but what is that penalty supposed to be? If it is supposed to be eternal damnation, then Christ should suffer it, but of course he does not suffer *that* eternally, since now he sits at the right hand of the Father, as the creed tells us. Even if one argues that somehow Jesus did suffer something equivalent to eternal damnation for all of us, though, it is still perplexing why most Christians maintain that our own damnation remains a real possibility for us since then it would be possible to suffer again what Christ already suffered in our place. A final difficulty Stump notes simply points out that nothing in the account she sketched really discussed how human beings are healed by Christ's saving work. Perhaps God's anger is somehow put on ice but we are still left with the problem of our sin, which is what has alienated us from God. What we need is reconciliation, not simply abatement of wrath. How does Jesus help to accomplish this, especially for us latecomers who look back two thousand years?

Our purpose here is not to rehearse Jesus' entire life, though we should emphasize the fact that it is Christ's living among us and not simply his dying among us that brings about our redemption. Nor is our purpose to offer a comprehensive discussion of the atonement. Rather, our purpose is to give some attention to a distinctively Catholic way of looking at the reconciliation achieved through and in Christ. We have said before that Christ is himself God's revelation, and we need to be wary of theologies that present reconciliation with God only as something that Christ does for us and not as something that Christ, however mysteriously, somehow *is* for us. St. John of the Cross claims that Jesus is "brother, companion, master, ransom, and reward."[26] It is good to remind ourselves that Jesus entered our human condition to teach us and to save us, and on the Christian story it is clear enough that we need saving from sin, a condition that gets worse the longer it is allowed to fester. But when Jesus has saved us he will not have gotten us any further than himself. He is the way and the truth, but he is also the life, and we can hope for no greater reward than union with him.

Martin Luther famously argued that a Christian is "justified by the merits of another, namely, of Christ alone."[27] It is often overlooked that the

---

26. See St. John of the Cross, *The Ascent of Mount Carmel,* book II, chapter 22, section 5, in *The Collected Works of St. John of the Cross,* trans. Kieran Kavanaugh, O.C.D., and Otilio Rodriguez, O.C.D. (Washington, DC: ICS Publications, 1973), p. 180.

27. See Luther, "The Freedom of a Christian," *LW* 31, p. 347.

Catholic Church, even in its own response to Luther and the Reformation, could agree with much (though of course not all) of what Luther had to say. The Council of Trent (1545-63), generally reckoned as the nineteenth ecumenical council, wrote, in its decree on justification, that "God touches the heart of man with the illumination of the Holy Spirit, but man himself is not entirely inactive while receiving that inspiration, since he can reject it; and yet, without God's grace, he cannot by his own free will move toward justice in God's sight."[28] What the Catholic Church was at pains to insist upon, at least in part, was the role for human freedom in cooperating with God's grace. It is interesting to note that, in 1999, when the Catholic Church and the Lutheran World Federation issued the *Joint Declaration on the Doctrine of Justification,* there was much agreement, although each tradition continued to articulate its faith in a distinctive way. For instance, the Joint Declaration noted how the Catholic Church prefers to use the term "cooperation," while the Lutheran community prefers not to do so. Despite this terminological difference, the Catholic Church is not insisting that humans can do something before the arrival of God's grace to merit such grace, nor is the Lutheran World Federation denying that the human being is fully involved in her faith.[29]

All Christians should be able to read Paul's insistence in Romans 3:21-26 without flinching and agree that one is justified by faith through grace. God's grace makes our faithful response possible. Without grace, such a faithful response is not possible. That grace is won for us by Christ's atoning work. What it ultimately achieves for us is union with Christ, the second Adam. When we were lost in sin, we were taken away from God by our first parents, who migrated from God's paradise to what they erroneously considered greener (metaphorical) pastures. Our lives were taken up into the reality of sin that the heads of our race, our first parents, chose. Throughout our lives we have all seconded their rebellious choices. But Christians claim now to be taken up into a new reality, namely, the reality of Christ. We are now under the guidance of the Good Shepherd (John 10:11), who guides us in the right path and lets us graze in the greenest pastures, those signified by union with Christ. Indeed, Christ is not only the Good Shepherd, but the vine from which we spring as the branches (John 15:1-10).

28. DH, 1525.

29. See paragraphs 19-21 in the Pontifical Council for Promoting Christian Unity, *Joint Declaration on the Doctrine of Justification.*

So much seems attested by a good deal of the biblical witness. There remain some differences between Protestants and Catholics on matters of how this justification becomes ours, though. In the *Joint Declaration* the Lutheran World Federation insisted that the human being's "sharing in the righteousness of Christ is always complete."[30] Catholics agree that our righteousness is fundamentally Christ's. He is our head, and the mediator of a new covenant between us and God. The grace received through baptism takes away all our sin, yet we continue to struggle with inclinations toward sin (Catholics call this concupiscence). The Council of Trent also taught that human beings increase in justification.[31]

To see this, suppose that I receive justification in baptism as an infant. While baptism cleanses me, I continue to grow up as a member of Christ's body, the church. Throughout this process, I find that I stumble into sin, as we all do. As I will discuss in the chapter on sacraments, some of those sins are more grievous than others. Even as I repent for all my sins, and receive God's forgiveness, I still suffer because of my attachment to sin. The struggle with sin is a lifelong process, and my continual growth away from sin and in Christ is an increase in justification. As we mature, we must grow deeper roots (Luke 8:13). To use another biblical analogy, mature Christians need to advance beyond milk to solid food (1 Cor. 3:2). Another way one might understand this increase in justification is to picture the reality of human life amid the flow of time. A popular rock band called Guster has a song called "Homecoming King" in which it sings "Stay right where you are, you'll be half of who you were."[32] The point seems to be that the very self of a person is not something that can ever be done growing this side of death. Since the self does grow throughout life, if one does not constantly seek to grow in accordance with time, then one will actually be getting worse by staying put. It should not be surprising that we need God's grace in this process just as we need it through every aspect of our lives.

Many Protestants wish to make a clear distinction between justification and sanctification (even though they often emphasize that the two processes are not "separate"), but the Catholic tradition does not usually insist upon such a hard-and-fast line between them. Lutheran theologian Bradley C. Hanson puts the distinction well: "In a Protestant context, justification has the restricted sense of full forgiveness of sin, while sanctifi-

---

30. Pontifical Council for Promoting Christian Unity, *Joint Declaration*, 39.
31. DH, 1535.
32. Guster, *Keep It Together* (Palm/Reprise, 2003).

cation is always in this life a partial transformation of sinners."[33] Catholics, too, know that people are usually not totally sanctified all at once, but they tend to see the process of growing into Christ as itself the further justification of the sinner. Nothing prevents Catholics from employing the term "sanctification" for the growth in holiness that Protestants discuss, but one should not expect Catholics to reserve the term "justification" merely for the forgiveness of sins for which Protestants often reserve it. Rather, the Catholic Church tends to see justification as, at times, an event (as in baptism), but also as a process whereby one "increases" in justification. Although these differences are no longer the occasion for fierce condemnation, it is important to remember that there are some distinctive aspects of each position. Lutherans tend to see justification as something imputed to us through union with Christ. Since this justification is always complete, one either is fully justified before God or one is not justified before God at all. The Catholic Church, however, tends to see justification as something imparted to us through union with Christ, as something that ultimately becomes really ours, though the degree to which we accept that grace in the transformation of our lives is often woefully incomplete.

This seemingly very slight issue makes a big difference (though not the only one) when it comes to doctrines like purgatory and even the atonement. The idea that one can be fully justified before God while one is still a sinner certainly works against spiritual pride in our own works, but it has some problems, too. Certainly Christ died for us while we were yet sinners (Rom. 5:8), but he did that to *heal* us. For God does not merely desire justice, but our good. Aquinas once pointed out that "we do not offend God except by doing something contrary to our own good."[34] Our delight in living the life of faith is enhanced by the acquisition of the tendency to love God and our neighbors more deeply, and we do this by the acquisition and deepening of the virtues such as faith, hope, and love. This love is the ground of Christian prayer, in which we commune with Christ.[35] When Catholics call even our growth in holiness an increase in justification, they mean that God is not "satisfied" until our transformation in love (which is also our deepest happiness) is complete.

33. Bradley C. Hanson, *Introduction to Christian Theology* (Minneapolis: Fortress Press, 1997), p. 244.

34. St. Thomas Aquinas, *Summa Contra Gentiles,* III.122.2, in *Summa Contra Gentiles: Book Three: Providence Part II,* trans. Vernon J. Bourke (Notre Dame: University of Notre Dame Press, 1975), p. 143.

35. *CCC,* 2565 and 2658.

There is another link that is important to consider. For Catholics, the word "law" carries a much more positive connotation than it does for Lutherans, for instance. For Lutherans, the "law" tends to mean "demand and accusation."[36] Although Catholics are familiar with this biblical way of referring to the Jewish law that Christ fulfilled (Matt. 5:17; Rom. 13:8), for Catholics, the moral law also has a positive sense that "prescribes for man the ways, the rules of conduct that lead to the promised beatitude."[37] What many Protestants call "sanctification" is the journey toward beatitude that Catholics link with the whole redemptive process. The simplistic theory of the atonement we discussed earlier has God's (the Father's) wrath put on ice by the Son's sacrifice. While it is true, as I will discuss below, that Jesus' death is a sacrifice, and the reality of sin does offend God, the sacrifice that culminated in Christ's death on the cross stems not from God's wrath but from God's love. God's love is the only thing that needs "satisfying" and God's love wants us to be as fully and deeply happy as we can be.

A Story of Redemption

From what I have said to this point, you'd be right to infer that there are some theories of the atonement that I do not think will be adequate representations of what Christ was doing in his life, death, and resurrection. Many centuries ago, some thinkers appear to have been tinkering with a theory according to which the devil had acquired rights over human beings by their fall into sin and that Christ was at burden to respect these rights and did so by dying for them on the cross. This theory is routinely rejected nowadays. As Gerald O'Collins argues, "Nowhere does the NT [New Testament] accept or even imply that Satan has any rights over human beings."[38] That also applies to the idea that God the Father requires the sacrifice of Christ's cross merely to placate his own wrath. St. John of the Cross may have called Christ a "ransom," along with a brother, companion, master, and reward, but there is no need for us to turn to the Mel Gibson movie (1996) by that name to unpack the term *ransom*.

Our redemption by Christ is a mystery, and as with other mysteries

36. Pontifical Council for Promoting Christian Unity, *Joint Declaration*, 32.
37. *CCC*, 1950.
38. Gerald O'Collins, SJ, *Jesus Our Redeemer: A Christian Approach to Salvation* (Oxford: Oxford University Press, 2007), pp. 120-21.

such as the Trinity, we should expect that some analogies will do a better job than others of illustrating the core Christian convictions. Stump is right to reject the view that the sufferings of Jesus occur *instead* of our sufferings, as if a just judge would ever accept an innocent person's offer, however honorable, to be a substitute for a wicked person. Nevertheless, there are some convictions that need to be honored about Christ's atoning work. First, Jesus' death was not a suicide. Jesus kept faith with his ministry by refusing to occupy some out-of-the-way corner of Israel until the storm of his persecution blew over. Rather, he went to Jerusalem as an observant Jew for his last Passover, even though he knew that this was the opportunity his opponents were looking for to seize him (Matt. 20:17-19; Mark 10:32-34; Luke 18:31-34). Jesus was conscious of Old Testament prophecies and how they would come to pass in his death, but it would be foolish to think he was, as a human being, positively orchestrating such things.

Jesus' death was also a sacrifice. It was not a sacrifice that we made, but one that he made. This is why the Letter to the Hebrews goes to such length to note Christ's unique high priesthood. On the one hand, Christ shares our human nature, and so his sacrifice is really for us. Yet, Christ also is divine, and so enters the true sanctuary in heaven to offer a definitive sacrifice (Heb. 9:24). But why? Why should Christ offer a sacrifice at all? Couldn't God simply forgive us? What does Christ's bloody sacrifice accomplish that nothing else could? Popular Christian writers Philip Gulley and James Mulholland claim that "the forgiveness of sin didn't require the death of Jesus. It only required God's resolve to forgive." They also argue that "atonement theology," as they understand it, is inconsistent with the message of Jesus and that Jesus' very death on the cross was not God's will at all.[39]

From a Catholic point of view (as well as the point of view of traditional Christian orthodoxy), this has gone too far. While St. Thomas Aquinas argued that Jesus' sacrificial death was not strictly necessary in that the omnipotent God could have "restored human nature in many other ways," it was the most fitting way for God to restore us.[40] Let us think a bit about why the redemption may have been so fitting through Christ's death on the cross, without trying to capture the mystery of the redemption. Before all else, it is important to remember that God sent his Son to earth out of

---

39. See Philip Gulley and James Mulholland, *If Grace Is True: Why God Will Save Every Person* (San Francisco: Harper, 2003), pp. 127, 128, and 135-36; quotation on p. 128.
40. *ST,* III.1.2.

love (John 3:16). In the final analysis God is not stingy, wrathful, angry, or vindictive. The enduring message of the Scriptures is that God is slow to anger and rich in kindness (Num. 14:18). Because of this, we should be very reluctant to accept a model of the atonement in which Christ's bloody sacrifice is accepted by an angry God the Father who only relents from torturing human beings because his Son placates his wrath by a suffering at least as bad as our suffering would have been. Christ did sacrifice his human life, and this was very painful, but he did so out of self-sacrificing love. The life, death, and resurrection of Christ did please God, but they pleased God precisely because they manifested his great love for us. The cry of Jesus that God had abandoned him on the cross (Matt. 27:46; Mark 15:34) should not be read as if God the Father were literally abandoning God the Son, but rather as the cry of a faithful Jew who invoked the psalms (Psalm 22, to be exact) to express the pain he felt in his human nature as he died for sinners, who in their ordinary lives of sinfulness experience God's hiddenness.[41]

While Christ is thus not to be understood as taking our exact penalty upon himself in our place, we might envision him as suffering for us vicariously so that we would understand the depths to which we had fallen by becoming guilty of his death.[42] Thus, when Peter delivered his speech at Pentecost, he narrated a bit of the history of salvation and then said, "Therefore let the whole house of Israel know for certain that God has made him both Lord and Messiah, this Jesus whom you crucified" (Acts 2:36). When the people listening heard this, we are told, they were "cut to the heart" and repented (2:37-38). In this view, a major part of our punishment is the guilt (and not just the knowledge) *that we killed our Lord*. This is captured in a powerful way when Catholics read the passion narratives on Palm Sunday, and join their voices to those in the Gospel that say "Crucify him!" In God's omnipotence, we could have been forgiven without Christ's sacrifice, but only because God could have been content with something that was not fully adequate for our reconciliation.[43] For us to be punished by the guilt of having killed our Lord, in whom we find our deepest happiness, is a significant punishment; but to give us an opportunity to be raised to life anew with him is a very great benefit, one that even surpasses the condition of humanity before our fall.

41. See *CCC*, 603.
42. See Mark C. Murphy, "Not Penal Substitution but Vicarious Punishment," *Faith and Philosophy* 26 (2009): 253-73.
43. See Ott, *Fundamentals of Catholic Dogma*, p. 179.

We cannot be too individualistic here. Christ's death was, humanly speaking, the inevitable result of having been sent into a world run through by sin. We have all been part of the regime of sin, and, as we noted before, we have all seconded that regime through our sinfulness. We are guilty *in Adam* in a manner similar to the way in which we receive salvation *in Christ* (see Rom. 5:15-21). The guilt of killing one's Lord is a much greater loss than incurring the loss of one's livestock, as in the Jewish covenant that Hebrews sees Jesus as succeeding, but it signifies a once-and-for-all-time loss that can only be recouped by dying with and rising with Christ. O'Collins writes, "Lovingly accepting for others the undeserved suffering that his sheer goodness faced in a wicked world, Christ removed the defilement of sin and restored a disturbed moral order."[44] There is no need to fixate on just how gruesome Christ's death would have been. Christ did not suffer every possible physical suffering. As Aquinas makes clear, some of these are incompatible, as are death by drowning and death by burning.[45] Nevertheless, we can rest assured that Christ's sufferings were quite enough.

After having died for us and our sins, Jesus "descended into hell," as the Apostles' Creed says. Ephesians 4:8-10 speaks of Christ's descent into the "lower [regions] of the earth" and ascent into the heavens. 1 Peter 4:6 also speaks of the Gospel being preached even unto the dead. The traditional rendering of what occurs when Christ "descends to hell" is that he enters the realm of the dead, not eternal damnation.[46] Once there, Christ, as the universal savior, rescues the fallen souls of the just people who had lived and died before his own death and resurrection.[47] Many lived with the longing to see the days of Christ and did not do so in their earthly lives (Matt. 13:17). They did, however, see the day of his redemption in his descent to the dead. Catholic theologian Hans Urs von Balthasar argued at length that we should see Christ as descending to hell itself and there experiencing a kind of rejection by God the Father that we would otherwise experience.[48] This, he suggests, is the only way to love "to the end" (John 13:1). Balthasar's understanding is not the standard Catholic view,

---

44. O'Collins, *Jesus Our Redeemer*, p. 178.

45. ST, III.46.5.

46. See St. John Paul, General Audience of January 11, 1989, paragraph 2.

47. *CCC*, 633.

48. See Hans Urs von Balthasar, "The Descent into Hell," in *Explorations in Theology IV: Spirit and Institution,* trans. Edward T. Oakes, SJ (San Francisco: Ignatius Press, 1995), pp. 401-14.

and controversy will persist regarding whether it is even an option for Catholics, but regardless of these concerns I simply find his view strange.

Our redemption sets us free for union with Christ, for sharing in the divine nature (2 Pet. 1:4), not as if my puny human self were to become the eternal God, but in such a way that Christ now lives in me (Gal. 2:20). We are thus adopted sons and daughters of God the Father because we are one with Christ through the working of the Holy Spirit. For Catholics, this happens primarily through the sacraments and prayer. We enter into the very life of the Trinity, not as a fourth person, but as nothing before God, who graciously grafts us onto the true vine, Jesus Christ (John 15:5). Christians often sing of Jesus as their very life, and so he is, but if Jesus descends to hell, then our life must be there, too. Christ is not just our life, but our happiness. Christ brings not just life but light (John 1:4) wherever he goes. God in Christ is our heaven. If he should descend to hell, there would be no stopping his love or his victory over sin and death, unless by our refusal to don Christ as the wedding garment (Gal. 3:27; Matt. 22:1-14).

Christ's resurrection is itself our resurrection (1 Cor. 15:22), insofar as we are saved by being joined to it. In a homily on the Eucharist, then Joseph Cardinal Ratzinger (Pope Benedict XVI) notes that bodies are sometimes boundaries (e.g., my nose occupies different space than yours) and sometimes vehicles for communion with others through communication. He claims that in resurrection the body ceases to be a boundary but retains its capacity for communion.[49] This may be a worthwhile way to understand how the resurrected Jesus enters through a locked door (John 20:26) and yet could share a meal with his disciples (Luke 24:41-43). It could also help us understand how we become, as church, the body of Christ.

Although, as I will argue in chapter 7, one can rebel against God and not accept the redemption Christ offers for our salvation, it remains the case that Christ died for all human beings.[50] It is interesting to consider the way in which Christ's universal role as savior of all humanity contrasts with the fact of his Lordship. While Christ is both Lord and savior of all humanity, is he the savior of all rational beings? If there is intelligent life on other planets, how would such beings relate to Christ's sacrifice? At all events, Christians should not be troubled in their faith by such questions.

---

49. Joseph Cardinal Ratzinger, "The Presence of the Lord in the Sacrament," in *God Is Near Us,* ed. Stephan Otto Horn and Vinzenz Pfnür, trans. Henry Taylor (San Francisco: Ignatius Press, 2003), pp. 79-80.
50. See Vatican II's *Gaudium et Spes,* 22.

Whether there are no other forms of intelligent life on other planets, solar systems, or galaxies, or whether there are such forms of life, Christianity will continue to preach the good news. Nevertheless, the question could rightly be put: What sort of good news should it preach were human beings, in some distant future, to be put into communicative contact with extraterrestrials? The *Catechism* tells us that, if the good news of the Gospel is that Jesus is the savior of all "men," then the "reverse side" of that news is the sobering truth of the doctrine of original sin.[51] The interesting thing on this front, of course, is that original sin is a condition that affects the human race and is passed through "propagation," as we noted in the last chapter. So, upon discovering an unknown community on earth that had never heard the Gospel, a missionary would do well to preach the good news of Jesus Christ. But would that be the right thing to do upon discovering an intelligent nonhuman population in another corner of the universe? A brief response will help us round out this chapter.

Jesus is Lord by virtue of being God the Son. God is Lord of all universes and therefore, so is Jesus. Furthermore, should an extraterrestrial community have a religion of its own, it will not do to try to reckon its God as another member of the Trinity, any more than a missionary to, say, India would have done well to expand the number of persons in the Godhead every time she heard of a new Hindu deity. The completeness of God's revelation in Jesus must suffice for us, and we will never get around the so-called "scandal of particularity," which goes with having the Lord of the universe become incarnate in any city, country, culture, time, or planet. It will always be remarkable that God did not choose to be incarnate in some "universal person" but in a particular Jew of first-century Palestine. This shocking truth is Christianity.

At the same time, there are several possibilities to consider here. One possibility is that any ETs we could discover might never have sinned and would thus not need redemption. This is no strange possibility. Catholic philosopher Josef Pieper notes how strange sin is in that, somehow, we culpably go against what is best for us.[52] Lamenting Israel's fall into sin, Jeremiah prophesies: "Be horrified at this, heavens; shudder, be appalled — oracle of the LORD" (Jer. 2:12). We like to say that various imperfections are "only human," but sin is no foregone conclusion. It is a radical and re-

---

51. *CCC*, 389.

52. Josef Pieper, *The Concept of Sin*, trans. Edward T. Oakes (South Bend, IN: St. Augustine's Press, 2001), p. 42.

bellious decision, one that other creatures may never have made. Another possibility is that, owing to the different ways in which God could have redeemed us even apart from the incarnation of Jesus, God could have used other methods to redeem ETs that did not require an incarnation at all. In fact, maybe the ETs would not even have the kind of solidarity human beings do in both sin and salvation and so an incarnation that showed solidarity with their race would not even be very fitting.

Aquinas once considers another possibility: that one divine person (or even another) could assume a nonhuman nature. Thus, either the Father or Spirit could assume an ET nature, or the Son could assume another nature in addition to the human nature. Contrary to what some might expect, Aquinas does not totally rule this possibility out, at least not on philosophical grounds.[53] This would have been possible for God, since even now Jesus Christ, the second person of the Trinity, is just one person with two natures. And it might be theoretically possible for a divine person to assume another nature or two, since then there would still be only one person. But there may be other reasons to expect this possibility not to work. Marie I. George notes that the question of ETs being redeemed by another nature seems to fly in the face of Colossians 1:20, which says that God wished all things to be reconciled in heaven and on earth by the blood of Christ's cross.[54] Another complication for Catholics is that Mary is reckoned the Queen of the Universe, and it's not clear that there could be more than one such queen.[55] This compels George to argue that the better hypothesis, on scriptural grounds, is to believe that the cross of Christ is redemptive in ways perhaps not fully known to us, even for sinful ETs, should they exist. Thus George writes, "If the ETs are redeemed by Christ's death, they belong to the same church that humans do. If the ETs did not fall, they would be in a situation similar to that of the good angels who along with human saints are counted as members of the same Church triumphant."[56]

In this chapter I have tried to explain why a first-century Jew could be as significant as the religion he founded claims he is. Jesus is significant primarily because of who he is, the second person of the Trinity, the Lord of all. To us, however, he is not just Lord but savior, the one who recon-

---

53. *ST,* III.3.7.

54. Marie I. George, "The Catholic Faith, Scripture, and the Question of the Existence of Extra-terrestrial Life," in *Faith, Scholarship, and Culture in the 21st Century* (Washington, DC: American Maritain Association, 2002), pp. 135-45, at pp. 142-43.

55. Vatican II, *Lumen Gentium,* 59.

56. George, "The Catholic Faith," pp. 144-45.

ciled the world to himself by his life, death, and resurrection. Christians are to share in all three of these by imitation of his example, self-sacrificing love, and participation in his resurrection. We are also privileged to become members of his mystical body, the church. Those who have joined themselves to him in an exemplary way are his saints. Preeminent among these is his mother, Mary. In the next chapter we consider what the church says about her and the rest of Christ's saints.

Chapter 5

Mary and the Communion of Saints

Before I became a Catholic I was having a conversation one day with one of my classmates in graduate school. She and I were both Christians and she was very interested in feminist thought. I don't remember the whole context, but I recall one point very clearly. We came to the matter of how Jesus came into the world and my friend was insisting that Mary needed to freely say yes to the angel of God when he announced that she would bear the Son of God. "If she isn't free, then she's raped," she said. As strange as it seems, I had just never thought of it that way. My first response was to try to distinguish her pregnancy from a typical pregnancy because there was no intercourse. But I couldn't make my argument stick. Christians hold that God is the Father of Jesus and that Jesus has a mother, namely Mary. She bore Jesus as an embryo. It was a real pregnancy. But it was also incomparably unique, since God chose Mary out of all of humanity to bear his one and only Son. That isn't something you do with just anybody, and it certainly isn't something you do *to* just anybody. But what did that mean? The question would stay with me for a while.

As a typical Protestant, I hadn't thought about Mary that much. Like most of the people in my former tradition, I just didn't see the need to accentuate her role. Now there's a good reason why someone might do this. After all, if Mary's heart is as pure as Catholics claim, then she wouldn't want the attention on her, but on God, and God the Son, Jesus. But the thing about Jesus' humanity is that, like all the rest of us, Jesus didn't live in isolation, but joined himself to the world, his society and family included. Christians rejoice when we celebrate Easter because we remember the triumphant moment of Jesus' resurrection and victory over death. But we also rejoice at his birth during the season of Christmas. That very fact is significant. Jesus' birth is preparation for his victory. But for that reason, so is the birth of John the Baptist, who Scripture foretold would prepare the way for the Lord. Why then wouldn't Mary's "yes" to God be an important aspect of preparing the world for Jesus? It seems clear that it would be important, and in this chapter we will address how important it is, especially for Catholics.

Jesus and Mary

It's not uncommon to walk into a Catholic Church and see a picture of Mary very prominently placed. It's also not uncommon to see candles lit around this picture (often the Virgin of Guadalupe in the United States and the Americas), and people kneeling to pray next to it. These people are not giving Mary what we're used to calling *worship*. In the Catholic tradition, what many associate with worship is better rendered with the word "adoration" (a word that itself translates the Greek word *latria*) and means acknowledging someone to be, among other things, the Lord and Creator of all, and infinite and merciful Love.[1] For this reason, adoration is an attitude that should be directed to God alone. Jesus, because he is God incarnate, deserves this kind of worship. "Veneration" (a word that translates the Greek word *dulia*), however, is a word that is used for a kind of reverence, respect, and desire to emulate that is appropriate to give to holy human beings. Veneration of other human beings is not uncommon in our everyday life. Americans have a day devoted to the memory of the Rev. Dr. Martin Luther King, Jr. On that day, it's common to celebrate his legacy, extol his dedication to racial justice even in the face of persecution, and it's also common to ask how we can follow in his legacy and carry it forward to some new issue we are facing. We have images of people like Dr. King on everything from banners to postage stamps, and we would think it perverse to desecrate such images or do anything disrespectful to them. In the Catholic Church, those who lived a life committed to the Gospel of Christ are worthy of similar reverence and respect. However, since Catholics also believe that the unity of the church is not broken by death, we can also petition them for prayers and assistance as they intercede for us in heaven. This is not idolatry any more than asking for the prayers of a respected spiritual leader here on earth would be. Notice also that we

1. *CCC*, 2096.

implicitly know this, since the very word "idolatry" has the Greek word we used for "adoration," *latria,* built into it. That is, idolatry is giving *latria* to an idol, that is, anyone other than God.

Still, Mary is unique among the saints. She is the mother of God the Son, and God sought her consent, which she lovingly gave, to bear and raise Jesus. No one else in all creation has such a close relationship to Jesus or to God's plan of salvation. As Thomas Howard writes, "They all bore witness to the Word. This woman *bore the Word.*"[2] Mary is entitled to the dignity we give to the saints, but an even higher degree of veneration. The church has traditionally called this *hyperdulia.*[3] Now, of course, Mary is still human, and however much we respect and love her, she remains human, but among God's creatures Mary carries some unique privileges. Mary is first among the saints in dignity, and what applies to the other saints applies to her in a more sublime way.[4] All the saints are holy, but Mary is "All-Holy" because she neither inherited original sin nor committed any personal sin.[5] All the saints intercede for us, but Mary's intercession is active in all grace, even though Christ is the only one who *produces* grace.[6] All the saints have entered into eternal glory, but Mary has entered, body and soul, into the kingdom of heaven, whereas the rest of the saints await the final judgment to be reunited with their bodies in heaven.[7] The Catholic view of the Virgin Mary is based on two fundamental convictions. The first is that Mary is fully entitled to the surprising title "Mother of God." The second conviction is that Mary consented to bear God in the flesh by a totally free act of her own will.

The first conviction comes out of the Christology we just discussed in the previous chapter. If Jesus is a divine person, and this person has a fully human nature which formed and grew in the womb of a woman, then this woman is his mother. Since a divine person is God, then Mary, as the mother of a divine person, should be given the title "Mother of

---

2. Thomas Howard, *On Being Catholic* (San Francisco: Ignatius Press, 1997), p. 181, italics original.

3. See Ludwig Ott, *Fundamentals of Catholic Dogma,* ed. James Canon Batible, trans. Patrick Lynch, 4th edition (1955; reprint Rockford, IL: Tan Books, 1960), p. 215.

4. See Vatican II, *Lumen Gentium,* 53, and Christoph Schönborn, "The 'Communion of Saints' as three states of the Church: pilgrimage, purification, and glory," *Communio* 15 (1988): 167-81, p. 175.

5. *CCC,* 493.

6. DH, 3274, 3370.

7. *CCC,* 974.

God." Karl Barth, whom we have mentioned in this book several times now, argued in a very influential way that this title, often given its Greek name of *Theotokos,* or "God-bearer," while an essential element of Christian orthodoxy, can only be read as a statement about Christ's person and not about the Virgin Mary.[8] From a Catholic (as well as Eastern Orthodox) standpoint, this seems a little strained. When the Council of Ephesus declared, in 431, that the "holy Virgin" was Mother of God, there were other ways of referring to the unity of Christ's person that were not charged with such significance for Mary.[9] No one could have ignored the double significance entirely, tinged as it obviously was with the church's love for Mary. Indeed, in my experience, every time the title "Mother of God" is mentioned, those who hurry to clarify that it is a Christological and not a Mariological term betray their anxieties about Mary that the Council of Ephesus felt little need to relieve. To be sure, the title "Mother of God" has a *primarily* Christological origin, but, as the *Catechism* notes, "What the Catholic faith believes about Mary is based on what it believes about Christ, and what it teaches about Mary illumines in turn its faith in Christ."[10] According to the church, then, Mariology is a part of Christology.

To see why Mariology can be considered a part of Christology, consider the widely held Christian belief (which is Catholic teaching as well) that Jesus was, as the creed states, "born of the *Virgin* Mary."[11] Why is it so important that Jesus be born of a virgin? What's wrong with God taking on human flesh through the ordinary route of sexual intercourse? While there is nothing wrong with the act of intercourse between a married man and woman that would result in a child, the suggestion that God himself might become incarnate through this method presents some difficulties. To see this, consider what would happen if Jesus were both the son of God and the son of Joseph right from the start. For one thing, that would ring oddly with the Scriptures. When Mary finds Jesus in the Temple after having lost him for days, she asks, "Son, why have you done this to us? Your father and I have been looking for you with great anxiety." Jesus replies to her, "Why were you looking for me? Did you not know that I must be in my Father's house?" (Luke 2:48-49). To be sure, Joseph was a father to Jesus

8. See Karl Barth, "Letter on Mariology," in Barth, *Ad Limina Apostolorum: An Appraisal of Vatican II,* trans. Keith R. Crim (Louisville: Westminster John Knox Press, 1989), p. 60.

9. DH, 252.

10. *CCC,* 487.

11. *CCC,* 496.

in an important way,[12] but many have heard in Jesus' statement here the recognition that ultimately he has only one Father in what we would call the "biological" sense, namely, God.[13] Two other facts seem to shed some light on this. First, it seems highly appropriate for Jesus to have only one father responsible for his generation; otherwise he is not born of the bond of two parties but three. Second, a virgin woman seems particularly appropriate for God's choice of a woman through whom to deliver his Son. God would not be just "using" Mary for this purpose but would be cooperating with her intimately. But with the Holy Spirit as an incomparably unique kind of spouse, neither Mary nor God would want Mary "divided" in her devotion to God (1 Cor. 7:24).[14] We will talk more about the implications of this later, but for now, it seems highly appropriate for Mary to have borne Christ as a virgin. The Christian church has said through the ages that Jesus is born of the Virgin Mary by the power of the Holy Spirit.

The Immaculate Virgin

The Catholic Church claims still other striking things about Mary. Among the most interesting and distinctive is that Mary was "immaculately conceived." While many Christian communities continue to teach the Virgin Birth, or, alternatively, the Virginal Conception of Jesus, the Catholic Church is the only Christian community that teaches that Mary was immaculate from the very first moment of her existence. Here is the dogma that was defined by Pope Pius IX (pope from 1846 to 1878): "The most Blessed Virgin Mary was, from the first moment of her conception, by a singular grace and privilege of almighty God and by virtue of the merits of Jesus Christ, Savior of the human race, preserved immune from all stain of original sin."[15] Recall again that Mariology comes from Christology. Jesus is the savior of all human beings who are saved, without exception, and that includes Mary. Even Catholics sometimes think that Mary did not need redemption because of the Immaculate Conception. Instead, the Im-

---

12. See Pope St. John Paul II's apostolic exhortation *Redemptoris Custos*, 21.

13. Hans Urs von Balthasar, "Mary in the Church's Doctrine and Devotion," in Balthasar and (then) Joseph Cardinal Ratzinger, *Mary: The Church at the Source*, trans. Adrian Walker (San Francisco: Ignatius Press, 2005), p. 105.

14. See Balthasar, "Mary in the Church's Doctrine and Devotion," p. 106, and *CCC*, 505.

15. *CCC*, 491.

maculate Conception is the *manner* of her redemption. Ordinary human beings inherit original sin, as we discussed earlier in this book, and we are redeemed from original sin after having already been infected by it. Mary, however, is redeemed through God's decision to exempt her from ever having original sin, because of what God knew Jesus, as the redeemer of humanity, would do. Mary's redemption "preserves" her from original sin, and our redemption follows after original sin. This is why Mary's redemption is sometimes called "preservative" and ours is called "consequent."[16]

But *why* would God do this? There are many suggestions that have been defended here. At bottom, all of these reasons have something to do with Mary's dignity as "Mother of God." Blessed John Henry Cardinal Newman (1801-1890) put forward many arguments for the doctrine. He suggested, on the one hand, that there was something fitting for the woman from whom Christ took physical form to be even holier than the prophets, noting that "the child is like the parent, and we may well suppose that by His likeness to her was manifested her relationship to Him."[17] Surely there is something unique about Mary's intimate role as mother to Christ. Still, I think there is some justice to the complaint, which I often hear from non-Catholics, that if we took the first suggestion too literally, it could require us to stipulate that Mary's parents, and their parents, and so on, would also need to be immaculately conceived. Of course, this is nonsense. The Catholic case does not rest on this first suggestion alone, though.

Newman also argued, somewhat more boldly, that the doctrine of the Immaculate Conception could be deduced from the very ancient title of Mary as the "second Eve."[18] This claim is historically important, and does shed some light on things. Mary's consent to bear Jesus is the consent that brings our Lord into the world. As Pope Benedict XVI argues, "without Mary the entire process of God's stepping into history would fail of its object."[19] Through Adam and Eve sin entered into the world, but they chose to reject the gifts God had given them. Through Mary, Jesus, the antidote

16. See Anthony J. Tambasco, *What Are They Saying about Mary?* (New York: Paulist Press, 1984), p. 49.

17. See John Henry Cardinal Newman, *Discourses Addressed to Mixed Congregations,* new impression (London: Longmans, Green & Co., 1921), p. 369.

18. See John Henry Cardinal Newman, *Certain Difficulties Felt by Anglicans in Catholic Teaching Considered,* vol. 2 (London: Longmans, Green & Co., 1898), p. 49.

19. See Joseph Cardinal Ratzinger (Pope Benedict XVI), *God Is Near Us: The Eucharist, the Heart of Life,* ed. Stephan Otto Horn and Vinzenz Pfnür, trans. Henry Taylor (San Francisco: Ignatius Press, 2003), p. 13.

to sin and our savior, entered into the world. The church merely says that Mary was given the same kind of gifts that Adam and Eve were given.[20] Would it be surprising if the medicine for sin entered the world through as pure a form as sin itself had entered it?

However, the argument for Mary's Immaculate Conception that I find the most promising is suggested in the brief statement made by the *Catechism:* "In order for Mary to be able to give the free assent of her faith to the announcement of her vocation, it was necessary that she be wholly borne by God's grace."[21] Picture the scenario in Luke 1:26-38. The angel comes to Mary and informs her that she will become pregnant by the Holy Spirit and give birth to the Messiah, who is God in the flesh. What happens next? Consider two imaginary cases with me.[22]

Case 1: Suppose that when Mary is greeted by the angel in Luke 1 she doesn't say "May it be done to me according to your word" but instead refuses. Why would she do this? Well, perhaps because, due to original sin, she is "totally unable to do any good and inclined toward all evil" as some Protestant traditions hold the rest of us to be.[23] This won't work, since God would know that she was unable to do any such good and so either wouldn't ask her in the first place or would be forced to coerce Mary to bear Jesus out of fear, and this harkens back to my friend's discussion about how Mary needed to be free because God is not a rapist. If God wishes for a truly free consent, there can be no fear of coercion in Mary's reply. She can be frightened, sure, but not *frightened into action by God.*

Then suppose we examine another hypothetical case:

Case 2: Suppose that God, knowing Mary's condition of original sin, decides to cleanse her of original sin sometime just before issuing this invitation (knowing Jesus' sacrifice in the future) so that she can give a fully free consent. I believe that this case will not work. The majority

20. See Vatican II, *Lumen Gentium,* 56.
21. *CCC,* 490.
22. This argument is based on my essay: Jack Mulder, Jr., "Why More Christians Should Believe in Mary's Immaculate Conception," *Christian Scholar's Review* 41 (2012): 117-34.
23. See Question and Answer 8 from the *Heidelberg Catechism,* in *Ecumenical Creeds and Reformed Confessions* (Grand Rapids: CRC Publications, 1988), p. 15.

opinion among Christian theologians from all three main branches of Christianity has been that redemption inaugurates a new life within us but that we still struggle with the old life. We still have disordered inclinations to disobey God because of original sin. Those of us who are Christians don't need much of a theological argument for this, since we experience it every day. But these disordered inclinations make us disinclined (and not eager) to accept God's will for us. Compare the Annunciation to a marriage proposal for a moment. While there wouldn't be anything wrong with a potential spouse who asked for some time to think upon being given a kind marriage proposal from a worthy suitor, the suitor wouldn't want his or her intended to positively struggle with *wanting* to be married and wanting *not* to be married to the suitor. But that is what Mary would be struggling with if she possessed these disordered inclinations to disobey God.

Even if Mary makes up her mind, in case 2, to accept this invitation as a blessing, there would still be a portion of her that would wish not to *have* to assume this burden. That isn't the kind of coercion that will make lawyers nervous, but it is a state of mind that a spouse would prefer to avoid in his or her beloved. God is asking Mary to be nothing less than the mother of his child. Cleansing Mary of original sin (however you conceive of it) and its psychological effects is to remove the disorder in her will. Since Christians will claim that God is our blessedness, when the right order is restored, human beings will prefer God's way to their own not because God is forcing them to do so, but because it is the best and most conducive path to their happiness. Thus, Immaculate Mary, while as free as Eve was, will be in a position to consent to God's invitation for all the right reasons.

The Orthodox tradition often objects that the Immaculate Conception seems to make Mary an exception to the ordinary way human beings relate to God in the Old Testament. The important Orthodox theologian Alexander Schmemann (1921-1983) writes, "The Orthodox Church rejects the dogma of the Immaculate Conception precisely because it makes Mary a miraculous 'break' in this long and patient growth of love and expectation, of this 'hunger for the living God' which fills the Old Testament."[24] The idea here seems to be that Mary's hunger should come from the Old Testament longing for God expressed especially well in the Psalms and

---

24. See Alexander Schmemann, *For the Life of the World* (Crestwood, NY: St. Vladimir's Seminary Press, 2000), p. 86.

Prophets, rather than being a momentary glimpse of redemption before Christ actually enters the world. From a Catholic point of view, and with respect, I have trouble understanding this complaint. To Catholics, this "break" is necessary for Christological reasons, namely, that God would desire, and his majesty would require, the most completely free consent of the one person that most closely resembles the spouse of God in all history. Mary *already is* an exception to the way that human beings customarily relate to God, and her redemption is the first herald of God's redemptive plan. The real question is what the exception requires.

The next question that one might ask about this unique doctrine on Mary is how the church decided it was a part of God's revelation, committed to us through Scripture and tradition. Now, as we've noted, most doctrines of the Catholic faith can be traced in some manner to a "seed" that grows into a fully grown doctrine through theological reflection. In this case, the clearest example of this is the greeting of Mary by the angel, which reads, "Hail, favored one," or more traditionally, "Hail, full of grace!" (Luke 1:28). As we've seen, when the church infallibly teaches certain doctrines as articles of faith it must continually be faithful to the scriptural witness. As the church grew to understand the nature of original sin, it became clear that Mary's being full of grace at that time was inconsistent with her remaining under the scourge of sin and its effects when her vocation was announced to her. Many Catholic thinkers down through the ages have said similar things about John the Baptist, who was "filled with the holy Spirit even from his mother's womb" (see Luke 1:15), though such people usually say that John was redeemed after conception, at the visitation (Luke 1:44), and this has never been proclaimed as a dogma for Catholics.[25] Scripture must continually be revisited, and if Mary is full of grace just as John is full of the Holy Spirit, this may very well mean something for both of them even prior to Jesus' arrival.

I've already mentioned some reasons for why I think the claim that Mary never inherited original sin seems right to me, but how did the history of the church come upon this doctrine? Certainly one possible answer is that the church came upon the answer because, given that it is correct and represents the truth about things, the doctrine answers to the actual experience of the revelation of God in Jesus and the experience of the apostles in some way. After all, the apostle John is often thought to have lived

---

25. See Newman, *Certain Difficulties Felt by Anglicans in Catholic Teaching Considered*, vol. 2, p. 47.

with the Virgin Mary in Ephesus some years after the crucifixion. What might he have known by virtue of his closeness to Jesus and Mary? On the other hand, the trouble with that appeal is that it suggests that it is a fact about tradition that everyone recognized until the unity of the church was broken in 1054 and later in the Protestant Reformation, and that just isn't the case. Indeed, even Aquinas could not affirm the Immaculate Conception in the thirteenth century.[26] This doctrine only unfolded in the Catholic understanding over a long period of time. That does not mean that the doctrine must be rejected. Indeed, it took the church centuries to formulate her views on the matter of original sin alone. Naturally, it wouldn't have made much sense for the church to say that Mary was free from original sin until that doctrine was understood clearly anyway. But even after the basic idea of original sin was understood in the Catholic Church, it would still be a long time before the church recognized Mary's Immaculate Conception. On this doctrine, as with many, it seems the church's understanding grew deeper and deeper through the years.

The history of this development is complex, but we can detail some of the highlights here. The first major development in the understanding of the church here seems to be St. Irenaeus's (c. 130-c. 200) discussion of Mary as the "new Eve."

> [Eve], having become disobedient, was made the cause of death, both to herself and to the entire human race; so also did Mary, having a man betrothed [to her], and being nevertheless a virgin, by yielding obedience, become the cause of salvation, both to herself and the whole human race. . . . And thus also it was that the knot of Eve's disobedience was loosed by the obedience of Mary. For what the virgin Eve had bound fast through unbelief, this did the virgin Mary set free through faith.[27]

Now, Irenaeus is a very early Church Father, who was instructed by St. Polycarp (d. 155), bishop of Smyrna, and Polycarp had been instructed in the faith by the apostle John himself, so this is the testimony of a leader of the church at a time when people could still recall quite a bit of the apos-

---

26. *ST*, III.27.2.

27. Irenaeus, *Against Heresies*, III.22.4, in *The Ante-Nicene Fathers*, ed. Alexander Roberts and James Donaldson, rev. A. Cleveland Coxe, 10 vols. (1885; reprint Grand Rapids: Eerdmans, 1953), vol. 2, p. 455.

tolic testimony from only a couple of generations ago. What can we learn from this early tradition on Mary? Irenaeus does not yet say that Eve was sinless as she helped bring sin into the world and Mary was sinless as she helped bring redemption into the world, but in later centuries, this parallel is not far from anyone's mind. Notice also that since Christ is the new Adam, or the "last Adam" (1 Cor. 15:45) in that he brings life to all those who follow him, Mary can be said to be the new Eve in that, like Eve, who was the "mother of all the living" (Gen. 3:20), Mary became the mother of all who have their new life in Christ (1 Cor. 15:22). Indeed, since the church is the body of Christ (Eph. 1:23), this is one reason Mary is called the "Mother of the Church."[28]

Another episode in our highlight reel on the history of Mary's Immaculate Conception is St. Augustine, who, in his *Nature and Grace,* famously exempted her from consideration in the matter of sin, "out of respect for the Lord," who, Augustine suggests, would have given Mary "an abundance of grace for entirely overcoming sin."[29] Even this text is controversial, and the debate about how to understand Mary's redemption raged for more than another thousand years in Catholic circles. All the while, parts of the church had long been celebrating feast days for Mary's conception. The question was whether there was anything extraordinary about the conception itself. Eventually Pope Sixtus IV (pope from 1471 to 1484), in 1483, forbade anyone to censure the view now known as the Immaculate Conception, and formally approved the feast for her conception, even though he stopped short of defining the doctrine of the Immaculate Conception himself.[30]

In my experience, many lay Protestants sometimes imagine that Martin Luther came along and quickly put a stop to all of this nonsense. In fact, however, Luther had a deep respect for the Virgin Mary. He prayed to her for assistance as he began to write on the Magnificat (Luke 1:46-55) and once called her "sinless."[31] The Council of Trent, which met after Luther died, exempted Mary from consideration from original sin in much the same way that Augustine did, though because of Pope Sixtus's decision around eighty years earlier this took on the significance of elevating the

28. See St. John Paul, *Redemptoris Mater,* 47.
29. See Augustine, *On Nature and Grace,* 36, in Augustine, *Four Anti-Pelagian Writings,* trans. John A. Mourant and William J. Collinge (Washington, DC: Catholic University of America Press, 1992), pp. 53-54.
30. DH, 1400.
31. See Luther, *The Magnificat, LW* 21, esp. pp. 298 and 327.

doctrine of Mary's Immaculate Conception. Eventually, in 1854, the doctrine was defined by Pope Pius IX, as noted earlier.[32]

After she was born, says the church, Mary remained sinless her entire life.[33] While the last point about Mary's remaining free from any actual sin for her whole life might seem surprising, it is worth noting that this is a belief that Catholics share with the Orthodox Church.[34] Christ's church carried on as one until about 1054, when there was a formal schism and the result was a split between East and West, which is now evident in the split between the Orthodox and the Catholic Church. The Protestant Reformation, which had its own precursors, was a response to the Catholic Church in the West, with Luther's own movement beginning at around 1517 with his *Ninety-Five Theses*. If Mary's remaining free from actually committing a sin her whole life long is a doctrine on which both East and West substantially agreed until after 1517, one needs to imagine how strange the rejection of it by Protestants looks to both Catholic and Orthodox Christians. Nor should we find it strange that Mary didn't broadcast her sinlessness widely to an adoring public so that all first-century Christians would know about it. Sinless individuals, after all, don't go around bragging about their sinlessness, so Mary's sinlessness is not likely to have been a widely known fact.[35]

We need to keep this in mind when we turn to another teaching of the Catholic Church regarding Mary, one on which both Catholic and Orthodox again agree, namely, the claim that Mary was "ever-virgin" or remained perpetually a virgin.[36] Mary was given the title "ever-virgin" in 553 by the Second Council of Constantinople,[37] and the doctrine of her perpetual virginity shows up again and again in teachings of the church after that point. St. Jerome (d. 420) famously defended this doctrine against a certain Helvidius who appealed to Matthew 1:25 to support his denial of it.[38] Helvidius read, in that text, that "[Joseph] had no relations with her

---

32. DH, 2803.

33. *CCC*, 493.

34. See Timothy (Kallistos) Ware, *The Orthodox Church*, new edition (London: Penguin, 1997), p. 259.

35. See Hans Urs von Balthasar, *Mary for Today*, trans. Robert Nowell (San Francisco: Ignatius Press, 1988), p. 70.

36. See Ware, *The Orthodox Church*, pp. 257-58, and *CCC*, 499.

37. DH, 437.

38. See Jerome, *On the Perpetual Virginity of the Blessed Mary against Helvidius* (Washington, DC: Catholic University of America Press, 1965), pp. 3-43.

until she bore a son" and found other such verses to claim that Mary had relations with Joseph after Jesus' birth. The two brightest lights of the Protestant Reformation treated the doctrine of Mary's perpetual virginity with respect, explicitly noting Helvidius's mistakes. Luther, rather famously, defended this doctrine and held it devoutly.[39] John Calvin (1509-1564), like Jerome, argued against Helvidius that Matthew 1:25 needn't be interpreted as a denial of Mary's perpetual virginity, though he did not explicitly espouse this doctrine.[40]

The other major biblical texts that appear to threaten Mary's perpetual virginity are ones that seem to discuss Jesus' siblings.[41] Although novelist Anne Rice, in her popular series *Christ the Lord,* has drawn on the tradition that Joseph had other children prior to his marriage to Mary, the Catholic Church, and especially Pope St. John Paul II, has often promoted the view that Joseph himself lived a virginal life.[42] As for the people the biblical text identifies as "brothers" of Jesus, the church favors the view that they were actually sons of the "other Mary."[43] Objectors to Mary's perpetual virginity need to consider that in various Semitic cultures, the word for "brother" has a wider use than to actually be born from the same mother or parents. Indeed, the Hebrew word for "brother" is also used in several episodes in the Old Testament in which we know that the meaning is not literally "brother." One example can be found in the story of Abraham and Lot, where Genesis 12:5 tells us that Lot was Abraham's "brother's son," but then in verses 13:8, 14:14, and 14:16, Lot is called simply "brother" (my translation of the Hebrew). The collaborative project between Protestants and Catholics *Mary in the New Testament* agrees with this much: "[I]t is not implausible that Jesus' relatives would have been remembered according to the way they were designated in Aramaic or Hebrew."[44] The point of this is simply that if there is an early and longstanding tradition that Mary was perpetually a virgin, and there is, we need to take this seriously.

Indeed, if we insist on reading the words "brothers" and "sisters" literally, then, according to Matthew 13:55-56, Jesus would have had at

39. Luther, *Sermons on the Gospel of Saint John, LW* 22, esp. p. 23.

40. John Calvin, *Commentary on a Harmony of the Evangelists, Matthew, Mark, and Luke,* vol. 1, trans. William Pringle (Grand Rapids: Baker, 2009), p. 107.

41. See Matt. 12:46-50; Mark 3:31-35; Mark 6:3; Luke 8:19-21; John 7:1-9; and Gal. 1:19.

42. See St. John Paul's General Audience dated 21 August 1996.

43. See *CCC*, 500, and Matt. 27:56 and 28:1.

44. See *Mary in the New Testament,* ed. Raymond Brown et al. (Philadelphia: Fortress Press, 1978), p. 66.

least four brothers and two sisters, some of whom became Christians (as in the case of James). Probably a few of them would have married and had children, and probably some of them would have children. People who deny Mary's perpetual virginity should thus find it surprising that this is one of the earliest Marian teachings of the church to gain a wide following, since, if Mary did have other children, descendants of Mary might have been around for some years after Jesus' death to contest this claim. The conviction of the church is rather that Mary remained a virgin throughout her life. No doubt part of the reason the church has cared so much about this doctrine is its high regard for the life of virginity,[45] and the conviction of the church that Mary is a model for holy living. Still another reason to take this doctrine seriously is that in saying "yes" to God's invitation to bear Jesus, Mary was realizing her unique dignity as the spouse of God. God is not the "love them and leave them" type, and when God impregnates a woman, we can expect that God means to continue an especially close relationship with such a person forever. If the church holds that Mary remained free from sin her entire life, then she cannot have had intercourse prior to marriage, but then neither can she have had intercourse after marriage, since this would be to abandon her unique spousal relationship with God.[46]

A Model and Source of Encouragement

Mary is honored because of her obedience and the holy life that God enables her to live. When Mary visits Elizabeth while both are still pregnant, Elizabeth says that she is blessed because she believed and faithfully received the word of the angel that she would bear the Messiah (Luke 1:45). It is sometimes noted that Jesus appears to scorn his mother when Jesus is told, "Blessed is the womb that carried you and the breasts at which you nursed," and he replies, "Rather, blessed are those who hear the word of God and observe it" (Luke 11:27-28). Another similar case appears at Luke 8:19-21, where Jesus is told that his mother and brothers have come to see him and he responds by saying, "My mother and my brothers are those who hear the word of God and act on it."[47] St. John Paul notes here that

45. See 1 Cor. 7:8.
46. See St. John Paul, *Redemptoris Mater*, 39.
47. See also Mark 3:20-35.

Jesus "wishes to divert attention from motherhood understood only as a fleshly bond, in order to direct it towards those mysterious bonds of the spirit which develop from hearing and keeping God's word."[48] Jesus cannot be directly dishonoring his mother, since doing so would itself be an imperfection, indeed, a violation of the Ten Commandments (Exod. 20:12). Instead, he is pointing to a new way of relating to Jesus and his body, the church, which need not exclude Mary and in fact includes her as the very first of those who bear this new relationship to Jesus by hearing the word of God and acting on it.[49]

Another suggestion is often made that Jesus is, at best, quite short with his mother at the wedding of Cana, calling her simply "woman" as if, as we might say, to "talk down" to her (John 2:4). If this is Jesus' intention, then it is surprising to see him consent to her request almost immediately. It is also surprising that Jesus' only other usage of this term for his mother is when he is dying on the cross and she has faithfully remained at his feet (John 19:26). Surely he does not mean to leave his earthly life by contemptuously addressing one of the only people to lovingly stand by him as he was beaten and killed, and when many others left. What, indeed, could he mean by this? It is certainly possible that in Jesus' cultural context (or even his own tender way as a son) to address his mother as "woman" simply does not bear the scorn that it might in American English.

Another possibility is suggested by St. John Paul. Note that all of these instances occur in the Gospel of John, a Gospel unique for its very high view of Jesus' claims to divinity and later, more theologized version of the Gospel events. If the Catholic Church is right that Mariology springs from Christology, then one who has a high Christology should also have a high Mariology. And there is no better candidate for a person to have a high view of Mary than the apostle John or the Johannine writer of this Gospel, since John is probably "the disciple whom Jesus loved" (as in John 19:26). At the cross, John was given by Jesus to Mary and Mary to John as son to mother and mother to son (John 19:26-27). Accordingly, St. John Paul suggests that Mary is being understood here as the "woman" who is now the mother of those who have their life in Christ, as opposed to "the woman" of Genesis 3:2, who was mother of all the living but helped to bring the stain of sin upon humankind.[50] There is no need to preclude the

48. St. John Paul, *Redemptoris Mater,* 20.
49. St. John Paul, *Redemptoris Mater,* 20.
50. St. John Paul, *Redemptoris Mater,* 24.

idea that the biblical text could have more than one meaning and that one of its meanings might be more than just literal.[51] Perhaps this is one of those cases. In any case, Catholics see Mary as a perfect model for all Christians, since she gave the first, and most definitive, "yes" to God's plan for all of our lives in her consent to bear Jesus.

But not only is Mary a model, she is a source of encouragement, since she lived a life of incomparable closeness to God and did not succumb to the temptation that overtook someone like Eve. She is also a source of encouragement because, according to Catholic doctrine, Mary has been fully assumed into heaven, body and soul. As we will discuss in chapter 7, most of us die and await the resurrection of our bodies even while we experience the joy of heaven or the loss of it in hell. Mary, however, according to Catholic teaching, was assumed into heaven upon the completion of her earthly life. Note that this is not to say that Mary did not die, and many people still have this misunderstanding. Mary probably did die,[52] and there are legends about her death that, while legendary, may contain a grain of truth to them. But when she died, her body was taken up to heaven with her soul and reunited with it. This is a difficult dogma to understand, but Pope Benedict XVI, before he became pope, wrote that in it "the Church proclaims that the entire greatness possible to a human being is fulfilled and verified in this woman, in utter independence of descent or class."[53] Mary was a poor and lowly woman, but Catholics look to her as already the fulfillment of all that God promises to us when all things will finally be made new.

Very early on, the Church Fathers grew fond of talking about Mary using terms like the "ark of the covenant" and the "spiritual throne."[54] The ark of the covenant in the Old Testament was thought to manifest God's presence in a unique way. Mary, the new ark of the covenant, brought forth Jesus after having cared for him in her womb. Because she gave Christ her very flesh and substance, something no one else can claim, there is something very fitting about Christ bringing the woman who cared for him so deeply into the fullness of heaven that we still anticipate.

51. See *CCC*, 115-19.

52. Ott, *Fundamentals of Catholic Dogma*, pp. 207-8.

53. See Joseph Ratzinger, *Dogma and Preaching* (Chicago: Franciscan Herald Press, 1985), p. 114.

54. See, for instance, St. Methodius, *Oration Concerning Simeon and Anna*, 5, in *Ante-Nicene Fathers*, vol. 6, trans. William R. Clark, ed. Alexander Roberts, James Donaldson, and A. Cleveland Coxe (Buffalo, NY: Christian Literature Publishing Co., 1886), p. 386.

Consider also this example from a local newspaper. Recently I read a section editor's eulogy for his deceased father.[55] The article opens by noting that the author's father was ready to die some years ago when his wife (the author's mother) died. But, the article goes on, the father's sons and daughters still needed him for a little while. Who better to console the grieving disciples than Christ's own mother? Indeed, Blessed Amadeus of Lausanne cited this very reason for Mary's continuing here on earth after Jesus' death.[56] Yet if the disciples longed to have her with them for a time, how much more would Jesus long to bring her near? Jesus' humanity may be glorified in heaven, but he remains human. While he might wish for his apostles to have the comfort of his mother, at some point he too might wish to draw her close as well.

Mary now rejoices in heaven, but it is a mistake to think that in heaven one's "work" is over while the rest of us here on earth work to return to the Lord. St. Thérèse de Lisieux (1873-1897) is quoted as saying, "I want to spend my heaven in doing good on earth."[57] To the saints, the service of God *is* paradise. Mary's earthly service to God and Christ continues even now as she cooperates in Christ's own mediation, petitioning her Son to help us, as we petition her.[58] If you find this strange, consider that Jesus' own ministry began at the pleading of his mother. Like the persistent widow of Luke 18:1-8, Jesus exhorts us to be persistent in our prayers to God. It seems no accident that Jesus should have begun his ministry at the wedding of Cana when at first it appeared he was not going to act to save the wedding by miraculously providing wine (John 2:4). Then Mary pleaded with him, and he performed his first miraculous sign. Let us not be fooled here. Of course God can give good gifts to us without our asking; God knows what we need before we ask for it (Matt. 6:8). But God *wants* us to ask (Matt. 7:7-11). God also created us to be social beings that lean on one another for all kinds of things. The deeper truth about us is that we are not isolated individuals but interdependent on one another. It is a sign of health to know when one needs help, and it is a sign of Christian health to know when one needs prayer. To ask our friends, our family, and our

55. Charles Honey, "Good Game, Keith Honey," *The Grand Rapids Press,* January 21, 2012.

56. See St. Bernard of Clairvaux and Amadeus of Lausanne, *Magnificat: Homilies in Praise of the Blessed Virgin Mary,* trans. Marie-Bernard Saïd and Grace Perigo (Kalamazoo, MI: Cistercian Publications, 1979), pp. 119-20.

57. *CCC,* 956.

58. *Redemptoris Mater,* 41.

spiritual role-models for prayer is right and good, and God wants us to do that. Catholics merely believe that death, since it is the entry into eternal life for Christians, is no reason to stop asking someone for prayer.

Mediation

So it is not idolatry if we turn to our ancestors in the faith, and especially Mary, whose role as mother to Christ means that she is also mother to Christ's mystical body, the church. Mary is our mother, too, then, and we can expect the Lord to listen to her requests just as he did while they were both on earth. Here is what Vatican II said about the matter:

> The maternal duty of Mary toward men in no wise obscures or diminishes this unique mediation of Christ, but rather shows His power. For all the salvific influence of the Blessed Virgin on men originates, not from some inner necessity, but from the divine pleasure. It flows forth from the superabundance of the merits of Christ, rests on His mediation, depends entirely on it and draws all its power from it.[59]

Mary is mother to us, just as we are in Christ, and she is Christ's mother. But we are also sons and daughters of our teachers in the faith, as Paul treats Timothy (1 Tim. 1:2). The Christian faith forms a family, and that family remains knit together whether its members are on earth, being purified in purgatory (see chapter 7 on this), or in heaven.

All of us in these three states of the church are joined in Christ's mystical body, the church. We all, according to Vatican II, "sing the same hymn of glory to our God."[60] But it would mean very little if we were somehow united as church but could not benefit one another in any way. Instead, we can exchange prayers for one another as we seek to grow closer to Christ. Those in heaven stand in no real need of our prayers, but their joy is not lessened by interceding for us. Souls in purgatory stand in need of our prayers, though there is no reason why they, too, cannot offer prayers for us, though they are not given the veneration accorded the saints in heaven.[61]

---

59. Vatican II, *Lumen Gentium,* 60.
60. Vatican II, *Lumen Gentium,* 49.
61. Ott, *Fundamentals of Catholic Dogma,* p. 323.

This exchange of spiritual goods does not contravene Jesus' atoning work. Rather, it is one of the ways in which Christ's atoning work reaches out to us. Jesus is indeed the "one mediator between God and the human race" (1 Tim. 2:5-6), but most Christians have long had an awareness of the fact that, as the body of Christ, we are sometimes called to act as his hands and feet. This is not mediation apart from or added to the mediation of Christ, but it is mediation *in* Christ.[62] All the saints, and indeed all of us, are capable of this subordinate share in Christ's mediating work. Mary's share is particularly striking since as mother to Christ her "yes" opened a way for Christ into the world. This is why Mary is understood as "mediatrix"[63] even though her mediation is in Christ and totally dependent on Christ. Also, as mother to the church, which is Christ's body, she has a special regard for all of the church. This does not mean that Mary or any other saint is omniscient, but it does mean that God sees to it that spiritual communion is really established between those of us on earth, those in purgatory, and those in heaven. As Christians, we know that the reality of heaven is greater still than the reality of this earth. Recall that God knows everything because God is in everything. Whatever knowledge God is pleased to give Mary and the rest of the saints is entirely dependent on God's will for them and us. At the same time, we should not find it surprising that in glory the saints' knowledge is different and more expansive than it would have been on earth, and that the saints' prayers are more powerful and fruitful, precisely because of their greater intimacy with God.

Becoming a Saint

At this point, it would be natural to ask: Fine, but how do you become a saint? My father likes to joke about the old sketch from *Saturday Night Live* in which the fictional Father Guido Sarducci claimed that the standards for saints' miracles were being relaxed and that two of one saint's miracles were actually card tricks. The reality, of course, is much different. Instead of just formally laying out conditions for becoming a saint, I want to offer the example of the first Nigerian beatified, Fr. Cyprian Michael Iwene Tansi (1903-1964). We have accounts of his life, but we also have

---

62. St. John Paul, *Redemptoris Mater,* 38 and 40.
63. DH, 3370 and 3916.

the loving testimony of Francis Cardinal Arinze, also a Nigerian, who is currently the Prefect Emeritus of the Congregation for Divine Worship and the Discipline of the Sacraments.[64]

Arinze's testimony is most interesting because he credits his priestly vocation first to God and then to Father Tansi. Arinze knew Tansi personally early in life and was convinced that he lived a holy life worthy of being recognized by the church as a saint. When the church recognizes that a person is a saint, it is simply a confident declaration that the person is in heaven. No one believes that heaven is populated only by those whom the church declares to be saints, but the declaration means that the person is worthy of veneration and that she or he is an example to the faithful. Now it happened that in 1967, three years after Tansi's death, Arinze was assigned to be archbishop of the archdiocese in which Tansi had been born. Since he was convinced of Tansi's holiness, Arinze organized a symposium in 1974, ten years after Tansi's death, to recall his memory. There those who knew him discussed his life and holiness, and all of the information was documented.

When Arinze came to Rome in 1979, he discussed Tansi's life with the cardinal prefect of the Congregation for the Causes of Saints (a congregation in the Roman Curia that investigates cases for sainthood). Arinze was informed that he needed to check with the diocese in which Tansi died, which he did, and that diocese allowed Arinze to proceed with the cause for Tansi's sainthood. Just to be clear, Tansi has not yet been canonized (formally declared a saint) but he has been beatified, which is the final step before canonization, and comes after the church formally recognizes the candidate's heroic virtue and first miracle attributed to the saint. Tansi's beatification took place on March 22, 1998, in Nigeria, over twenty years after the 1974 symposium, and this is regarded as a very quick cause for sainthood. Most causes for sainthood take much longer.

In the meantime, the Nigerian people had been growing increasingly devoted to the memory of Father Tansi, and his remains were returned to the cathedral of the diocese in which he had been born. Arinze relates a miracle attributed to Tansi's intercession at this point. Note that most of the miracles attributed to saints occur posthumously through their intercession; it has nothing to do with card tricks! The story occurs in 1986,

---

64. See Francis Cardinal Arinze, *God's Invisible Hand: The Life and Work of Francis Cardinal Arinze: An Interview with Gerard O'Connell* (San Francisco: Ignatius Press, 2006), pp. 108-23 and 249-54.

when a girl of around twenty had a serious illness in her stomach, and the specialists who had examined her at the hospital in Onitsha concluded that nothing more could be done for her. A nun responsible for the girl's care heard about the remains of Father Tansi and took her there. The crowd prevented them from getting near the coffin, but the nun persuaded the monsignor (honored priest) in charge, and he allowed the girl to touch the coffin. After she fell upon the coffin, she immediately got up and walked, as she was not able to do before. Then she went to Mass and ate a full dinner, whereas formerly she had not been able to eat. The doctors who had concluded that nothing could be done for the girl later examined her and concluded that she was in fact the same person they had examined earlier and that she was now healed.

The event was documented carefully and, along with the testimony that Father Tansi had lived a life of "heroic virtue," as is required, it was sent to Rome for a judgment. Arinze, in reflecting on the need for a miracle in such causes, notes:

> It is an intervention on the part of Divine Providence. It isn't just hard work on the part of the promoter of his cause: because if God decided not to do a miracle, you could write as many books as you like, you could speak and hold conferences, but there would be no beatification if there were no miracle. So it goes beyond anything that men can put together.[65]

God is not a rubber stamp. Before the church will make a judgment as to whether someone should be honored and imitated as a saint, it waits for evidence that God has reached the same conclusion.

The Congregation then examined the case for the claim that Father Tansi lived a life of heroic virtue, which involved the judgment of Congregation officials, a number of theologians and consultors, and then the vote of the Congregation members themselves. This claim to heroic virtue was approved on July 11, 1995. The miracle then went through the same stages of approval and was approved on June 25, 1996. Ordinarily, in order for canonization to take place, which is when the person is formally declared a saint in heaven, another miracle must be attributed to the person or his or her intercession and it must be duly examined just like all of the other issues. However, recently, Pope Francis has allowed the causes for saint-

---

65. Arinze, *God's Invisible Hand*, p. 253.

hood of Pope St. John XXIII (pope from 1958 to 1963) and St. John Paul to proceed without a second miracle.

Being a saint is something to which we are all called, and it certainly does not mean that one is anything other than human. It means that one is *really* human, that one has lived a life worthy of her role as God's creature and servant. We look to our role-models just as we do in other areas of our life. This does not distract us from Jesus. Rather, the devotion to the memory of the saint, the petitioning for prayers by this saint to our one Lord, Jesus Christ, simply emphasizes the importance of the communion of saints that all Christians profess in the Apostles' Creed.

Chapter 6

The Seven Sacraments

My two kids have a favorite thing to do after Mass. While they love to run around and play with their friends, they also love to dip their fingers into the holy water font and perform the sign of the cross. My son is still pretty small, so he has a tendency to reach deeply into the font and almost topple over into it. He often gets pretty wet. During the Sunday Masses of the Easter season (the seven weeks from Easter Sunday to Pentecost), the priest often performs the rite of sprinkling. This basically involves him offering a prayer and then taking some palm leaves and walking through the congregation while flinging holy water on everyone present. It's not hard to see that our priest enjoys it. The sprinkling of holy water (outside of baptism) is what is known as a sacramental. Sacramentals do not directly confer the special graces that the sacraments (such as baptism and Eucharist) do. However, the sprinkling of holy water or other sacramentals do, through the prayers of the church, prepare us in a unique way to enter into the sacraments and to cooperate with the grace given there.[1]

Just as God chose to use people to accomplish his purpose in salvation, so God chose to use tangible objects as vehicles of grace. As Pope Pius XII indicates, it was certainly possible for Christ "of Himself to impart these graces to mankind directly; but He willed to do so only through a visible Church made up of men, so that through her all might cooperate with Him in dispensing the graces of Redemption."[2] The church is Christ's body (Eph. 5:23), and a body "is given the proper means to provide for its

1. *CCC*, 1668-70.
2. See Pius XII, *Mystici Corporis Christi*, 12.

133

own life, health, and growth, and for that of all of its members."[3] It is fitting that God would provide for the needs of the church in ways that would recognize it as a body.

The church knows that grace can be communicated through visible and physical as well as invisible and spiritual means, and this is what sacraments do. Sacraments are instituted by Christ as power that comes forth from his body. The sacraments "make the Church," as the *Catechism* says.[4] The church's life is sacramental; we are to become members of Christ's body and one spirit with him (1 Cor. 6:17). When I was young my friends and I often wondered why we "had" to go to church. Happily, we liked each other's company, so seeing one another at church seemed like a pretty good reason. But mere fellowship as a reason for going to Mass leaves something to be desired. During Mass the Eucharist is offered as a supper and sacrifice and the unity of those gathered manifests the unity of Christ's body.[5] The real reason for going to church is sacramental; it is because Christ instituted sacraments so that we could be joined to him through them. This is why the sacraments "make" the church.

But the church is not just made by the sacraments; the church is herself the fundamental sacrament of Christ's action at work in us through the Holy Spirit. That the action is Christ's is important. As long as the action is not a mockery and the minister of the sacrament is authorized to do it, the sacrament is valid. The person receiving the sacrament should be properly disposed or prepared for it,[6] but the work of the sacrament itself is the instrument through which God dispenses grace. One of the reasons this is important is because the work of Christ in the sacraments does not depend on the worthiness of the minister. The people of God still receive the grace of the sacraments even if the minister is morally corrupt.

The task for the rest of this chapter is to discuss the seven sacraments of the Catholic Church. It is well known that Martin Luther and most of the Protestant traditions with him held that there were only two sacraments, namely, baptism and Eucharist. The Catholic Church, along with the Orthodox Church, however, insists that there are seven. The first group, the sacraments of Christian initiation, includes baptism, confirmation, and Eucharist. The second group, the two sacraments of healing, are penance

---

3. Pope Pius XII, *Mystici Corporis Christi*, 18.
4. *CCC*, 1116, 1118.
5. Vatican II, *Lumen Gentium*, 11.
6. *CCC*, 1118.

(or reconciliation or confession) and the anointing of the sick. The third group, which the *Catechism* calls "sacraments at the service of communion," includes holy orders and matrimony. I will follow this order with two exceptions. I will place the sacrament of penance between baptism and confirmation in the order of our treatment here because it parallels the order of my experience as someone who entered the church as an adult a bit better, and I will treat the anointing of the sick at the end of the chapter.

Baptism

Every Christian is adopted. Christianity is a religion based on adoption. Jesus is the only begotten Son of God, and yet Christ became a man so that we might share in the very life of God.[7] We do this through Christ and in Christ, but even now Jesus is both God and human. He never took off the human nature he took on; he did not revert to being "merely" God upon his Ascension. Jesus is Lord of the universe and head of his body, the church, but he is also our human brother. On this St. Paul writes,

> For those who are led by the Spirit of God are children of God. For you did not receive a spirit of slavery to fall back into fear, but you received a spirit of adoption, through which we cry "*Abba,* Father!" The Spirit itself bears witness with our spirit that we are children of God, and if children, then heirs, heirs of God and joint heirs with Christ, if only we suffer with him so that we may also be glorified with him. (Rom. 8:14-17)

John the Baptist began a ministry in which he preached repentance. He always acknowledged that his role was only preparatory. He claimed that "one mightier than I is coming after me" and that "I have baptized you with water; he will baptize you with the Holy Spirit" (Mark 1:7-8). Early in the apostles' ministry, some Christians were discovered who had never received a baptism other than the baptism of John (Acts 19:1-7). When this was discovered, they were baptized in the name of the Lord Jesus. Clearly it was thought that the baptism of Jesus was decisively different from the baptism of John.[8] How does the church understand that difference?

7. *CCC,* 1.
8. DH, 1614.

While John's baptism was merely a baptism of repentance, Catholics understand the sacrament of baptism instituted by Christ as the sacrament of regeneration. In Jesus' discourse with the Pharisee Nicodemus he notes that "no one can enter the kingdom of God without being born of water and Spirit" (John 3:5). In baptism we are born again; we become a new creation in Christ, and are adopted into the family of God. A rebirth requires a death, however. In baptism, the old self dies. Ancient Near Eastern societies like that of Israel were terrified of the destructive power of the sea. To be baptized is to descend into the death of Christ and yet to rise up out of it cleansed. Baptism clothes us in Christ (Gal. 3:27). To a Catholic there is no getting around the mystical character of the identification with Christ in baptism. We may fall away from the dignity of our baptism, but it grafts us onto Christ in an unrepeatable way. After baptism, we are sons and daughters of God even if we choose to fall away. By virtue of this identification, we also share in the ministry of Christ's kingdom, as well as in his offices of prophet and priest.[9] Although the ordained priesthood is different from the "common priesthood of the faithful," there is a sense in which all the faithful have a share in Christ's priesthood (see Rev. 1:6) and in that limited sense, Martin Luther was right that there is a priesthood of all believers.[10]

Baptism is not magic, but it is a divine grace and not merely a symbol. Through it, "all sins are forgiven, original sin, and all personal sins, as well as all punishment for sin."[11] The punishments for sin will be discussed in the next chapter, but the basic idea is that our sins carry with them unhealthy attachments to creatures, and baptism cleanses us even of this, though we still struggle to keep ourselves from sin even after baptism.[12] Because of the astonishing grace available in the sacrament of baptism, many early Christians waited too long for their own baptism because they hoped to have its grace somewhat closer to their death. This included the emperor Constantine, who died in 337, just after his baptism. His motives remain controversial.

Regardless of Constantine's case, was it wrong of many in the early church to postpone baptism? Surely it is not right to postpone baptism merely to get a profligate life out of your system. Nevertheless, baptism's validity does not depend on one's holiness. God wills for all to be saved and

9. See Vatican II, *Lumen Gentium*, 9-13.
10. See Luther, *The Babylonian Captivity of the Church, LW* 36, p. 116.
11. *CCC*, 1263.
12. See *CCC*, 1426 and 1472-73.

even those who have committed serious ("mortal") sins are welcomed at the baptismal font. Sin does not impede the sacrament, nor does it deprive it of its grace. However, if one is merely using baptism as a "get out of jail free card" and has no intention of changing one's sinful way of life, it will not work. Susan K. Wood writes, "Unrepented mortal sin is an impediment to the grace of the sacrament, but not to the sacrament itself."[13] The unrepentant Mafia boss will not need to be rebaptized, but he will need to repent, should he hope to be welcomed into God's heavenly kingdom. This suggests that baptism, in order to be properly received, requires repentance and faith. This is true, though rebaptism is not required even if both are absent, and when both are present, the faith required is not a "perfect and mature faith" but the beginning of faith, a faith that may well cry both to the Lord and to his church, "I do believe; help my unbelief!" (Mark 9:24).[14]

What then about infants who cannot manifest even the beginnings of personal faith? The Catholic Church, along with the majority of Christian traditions, maintains that infant baptism is permitted and encouraged. In such cases, the faith of the church substitutes for the infant's personal faith. In the Baptist tradition, infant baptism is rejected as illegitimate; thus Baptist theologian Paul E. Robertson writes that "the issue is not one of rebaptism but of one's legitimate baptism, which is to be a believer's baptism by immersion."[15] From the Churches of Christ denomination, John D. Castelein dismisses the idea that infant baptism is a witness to the priority of God's grace because he insists that when we were still sinners (Rom. 5:6) Christ died for us, not baptized us. Castelein even goes so far as to suggest that infant baptism is the main reason why Western Europe is deserting Christianity.[16]

How shall we resolve this dispute? The issues are biblical and theological. It is often noted that Scripture speaks in several places of whole households being baptized (Acts 16:15, 33), and there is nothing said to

13. Susan K. Wood, *One Baptism: Ecumenical Dimensions of the Doctrine of Baptism* (Collegeville, MN: Liturgical Press, 2009), p. 36.

14. *CCC*, 1123.

15. See Robertson's response to Jeffrey Gros in *Ancient Faith and American-born Churches*, ed. Ted A. Campbell, Ann K. Riggs, and Gilbert W. Stafford (New York: Paulist Press, 2006), pp. 199-204, at p. 202.

16. John D. Castelein, "Christian Churches/Churches of Christ View," in *Understanding Four Views on Baptism*, ed. John H. Armstrong (Grand Rapids: Zondervan, 2007), pp. 129-44, at p. 138.

exclude children. Given the fairly early testimony about infant baptism in the centuries that follow, it is surprising that the church would have gone astray in its understanding of so fundamental a sacrament so quickly, especially since Christian initiation was a much more guarded business than it is in our day. The evidence from Scripture that baptism incorporates one into the church is strong. St. Paul writes that "in one Spirit we were all baptized into one body," which of course is Christ's body, the church (1 Cor. 12:13). The evidence is also strong that baptism is tied to salvation (John 3:5). This grounds the early understanding of the Church Fathers that outside the church there is no salvation, though we discussed how the contemporary church understands that claim in the introduction to this book. Thus, in baptism, we find the work of God for our salvation. As Lutheran scholar Martin E. Marty explains, "If baptism is part of what God does, not of what man does . . . then the priority does not fall on what man consciously brings."[17] Adults do ask for baptism, and only living individuals can be incorporated anew into the family of God, but the work is primarily God's. If this is so, why wouldn't infants be eligible for it?

A Catholic understanding of grace is a sacramental understanding of grace. This does not mean that God can offer grace only inside a sacramental context, but it does mean that the sacramental context is the ordinary context God chose for doing so. The Scriptures seem to attest to this view. If baptism is for incorporation into Christ's body, it is difficult to understand Jesus' own claim that the kingdom of heaven belongs to little children (Matt. 19:14) if they are not included in his body. Doubtless these brief remarks will not serve to convince anyone who rejects infant baptism, but in any case the point here is not to persuade but to explain why the Catholic Church holds what it does.

Through baptism a person becomes a branch on the vine that is Jesus (John 15:5). We must remain on the vine or wither and die, but a branch we are after baptism. This is why baptism cannot be repeated. How, then, does one baptize in such a way as to be unrepeatable? What do you have to *do*? For one thing, the ordinary minister is a bishop, priest, or deacon. However, in a case of emergency, anyone can baptize, even a non-Christian. The (ordained or lay) minister must use the required formula and have the intention of doing what the church does in baptism. The formula, as we discussed in chapter 3, is according to Jesus' own mandate. Baptism must be administered in the name of the Father, and of the Son, and of the

17. See Martin E. Marty, *Baptism* (Philadelphia: Fortress Press, 1977), p. 24.

Holy Spirit (Matt. 28:19).[18] This formula was understood to be required already by Tertullian (d. 225), the first Church Father to write a treatise on baptism.[19] According to the Catholic Church, in addition to the right form, or formula, which includes the invocation of the Holy Trinity, the right matter, the right intention of the minister, and the right disposition of the recipient are also required.[20] Right matter requires water, but the Catholic Church has not said exactly how much water is to be used. Many Catholic parishes choose to immerse catechumens three times or pour water over their heads three times. As a rule, one gets pretty wet. This is the sacramental way in which God adopts us as his own.

Any baptism in which the matter (water), form (Trinitarian invocation), intention (of doing what the church does), and disposition of the recipient (to join Christ's church) are intact is a valid baptism, one that will not need to be repeated. If there is genuine doubt about the validity of the baptism, then a conditional baptism may be administered, which is a baptism offered in case the earlier one was not valid.[21] However, the idea that one must first check on the holiness of the minister before declaring a baptism valid is a heresy known as Donatism. Donatism originally sprang up as a schismatic group that broke off from the Catholic Church because one of the celebrants of a sacrament of ordination in North Africa had succumbed to persecution by surrendering the Scriptures. The Donatists objected to this and declared the ordination invalid. The schism lasted some years and eventually some Christians received their only baptism in that sect. When these people asked to join the Catholic Church from which the Donatists separated, what was the church to do? Thanks in large part to the work of St. Augustine, it was decided that there would be no rebaptism because the true agent at work in the sacrament is Christ himself, even if he chooses to work through an unworthy (or schismatic) human minister.

Given this precedent, why did the church decide, in 2001, that the baptisms of Latter-day Saints (LDS), or Mormons, are not valid?[22] After

18. *CCC*, 1240.

19. Tertullian, *On Baptism*, 13, in *Tertullian's Homily on Baptism*, trans. Ernest Evans (London: SPCK, 1964), p. 31.

20. See Fr. Luis Ladaria, SJ, "The Question of the Validity of Baptism Conferred in *The Church of Jesus Christ of Latter-Day Saints*," *L'Osservatore Romano*, weekly edition in English, 1 August 2001, p. 5.

21. *CCL*, 869, §1.

22. See Congregation for the Doctrine of Faith, "Response to a 'Dubium' on the validity of baptism conferred by *The Church of Jesus Christ of Latter-day Saints* called *Mormons*."

all, they too are administered using a Trinitarian invocation. The trouble the Congregation for the Doctrine of Faith emphasized is that the Trinitarian formula used by the LDS community seems to refer to something quite different from the Trinity to which the Catholic Church means to refer. For instance, the *Doctrines and Covenants,* an LDS scripture, notes that "the Father has a body of flesh and bones as tangible as man's."[23] The same text seems to claim that Jesus was not God until he received of the fullness of divinity.[24] Even the Father was once mortal and not divine, according to their view.[25] Recent efforts have been made by LDS thinkers to claim that their view of the Trinity should be seen within the Christian tradition. Notwithstanding these efforts, the Catholic Church came to the conclusion that "[t]he teaching of the Mormons has a completely different matrix."[26] The LDS community regards its baptism as originating with Adam's baptism by God,[27] something completely foreign to the Catholic Scriptures, and this seems to create a very different sacramental context. To me, the view that the Mormon minister intends to do something different from what the Catholic Church intends to do seems justified.

Confession

When I was on a path to becoming a Catholic, my baptism in the Reformed Church in America was accepted without any problem. Nevertheless, I experienced my journey to the Catholic Church as a deeper incorporation into Christ's body and God's family. As I said in the introduction to this book, this is not to say that I "found" Jesus anew, but it is to say that I found a context where my faith could flourish when I had been struggling to do so elsewhere. I was never particularly rebellious as a child, but I experienced parts of this journey in ways similar to how the Prodigal Son might have experienced his return to his family from a period of wandering (Luke 15:11-32). This is an important story for understanding the sacrament of

23. *Doctrines and Covenants,* 130:22 at http://www.lds.org/scriptures/dc-testament/dc?lang=eng. Accessed 14 July 2014.

24. *Doctrines and Covenants,* 93:12.

25. See Blake Ostler, *Exploring Mormon Thought: The Attributes of God* (Salt Lake City: Greg Kofford Books, 2001), p. 80.

26. See Ladaria, "The Question of the Validity of Baptism."

27. See *The Pearl of Great Price*'s Moses 6:64-65 at http://www.lds.org/scriptures/pgp?lang=eng. Accessed 14 July 2014.

penance, reconciliation, or more commonly, "confession." The Prodigal Son was a part of the father's family, and even though he had deserted his family, he was immediately greeted not as a worker but as a member of the family when he returned. One is already a member of the family in the confessional, even if one has wandered since baptism.

People often bristle at the idea of confessing one's sins to a priest. Why not just be sorry by yourself, or perhaps say that you are sorry to the person you wronged? Maybe you have such a sense of the Christian community that you even find it worthwhile to confess various sins to another member of that community, but why does it have to be a priest? After all, Martin Luther thought confession was very valuable, but thought that any Christian had the ability to hear another's confession.[28] Why do Catholics make such a fuss about confessing one's sins to a priest?

To answer this, we need to talk about church history for a bit. As we've noticed throughout this book, doctrines of the Catholic Church do not come pre-packaged in the Bible. They require theological development over centuries. Confession is perhaps the clearest example. It is now often called the sacrament of reconciliation, but early on in the church's history it was a vexing question whether someone who committed an especially serious sin after baptism could even be reconciled. To begin with, there are important passages in Scripture that suggest something like confession. The apostles were commissioned to go and preach the Gospel, and when they were, they were told, "[w]hose sins you forgive are forgiven them, and whose sins you retain are retained" (John 20:23). *The Didache,* an early Christian text possibly from the late first century, implores Christians to confess their faults,[29] and St. Clement's letter to the Corinthians in the year 96 exhorts its readers to "pray now make submission to the clergy. Bend the knees of your hearts and accept correction."[30] This does not mean that one should not be repentant to God, or that the clergy are the source of forgiveness. As the *Catechism* makes clear, ultimately only God forgives sins.[31]

Nor was this sacrament as formalized in the early centuries as it has become now. In the introduction to this book, we mentioned the time of the middle third century, when the Christian church was still a minority everywhere in the western world, but it had a stronger presence in North

---

28. Luther, *Babylonian Captivity of the Church, LW* 36, p. 88.

29. *The Didache,* 4, p. 193.

30. Clement, *1 Corinthians,* 57, in *Early Christian Writings,* trans. Maxwell Staniforth, revised and edited by Andrew Louth (London: Penguin, 1987), p. 46.

31. *CCC,* 1441.

Africa. One of the most important sees was in Carthage, and its bishop was the newly elected Cyprian (later to become a saint). In the year 249, the Roman emperor Decius decided that he would require everyone to offer a sacrifice to the Roman gods, in an effort to secure their blessings for his rule. Christianity, which was still regarded as a pesky upstart religion by the Romans, was hardly going to allow its adherents to sacrifice to idols. But of course many Christians did sacrifice. There were other Christians who suffered torture and death, though, and there were many people in between these extremes. Some of those who sacrificed did so to protect the rest of their families. Some only offered incense, thinking that it was worse to sacrifice. Some were led by their own bishop to offer sacrifices. Some of the wealthier Christians purchased certificates (or bribed officials to obtain them) that said that they had sacrificed to protect themselves, even though they never did. Indeed, some of these wealthier Christians may not have fully understood the nature of the certificate. Moreover, some Christians sacrificed but publicly denounced their earlier decision before the Romans, and suffered for this.[32]

Trying to figure out what to do about the various forms of disobedience was a very difficult problem for Cyprian. It wasn't a question of simply asking whether those who succumbed to persecution were sorry. It was also a question of how to reintegrate them into the life of the church. Some argued that there could be no return to the church after such a fall; some argued that a return to the church could be had on the cheap. Cyprian aimed for a middle course. What would it say if someone who rushed off to sacrifice to the Roman gods was knowingly allowed to rejoin the church alongside those who had been mocked, beaten, tortured, and perhaps ultimately killed in faithfulness to Christ's commands without even so much as a question about their loyalties? Instead, it was decided that someone had to speak for God's church, and had to decide when these people could be allowed to rejoin the church in Communion. Cyprian, with the rest of the church, asked that the sinner do what is called penance.

In the early church, penance could often be public, difficult, and would occur before one could fully reenter the sacramental life of the church. Although the practice of penance has evolved in the church over the centuries, in the contemporary Catholic Church, the penance is given

---

32. See Cyprian, *The Lapsed,* in *The Lapsed and On the Unity of the Catholic Church* (both works in one volume), trans. and ed. Maurice Bévenot (New York: Newman Press, 1956) (*Ancient Christian Writers,* vol. 25).

after the priest absolves the penitent of her sin. Pope St. John Paul II makes it clear that penance is not payment for sin.[33] Penance is, however, a way of instilling within one's heart the proper habits of a Christian. Nowadays, in more ordinary cases of penance, one is asked to say a few prayers while meditating on a particular Christian truth, or to read a particular Scripture while meditating. The church does not ask for public penance anymore, but when sins are particularly grievous, the priest may rightfully ask the sinner to admit his or her guilt to the parties he or she injured, or, in especially serious cases, "turn himself in" to the local authorities. Still, the priest must observe the "seal" of confession and cannot tell anyone what sins have been confessed for any reason at all.[34] Penance following sacramental confession is also a way of healing the "wound of sin" that each of us experiences when we prefer merely earthly goods to God.[35] We will discuss this more in connection with purgatory in the next chapter.

There are basically four parts to the sacrament of reconciliation, namely, contrition, confession, satisfaction, and the absolution by the priest. We've already discussed satisfaction, which is also called penance. Let us discuss contrition. The reconciliation this sacrament brings is not magic; you have to be truly sorry for your sin to be absolved. This requires that you hate your sin and resolve to sin no more.[36] One needs to prepare for one's confession by what is known as an examination of conscience. This should be done by considering one's sins in the light of Scripture. In the process, one should grieve over one's sins and wish to repent of them. Obviously, it is best to be sorry for a wrong committed against a person because you love her or him and wish to be reconciled. When you confess your sins because you love God in this way, it is what is called "perfect contrition." That doesn't mean that your love is already as intense as it could be, but it means that you have the best reason to be sorry. The church also recognizes that some might confess because they are afraid of hell, or for other less-than-ideal reasons. This is called "imperfect contrition" or "attrition."[37] In the 1999 movie *The Mummy,* the character Beni is being approached by the titular resurrected mummy intent on killing him. Beni is afraid, but not very devout. He pulls out a cross necklace to pray to the Christian God, a Buddhist statue to pray to the Buddha, and a Star of David

33. St. John Paul, *Reconciliatio et Paenitentia,* 31.
34. *CCL,* 983, §1.
35. See St. John Paul, *Reconciliatio et Paenitentia,* 31.
36. DH, 1673 and 1676.
37. *CCC,* 1453.

to pray as a faithful Jew might, but he isn't a faithful Christian, Buddhist, or Jew. This is not the situation of imperfect contrition. One who is imperfectly contrite does not confess on the *off chance* that hell awaits her. She faithfully *believes* that hell awaits the unrepentant sinner and so she confesses. Luther found the acceptance of attrition unacceptable because he considered it a fraud.[38] Yet I find it very comforting. The fear of the Lord is the beginning of wisdom, and the fact that I might have been led by the Holy Spirit to fear the right sort of thing (hell) seems a step in the right direction, and Catholics believe the sacrament can perfect this attrition.[39] Attrition is not a halfway house, but a gift from God. If one isn't minimally sorry, one is simply in the wrong place. But attrition is real sorrow for motives that need perfecting. Similarly, if you're unwilling to address the wrong you've committed, then you're not really sorry in the first place.

But what actually happens in the confessional? After being welcomed to the sacrament by the priest, the penitent usually begins by noting how long it has been since his or her last confession. Then he or she proceeds to indicate what sins his or her prayers and examination of conscience have revealed. Some sins are more serious than others, and the Catholic tradition holds to a distinction between mortal and venial sins, which we will discuss briefly below. Apart from extraordinary circumstances, it is required to confess any serious sins of which a person is conscious in the sacrament of reconciliation. The church requires that this be done at least once a year, though more frequent confession is helpful and highly recommended. One can also confess less serious sins and doing so can be very helpful. One should not hold anything back. Personally, I've never had a bad experience in the confessional. Most priests are wonderful, prayerful men who deeply want to help and who confess their sins regularly as well. Once one has given one's confession, the priest will require an act of contrition. There are several one might use, but I like this one:

> O my God,
> I am heartily sorry for having offended you,
> and I detest all my sins,
> because I dread the loss of heaven
> and the pains of hell;
> but most of all because they offend you, my God,

38. Luther, *Babylonian Captivity, LW* 36, p. 84.
39. St. John Paul, *Reconciliatio et Paenitentia*, 31.

who are all good and deserving of all my love.
I firmly resolve, with the help of your grace,
to confess my sins, to do penance,
and to amend my life. Amen.[40]

The priest then grants absolution by using a formula that explains his sacramental work in the light of the ministry of the church, the Holy Spirit, the reconciling ministry of Jesus' life and death, and God the Father's love and mercy.[41]

We noted that only God can forgive sins, but here we have a priest absolving a person of her sins. How is this possible? One thing to note is that this, as in many other things, is an example of what Alan Schreck calls the "incarnational principle" of Catholicism.[42] God is the principal actor, but God uses human people and even things to accomplish his purpose. As he does in all the sacraments, the priest acts *in persona Christi,* or in the person of Christ, in this sacrament. The priest does not merely pray for absolution; he *gives* it, in the person of Christ, to the penitent.[43] This sacrament is for reconciliation to Christ's body. It is not a rebaptism, but it is giving life anew to a dying branch on the vine of Christ. It is remarkable that Jesus told his disciples that when they forgave someone, that person's sins were truly forgiven (John 20:23), but so he did, and it is Jesus, in his reconciling ministry, who ultimately forgives sins. Priests are called to participate, in a radical and mystical way, in this ministry, and that is what the sacrament of reconciliation offers us. This is why we confess to priests.

We still need to say something about the distinction between venial and mortal sins. As we continue to point out, not everything that Catholics believe is to be found *explicitly* in Scripture. However, the things that Catholics believe have some kind of "seed" in Scripture. This kind of seed is just like any other kind of seed; you water it, feed it, give it ample sunshine, and it will eventually grow into a full-fledged flower. In the case of Catholic doctrines, you will usually find something similar to be true of their origin in the Bible and subsequent reflection on it. A little precious morsel of testimony in the Scriptures is all a doctrine needs, with careful

40. James Socias, ed., *Daily Roman Missal* (Chicago: Midwest Theological Forum and United States Conference of Catholic Bishops, 2004), p. 2253.
41. *CCC,* 1449.
42. See Alan Schreck, *Catholic and Christian* (Cincinnati: St. Anthony Messenger Press, 2004), p. 7.
43. See St. John Paul, *Reconciliatio et Paenitentia,* 29, and *ST,* III.84.3.

and painstaking reflection, to develop into a doctrine of the church herself. The distinction between venial and mortal sins developed along such lines.

The seed is to be found in 1 John 5:16-17, which reads, "If anyone sees his brother sinning, if the sin is not deadly, he should pray to God and he will give him life. This is only for those whose sin is not deadly. There is such a thing as deadly sin, about which I do not say that you should pray. All wrongdoing is sin, but there is sin that is not deadly." Although the original meaning of this passage is subject to some dispute,[44] the church herself took time to discern the divisions within sin. What cannot be denied is that a distinction is being made between sins. First, there is such a thing as deadly sin, and second, there is such a thing as sin that is not deadly. What that division amounted to would take time to discern precisely. It would seem obvious that deadly sin is worse, in some sense, than sin that isn't. So what could that mean?

The Catholic Church interprets this passage as the kind of "seed" that later gave rise to the distinction between mortal (deadly) and venial (less serious) sin. The basic idea is actually pretty simple. Sin is the prideful desire to separate one's self from God and to live according to one's own lights and one's own desires. Sin is thus the desire to wound and the action of wounding one's relationship with God. Some actions, like an intentional physical attack, disrupt a friendship so completely that a radical reconciliation is needed. But not every act is like this.

Married people often get frustrated with their spouses, and sometimes we say things that we know we shouldn't. Sometimes it is as simple as saying something that didn't need to be said. For example, suppose that a married couple is driving along on a busy highway and listening to one of the passenger's favorite songs. As it happens, they miss an important exit, and have to take a detour that makes them late for an event. The driver, let us say, is often frustrated by lateness, and blurts out, "We wouldn't have been late if you hadn't been so engrossed in your song" to his wife. His snap hurts his wife and wounds their relationship. The driver needs to think a bit more here. It may well have been the case that, if his wife had not been so engrossed in the song, she may have alerted him to the exit. But he is the one doing the driving, and should also be paying attention to the road. In any case, anger won't accomplish anything, and there is no need to lay the blame at the feet of his wife. Suppose that the couple

---

44. See Raymond E. Brown, *The Epistles of John* (Garden City, NY: Doubleday, 1982), pp. 615-17.

is dancing later on that evening (perhaps it was a wedding reception that they were late for) and the husband is generous and kind to his wife during this time. Perhaps he later apologizes for his earlier snap. Or, perhaps they ultimately both forget about it, as they enjoy their time together that evening, and the husband, if he ever thinks of it again, is sorry for the snap. This is an example of a crack in a relationship that is less radical and that can be repaired with grace and love. It may also be a fitting (albeit fictional) example of a venial sin.

The church believes that it is very difficult to stay clear of these kinds of venial sins for very long.[45] Venial sins are the kinds of sins that *wound* the relationship between God and the human being, but they don't *destroy* the relationship. The thing to do is to be sorry and move on. It is highly appropriate to clearly apologize, but the relationship doesn't always mend because of an explicit apology, or, in the case of a Catholic, in the case of an explicit trip to the confessional. That's why venial sins are very appropriate to confess before a priest in a confessional, but failing to do so or remember one or another venial sin does not deprive one of reconciliation. Interestingly, one might also apply this to sacramentals like holy water, which, as we said in the beginning of this chapter, dispose a person to receive grace in the sacraments. If the wife in our example is especially caring and kind, lovingly finding a way to urge the husband out of his tendency to sulk or dwell on his lapse, her action can be like God's love reaching out for us to bring us to full reconciliation in the sacraments. The snap the husband made above wounded his relationship with his wife. Yet she loved him before he sought reconciliation and urged him to seek it. This parallels our sacramental context nicely.

Mortal sins are quite different from venial sins. God is still seeking us, as God always is, but when we sin in a mortal or serious way, we damage a relationship so severely that it cannot be passed over; it must be confronted and dealt with in a resolute way by both parties. This is why the *Catechism* tells us that mortal sin necessitates an entirely new initiative of God's grace to restore the relationship. There are three conditions any sin has to meet to become a mortal sin. They are listed below:

1. The sin must be a very serious matter — not simply a brief snap at one's wife in an otherwise harmonious relationship.
2. The sin must be committed when one possesses full knowledge of

45. *CCC*, 1863.

its seriousness, and the decisive rift it would cause in one's relationship to God. The *Catechism* makes it clear that if we do possess this
knowledge and convince ourselves that we do not, that makes it
more rather than less serious.

3. The sin must be committed with deliberate consent, which means
   that, whatever other pressure might be exerted upon a person to
   commit the sin, there is at least a decisive moment when the participation in the sin is up to the person, and thus constitutes a free
   choice.[46]

Mortal sins are classically the kinds of sins that are so decisive that they
can determine one's eternal destiny if one does not repent of them before
death. However, the church is not interested in consigning people to eternal torment, and she does not claim to be able to search out each sinner's
heart so that it is clear whether or not a particular sin met all three conditions and was mortal or not. To do that is ultimately the job of the sinner
and God, though it is especially fitting to discuss this kind of thing with
one's priest in the confessional, and even better to have a regular priest,
usually called a confessor, with whom one meets and who knows the person's habits and the things with which the sinner particularly struggles.
Sacramental confession communicates life-giving grace to us when we
fall away and renews us with grace to remain in Christ. It is a visible and
tangible way to experience the forgiveness that we know God offers us.

Confirmation

The next sacrament we will discuss briefly is the sacrament of confirmation. The Catholic Church herself holds many rites within her, and some
of the liturgical traditions in them vary. In the Latin rite of the Catholic
Church (which is by far the largest and is likely to be the one with which
most readers of this book are familiar) this sacrament is administered to
a baptized Christian whose baptismal grace is thereby confirmed and
strengthened. In Eastern Catholic churches this sacrament is administered
along with baptism. The development of the sacrament took place over
centuries and with some variance in its practice across the different traditions within the Catholic Church. But the origin of the sacrament itself is

---

46. *CCC,* 1856-60.

in the laying on of hands to impart the gift of the Holy Spirit.[47] Later, the anointing with chrism oil by the bishop, or at least blessed by the bishop, and administered by a priest, was added to the practice. This has the effect of linking the mature Christian to Christ, whose name means "anointed one." Luther rejected this as a sacrament, since he thought its institution by Christ was not attested well enough by Scripture.[48] So let us begin by discussing its scriptural foundation.

What confirmation does is increase the gift of the Holy Spirit. This had been foretold even in the Old Testament in passages that seem to be talking about the time of the Messiah (e.g., Joel 3:1). If we look for a time when the apostolic community received the gift of the Holy Spirit in Scripture, it is not difficult to find: it occurs at Pentecost in the second chapter of Acts. What appeared to be tongues of fire came to rest on each of those present and they received the Holy Spirit. Though Jesus had ascended into heaven at this point, he had promised this gift to them. St. Thomas Aquinas writes, "We must say that Christ instituted this sacrament not by bestowing but by promising it."[49] Thus, Jesus told the apostles, "I tell you the truth, it is better for you that I go. For if I do not go, the Advocate will not come to you. But if I go, I will send him to you" (John 16:7). After that time, the apostles treat the reception of the Holy Spirit as a distinct event to follow baptism, as when Peter and John go to the new believers in Samaria who had as yet only been baptized and pray that they might receive the Holy Spirit. This happens through the laying on of hands (Acts 8:14-17). St. Cyprian, in commenting on this passage, clearly connects this passage to the practice of the church less than 200 years later, noting that by the imposition of hands, baptized Christians receive the Holy Spirit and are "perfected."[50]

Of course, confirmation does not make people perfect so much as it perfects or completes the grace of baptism by which they were incorporated into the church. Catholics understand the Christian life as fundamentally sacramental, and they understand grace to be communicated through sacraments. There are many ways in which we experience grace, but the special graces of the sacraments empower us not just to live the Christian

47. *CCC,* 1288.

48. Luther, *Babylonian Captivity, LW* 36, p. 91.

49. *ST,* III.72.1, reply to objection 1.

50. See Cyprian, Letter 73.9.2 in *The Letters of St. Cyprian of Carthage,* vols. 1-4, trans. and annotated G. W. Clarke (New York: Newman Press, 1984-89) (*Ancient Christian Writers,* vols. 43, 44, 46, and 47), vol. 4, p. 59.

life but to do so boldly. In this respect it is no accident that the apostolic community "went public" after Pentecost. Until that time, the community was quiet and small, but after Pentecost, the apostles began to proclaim the Gospel to the world. Christianity is also a religion that is indelibly formed by its early experience of persecution. Confirmation is said to give "special strength" to enable Christians to confess Christ boldly and "never to be ashamed of the Cross."[51] It is true that with more strength comes a greater obligation to serve God's church, and the choice to be confirmed should be prayerfully considered. Even with this grace, however, we know that Christians will always choose whether to fall away or to stand firm in the faith, but this sacrament is a permanent act of grace that binds us more firmly to Christ, who always calls us back even after our failures.

The Most Holy Eucharist

The "source and summit of the Christian life"[52] is a fitting description for the Eucharist, the centerpiece of our discussion in this chapter. This sacrament is the high point of the church's liturgy and the wedding feast of the Lamb. As the angel in Revelation says to the apostle John, "Blessed are those who have been called to the wedding feast of the Lamb" (Rev. 19:9). In offering the newly consecrated Eucharist to worshipers present, the priest says, "Blessed are those called to the supper of the Lamb." The convergence between the two is not an accident. I know of no decision by the church as to whether we eat earthly food in heaven, but Aquinas tells us that we do not.[53] If it should turn out that Aquinas is right, it would be fitting. Vatican II tells us that even now, by nourishing us through his body and blood in the Eucharist, Christ makes us to share in his glorious life. Thus the world's ultimate restoration, and ours, has already begun.[54] In that ultimate restoration, we will have no need of lamp or sun, for the Lord will be our light (Rev. 22:5). Just so, Jesus is the bread of life, and we who come to him will never hunger (John 6:35). In the Eucharist, Jesus gives us his body and blood as a real participation in the heavenly banquet, even though for us right now it is only temporary.

51. *CCC*, 1303.
52. Vatican II, *Lumen Gentium*, 11.
53. St. Thomas Aquinas, *Compendium Theologiae*, I.1.156 (see *Aquinas's Shorter Summa*, trans. Cyril Vollert, SJ (Manchester, NH: Sophia Institute Press, 2002), p. 177.
54. Vatican II, *Lumen Gentium*, 48.

Every Christian community has some version of this sacrament simply because the Lord's command to do it in remembrance of him is so clear. Indeed, the institution of the Lord's Supper is in every Gospel except John, where Jesus' "bread of life" discourse (John 6:22-59) is so prominent that it's hard to lose sight of the Lord's Supper anyway. In that discourse, Jesus assures his listeners that they must eat his flesh and drink his blood, for those who do, remain in him and this is the way to have life. At that point, Jesus asks his listeners if this is shocking to them. We know that some did find it shocking, since some left him because of this teaching (John 6:66). Jesus said that he eagerly desired to eat the Passover, the feast of unleavened bread, with his disciples (Luke 22:15), and at that feast, he blessed bread and told his disciples "this is my body" and of the cup, some version of "this is my blood of the covenant" or "this cup is the new covenant in my blood" (Matt. 26:26-28; Mark 14:22-24; Luke 22:19-20; 1 Cor. 11:24-25). Given early Christian history, it seems unlikely that this was just a metaphor. The biblical text confirms Jesus' seriousness and St. Ignatius of Antioch, among other ancient figures, gives a ringing condemnation of people leaving the Christian community "because they will not admit that the Eucharist is the self-same body of our Saviour Jesus Christ."[55]

Catholics believe that the Eucharist is, in fact, just that. This is an astonishing claim. How could bread and wine be transformed into something quite different even while it looks, tastes, feels, smells, and sounds exactly the same? Catholics will insist that this is a mystery, and it is. But we should recall that something's being a mystery does not mean it is allowed to be nonsense. In the same way, while the Eucharist is a mystery, and it cannot be proven true using methods in the natural sciences, it nevertheless is something that can be partially understood. The idea is not to explain away a mystery; it is simply to say enough about what happens so that the believer knows why the Eucharist matters for her spiritual life, which includes freeing us of the doubt about whether it is even coherent. One of the first key mysteries of the Eucharist is how Christ is present in it.

Let me attempt this partial explanation. Suppose that we are studying tadpoles in a laboratory and want to keep track of the rate of their growth into adult frogs. To be sure of which one grows at which rate, we mark each tadpole and give it a name, so that we can distinguish it from the others. Suppose we call one of our tadpoles "Tony." Tony grows at a normal rate and soon enough becomes an adult frog. When this happens, his features

---

55. Ignatius of Antioch, *Epistle to the Smyrneans*, 7, in *Early Christian Writings*, p. 102.

are almost entirely different. He walks on legs, rather than swimming with his tail. The color of his skin is different. His face has changed completely. He no longer has gills. The marvelous thing, however, is that he is still Tony. He still has the same identifying mark and his name has remained the same throughout his short life. If you will, he is the same "substance," despite that fact that these sensible features (we call these "accidents") have changed as he grew. This is a normal case of growth in nature. The accidents change, but the substance remains the same.

The Eucharist involves an extraordinary change that happens in exactly the opposite way. The church at the Council of Trent insisted on "that wonderful and unique change of the whole substance of the bread into his body and of the whole substance of the wine into his blood."[56] Catholics have often been taught to call this "transubstantiation." This is not simply a change from how we regard the sacrament, but a change in the sacrament itself. Aquinas was widely influential even to the present day in discussing how this might be possible.[57] He argued that the substance of the bread changes into the body of Christ, so that Christ is really present under the species (or accidents) of the bread. That is to say, the Eucharist, after it has been consecrated using Jesus' own words, looks like bread, but it really isn't anymore. It also smells like bread, tastes like bread, nourishes like bread, and all the rest. But it is not bread any longer. What has changed are the substances of bread and wine; the invisible anchors of reality in the things themselves have changed so that they are now really Christ, who, though he is in heaven, communes with us substantially and entirely in a mysterious way through the Eucharist. In this way, the Eucharist brings us substantially as close to Christ as we can be in this life. We ingest the body of Christ under the appearance of bread and wine, but Christ is the stronger one; it is not so much that Christ enters us, but that we enter Christ and are grafted more and more onto his mystical body.[58]

If we were to say that this "transubstantiation" occurred in Tony, we would be forced to say that the individual frog had changed, but the appearance of Tony remained. This suggests that Tony's soul changed, but his body remains the same. The problem with this statement is that it misunderstands the nature of the soul. Souls are not like shadows that fall in and

56. DH, 1652.

57. *ST,* III, Questions 73-83.

58. See Joseph Cardinal Ratzinger (Pope Benedict XVI), "The Presence of the Lord in the Sacrament," in *God Is Near Us,* ed. Stephan Otto Horn and Vinzenz Pfnür, trans. Henry Taylor (San Francisco: Ignatius Press, 2003), p. 78.

out of bodies as they do sometimes in Hollywood movies. Souls, in living organisms, actually make the individuals be what they are. If Tony's soul switched with the soul of another tadpole, the accidents of Tony would *not* remain, because the new soul would really change the appearance of Tony. In a similar way, if the accidental features of the bread remained united to the substance into which the bread was changed, we would have to say that Christ, in his glorified heavenly existence "looks like bread" or that Jesus is approximately an inch in diameter. None of these things are true.

The accidents do, however, continue to behave as they would in any other substance by God's miraculous power. When we take the body and blood of Christ, the whole Christ is present under the sacramental accidents or "species" because the substance of Christ's living body and Christ's living blood is what is truly present. Communion is not a different part of Christ in Singapore than it is in Stockholm or Sacramento. Substance is not about place. Place, too, is an accident, and Jesus' body is *located* in heaven. But the substance of Christ's body is present under the accidents of the bread and wine, which remain.

The sacramental species of wine still have the ability to intoxicate a person. The sacramental species of the bread still nourish a person. But Jesus' body does not look, taste, feel, smell, or sound the way that bread does. That is why the church says that the accidents of bread, while they remain present to us, are not united to the body of Christ in the way that Tony's skin color is united to him. The accidents remain in existence, signifying to us something clear and definite that we can see and partake of, while the real substance is Christ's body. The accidents, Aquinas says, remain without a subject simply through God's power.[59]

Catholics believe that they eat and drink the body and blood of the Lord, but they are not being cannibals in doing so. Christ's body is not present in the same way that my body is present when another interacts with me. In ordinary encounters my substance and accidents are present. But in the Eucharist Christ is present in the mode of substance, even though his accidental features (hair color, eye color, size, and so on) remain in heaven. One might object that this "substance" is very strange. After all, don't we know that reality is constituted by atoms and subatomic particles

---

59. *ST,* III.77.1. See also the United States Conference of Catholic Bishops' document, "The Real Presence of Jesus Christ in the Sacrament of the Eucharist: Basic Questions and Answers," question 3, at http://www.usccb.org/prayer-and-worship/the-mass/frequently -asked-questions/the-real-presence-of-jesus-christ-in-the-sacrament-of-the-eucharist-basic -questions-and-answers.cfm. Accessed 14 July 2014.

and so on? Well, yes, reality is constituted by those things, but even of those things we can ask, why are they those things rather than some other things? Let me explain.

We now know that the atom has subatomic particles, such as protons, neutrons, and electrons. We also know that subatomic particles are composed of still smaller particles. These smaller particles are of different types and have features that distinguish them one from another. Suppose you get all the way down to a quark. No matter how far down you go, even to the smallest particle we can measure, there is still something about that thing that could have been different. Sure, that difference might have a big impact, but it could still have been different. All that means is that even the smallest particles have accidents. They could spin in different ways than they do or have other qualities than they have. Again, that means that there is still something that changes (the accident) and something that undergoes the change (the substance). The fact that larger things (like trees) are constituted by smaller things (like quarks) doesn't change the fact that what is true of larger things could just as easily have been different. Larger things, too, can have substances and accidents. The deeper reality of being is that each thing is what it is, even though it could have been some other way, and that fact will not be explained away by empirical science.[60] The substance is this deeper reality, and it changes in the Eucharistic consecration.

Just as things could have been different in creation, things could also have been different in the sacramental order. Jesus chose to use bread and wine as the matter for the Eucharist. When Jesus commands us to do "this" in his remembrance, there must be a "this" to do. It was not some generic meal that Jesus instituted but a particular meal with particular food that has come down to us. This is why non-wheat substitutes for bread are not considered valid matter for this sacrament.[61] Likewise, the priest must consecrate a chalice of real wine, not simply grape juice or some other beverage. In the early church, this also had practical consequences. An error known as "aquarianism" held that one could replace the wine with water. The reason one would want to do that is that the Mass was ordinarily

---

60. See Joseph Cardinal Ratzinger, *God Is Near Us,* p. 85.

61. See the Congregation for the Doctrine of Faith's *Circular Letter to all Presidents of the Episcopal Conferences concerning the use of low-gluten altar breads and mustum as matter for the celebration of the Eucharist* (24 July 2003) at http://www.vatican.va/roman_curia/ congregations/cfaith/documents/rc_con_cfaith_doc_20030724_pane-senza-glutine_en .html. Accessed 14 July 2014.

celebrated in the morning, and for one to have alcohol on one's breath that early in the morning would expose one to suspicion of being a Christian when being a Christian was a punishable offense.[62] The church has resisted this error, because just as Jesus' life, death, and resurrection as a first-century Jew raises the "scandal of particularity" so also does the Eucharist. The Eucharist cannot be replaced by tea and crumpets or anything else; whether in the United States, the Philippines, India, Japan, or even space, the Christian church celebrates this particular sacrament to remember her Lord, a particular man.

This man suffered, died, and rose again, and while the Eucharist is not just a memorial of Christ's passion and death, it is that too. The Catholic Church understands that the Eucharist is a sacrifice as well. The *Catechism* tells us "[t]he Eucharist is thus a sacrifice because it *re-presents* (makes present) the sacrifice of the cross, because it is its *memorial* and because it *applies* its fruit."[63] The church prays to the Father to send the Holy Spirit so that the Spirit may transform the bread and wine into the body and blood of Christ.[64] In offering Christ's real body and blood to God the Father, the church, as Christ's body, offers no more and no less than Christ's once-and-for-all sacrifice on the cross. In this connection it is interesting to note that in 2004, the Christian Reformed Church denomination voted to print its version of the 1563 *Heidelberg Catechism* to include brackets around several paragraphs that attack the Catholic Church's doctrine of the Eucharist in Question and Answer #80.[65] The bracketed text claims that the Mass is a denial of the uniqueness of Christ's sacrifice and is itself a "condemnable idolatry." Happily, this view is no longer binding on members of the Christian Reformed Church. Catholics hold to the uniqueness of Christ's sacrifice, but we also hold that we participate in it in a unique way every time Mass is celebrated.

The Eucharist, under the species of bread, can be transported and brought to those who are unable to come to Mass. This practice both confirms and is confirmed by the Eucharistic piety of the church. Consider that now many dioceses will broadcast a Mass so that anyone may watch it, especially those who cannot leave their homes, or cannot do so easily.

---

62. See Raymond Johanny, "Cyprian of Carthage," in *The Eucharist of the Early Christians,* trans. Matthew J. O'Connell (New York: Pueblo, 1978), pp. 156-82, at p. 160.

63. *CCC,* 1366.

64. *CCC,* 1353.

65. See http://www.crcna.org/welcome/beliefs/confessions/heidelberg-catechism. Accessed 14 July 2014.

Someone who faithfully watches Mass, or even someone who faithfully longs to attend, is partaking in an important way in the life of the church. Yet partaking of the Eucharist is itself a concrete manifestation of the mystical body of Christ, the church. Bringing the Eucharist to someone who is ill so that she may participate even more fully in the Eucharistic sacrifice is a compassionate and thoughtful way to express the unity of Christ's body. When the Eucharist is transported, it must be treated with the utmost care and respect. Why? It is because the Eucharist does not cease being the body of Christ simply because it is moved. If the Eucharistic sacrifice in which our faithful but homebound parishioner wishes to participate were to simply stop being the Eucharist when it left the building, then it would cease to be a participation in the life of the church. Traditional Lutherans often insist that the Eucharist must be reconsecrated when brought to a homebound parishioner.[66] To a Catholic this seems strange, since something definitive and permanent has already happened to the elements, namely, a substantial change. Because this is definitive and permanent, Catholics also not only treat the Eucharist with care but worship Jesus in it. Thus most parishes will set aside some of the Blessed Sacrament for adoration and there are even devotional liturgies associated with this practice.

Many other Christian groups object to this. In fact adoring Christ in the Blessed Sacrament is a touchstone for controversy with other Christian groups. It is an important devotional practice for Catholics, and the denial of this practice was definitively rejected by the Council of Trent.[67] There are real concerns here, since prior to the Protestant Reformation, it was very rare for Catholics to partake of the Eucharist itself even though they would adore it elsewhere. Since that time, adoration of Christ in the Blessed Sacrament has focused not just on worshiping Christ present in the sacrament, but desiring to be united to him in eating his body and drinking his blood in Holy Communion, and this is a worthy change. Nevertheless, Catholics rightly worry that the denial of adoration has effects for one's basic doctrine of Eucharistic presence. As Lutheran theologian Robert W. Jenson puts it, "Disagreement about what the elements are after the celebration does in fact turn out to unravel consensus about what they are during it."[68] Luther himself claimed that, just as Christ is both God

66. See Roland Ziegler, "Should Lutherans Reserve the Consecrated Elements for the Communion of the Sick?" *Concordia Theological Quarterly* 67 (2003): 131-47.

67. DH, 1656-57.

68. Robert W. Jenson, *Unbaptized God: The Basic Flaw in Ecumenical Theology* (Minneapolis: Fortress Press, 1992), p. 29.

and man, the Eucharist is both Christ's body and bread.[69] But if, as Luther claims, the Eucharist is both body and bread, then why can the one depart at the end of the liturgical celebration and not the other? It is easy to insist that the unity is tighter than that (as some Lutherans do), but harder to come up with an explanation for how it could be without appealing to something like transubstantiation. Certainly this is a mystery of faith, but for Christians, mystery cannot be nonsense, and so we must continue to consider what *could* be happening in this miraculous sacrament. A major stumbling block for dialogue across Christian traditions here is that Catholics deny that the Eucharist is really bread (or wine) any longer. But doing so may be necessary in order to understand the church's faith that a definitive change has occurred, one that makes it possible to administer the Eucharist to the sick, homebound, and even dying without reconsecrating the hosts. In 1995, the church building at my parish in Michigan burnt down. This was an occasion for grief and sadness, but even now, to hear parishioners who were there tell of it, there is palpable relief in their voices when they say that the Blessed Sacrament was spared in the fire.

While the Eucharist is what it is, namely, the body and blood of Christ, regardless of where it travels, the disposition of the recipient is important as well. As St. Paul relates, anyone eating the bread and drinking the cup without "discerning the body" eats and drinks judgment on himself (1 Cor. 11:29). Paul encourages us to examine ourselves before partaking of the Eucharist. There are basically three types of obstacles to communion: (1) not being morally prepared or in a state of grace, (2) not having Catholic faith in the nature of the sacrament, and (3) not being in full communion with the body of Christ, the church (especially through a lack of apostolic succession). Let's consider them in this order.

First, one might simply have committed a serious or mortal sin. God is full of grace and mercy, but the first place to go to receive that grace and mercy in this situation is the sacrament of reconciliation (or confession). All sin wounds the body of Christ, and if one is conscious of a mortal sin, one should first be reconciled before communing (see Matt. 5:24). We are all conscious of smaller failings, and the Eucharist is a healing balm for venial sins,[70] but mortal sins should be confessed before receiving the body and blood. This raises a particularly vexing issue, one that has been raised in the United States frequently in recent times, namely, what is one to do

---

69. Luther, *Babylonian Captivity, LW* 36, p. 35.
70. *CCC*, 1394.

when someone "obstinately persists in manifest grave sin"? The church teaches that such a person cannot be admitted to Eucharistic Communion.[71] The reason this case is so vexing is because many politicians, both in the United States and abroad, publicly dissent from the church's teaching on the morality of abortion, a matter on which the church has given a solemn decision. Now the question of the circumstances under which one might still vote for a politician who supports laws allowing abortion despite his or her position on that issue is controversial, but to actively defend and champion laws allowing abortion or vote for people because they do so is problematic for Catholics.

The question of what a politician should do if she or he is in these circumstances is simple (if still spiritually difficult). He should pray for discernment and refrain from presenting himself for Communion until he can confess this sin and turn away from it. The question of how a bishop or priest should handle this is more difficult. The history of the church gives us two different tendencies. First, there is the example of Cyprian, who shows us that refusing people admittance to Communion was entirely common in the early church in the case of widely known and serious public sin. Indeed, St. Ambrose (339-397) famously ordered Emperor Theodosius I (346-395) to repent for his part in a massacre of his subjects before he could receive Communion. At the same time, it is important to emphasize that sin which would incur a denial of Communion should be public and open. One should never be denied Communion on questionable evidence or even on evidence that is known to the priest but not the congregation.[72] Secret sin is the secret sinner's problem, as is her secret decision to commune in a state of sin. Most of us are not even in much of a position to create a public scandal by our sin, unless we choose to publicize it. But public figures like judges, legislators, and so on are different cases.

It's important to note that public outcry over denial of Communion is often generated more by unpopular Catholic teaching than it is by a sense that Communion should never be denied. I am not alone in thinking this. Archbishop Charles J. Chaput gives us two interesting cases for reflection here. The first is from 1962 when Archbishop Joseph Rummel of New Orleans excommunicated three public figures for protesting against the desegregation of New Orleans Catholic schools. *The New York Times* lauded Rummel for his obvious courage. In 2004, Archbishop (now Cardi-

---

71. See St. John Paul, *Ecclesia de Eucharistia*, 37, and *CCL*, 915.
72. See *ST*, III.80.6.

nal) Raymond Burke (then of St. Louis) drew the ire of the national media for first asking three Catholic politicians who supported keeping abortion legal not to present themselves for Communion and then instructing his priests to withhold Communion from them.[73] I am not, nor will I ever be, a bishop, and I do not envy bishops their job. I will simply report that Chaput's statement about what he would do if a hypothetical Catholic official acting against church teaching on a grave moral issue presented himself for Communion seems like a sensible one to me. He indicated that he would find out whether this person belonged to his diocese. If not, then he would do nothing. If the person did belong to his diocese, he would discuss the matter with him. If that did not succeed in getting him to change his view, then he would ask the official not to present himself for Communion. If the hypothetical official persisted, Chaput said that he would publicly ask him not to receive Communion and publicly explain why he had done this. If the official still persisted, then, and only then, would Chaput withhold Communion from him.[74]

The Eucharist is called Holy Communion, and it is no accident. Union with Christ in the Eucharist is not a private matter, but a public union with other Christians. There is one faith, one Lord, and one baptism (Eph. 4:5) and so unity of faith or belief travels with sacramental unity. Members of Orthodox churches are welcomed to partake of the Eucharist at a Catholic Mass given suitable circumstances and the approval of the church authority. Indeed, under certain exceptional conditions, non-Catholics who share Catholic faith in the nature of the Eucharist, with the permission of the relevant authority, can receive Communion.[75] However, this is the exception, and not the rule. The Catholic Church has rejected the idea that Communion should be entirely open, as have the Orthodox churches, and the Lutheran Church–Missouri Synod denomination.

The founding denomination of the college where I teach is also the denomination in which I was raised. Every year, the college's Campus Ministries staff gives a Communion service to begin the academic year. I usually attend it, but as a Catholic I am not permitted to receive Communion there. Despite the exceptional cases noted above, "intercommunion" is not possible between Catholics and most other Christians.[76] This is chiefly the

73. Charles J. Chaput, *Render unto Caesar* (New York: Image, 2008), pp. 55-58.
74. Chaput, *Render unto Caesar*, pp. 227-28.
75. St. John Paul, *Ecclesia de Eucharistia*, 46.
76. *CCC*, 1400.

case with traditions originating from the Reformation. While I am happy to be Catholic, I still experience the division in our Christian communities as painful, though this does not mean that I think the celebrations of other communities are merely parodies. They, too, are holy celebrations of our Lord's passion and death, and our life with him. The main reason that there cannot be intercommunion is that the Catholic Church prizes apostolic succession as an indispensable component of priestly ministry.[77] Without this, the priest cannot truly be ordained to the priesthood, and so the priest cannot truly act *in persona Christi* when he celebrates Mass. To say more about why this is so, we now turn to the priesthood, or the sacrament of holy orders.

Holy Orders

In his encyclical *Ecclesia de Eucharistia,* St. John Paul clarifies some aspects of what it means for the priest to be *in persona Christi.* He first points out that the priest does not merely stand in for Christ, but is in a sacramental identity with Christ. Christ works in and through the priest. St. John Paul goes on to note that the Eucharist which the priest celebrates is *"a gift which radically transcends the power of the assembly."* Yet, he also makes it clear that the assembly itself cannot provide an ordained minister, since "[t]his minister is a gift which the assembly *receives through episcopal succession going back to the Apostles."*[78]

The contrast with Luther's view of ordination can hardly be more striking. To show this, it is worth quoting a passage from Luther at length. He writes:

> ... suppose a group of earnest Christian laymen were taken prisoner and set down in a desert without an episcopally ordained priest among them. And suppose they were to come to a common mind there and then in the desert and elect one of their number, whether he were married or not, and charge him to baptize, say mass, pronounce absolution, and preach the gospel. Such a man would be as truly a priest as though he had been ordained by all the bishops and popes in the world.[79]

77. St. John Paul, *Ecclesia de Eucharistia,* 46.
78. St. John Paul, *Ecclesia de Eucharistia,* 29.
79. Luther, *To the Christian Nobility of the German Nation, LW* 44, p. 128.

Many of my Protestant friends ask me why the Catholic Church persists in putting up "fences" around the communion table. Although they are far too polite and kind to put it this way, I suspect that a version of their question could be put like this: "Where does the Catholic Church get the nerve to exclude me from Communion?" But just as a Protestant wonders about the nerve of the Catholic Church, a Catholic reads the above passage from Luther and wonders where *he* got the nerve to shift the understanding of ordination so as to reject the heart of apostolic succession. In this passage, Luther clearly allows the community, even if only in a fanciful scenario, to elect and charge one of its own to priestly ministry. This difference is at the heart of the sacrament of Holy Orders in the Catholic Church.

In Genesis 14:18-20, before God named him Abraham, Abram was met by Melchizedek, the king of Salem. Melchizedek is called "a priest of God Most High" (v. 19), and he brings out bread and wine and blesses Abram. This episode is brief, and Melchizedek is only mentioned again in the Old Testament in Psalm 110:4, where the psalmist writes, "You are a priest forever in the manner of Melchizedek." The reason I mention this is because the New Testament had to confront a nagging theological problem: Jesus was surely the Great High Priest, but how could he be a priest, since he was not a Levite and so could not inherit the Jewish priesthood of Aaron, Moses' brother? The writer of the Letter to the Hebrews solves this problem by linking Jesus with the priesthood of Melchizedek. Thus he quotes the psalmist, applying "You are a priest forever according to the order of Melchizedek" (Heb. 5:6) to Jesus. Without this linkage, Jesus could not be the fulfillment of the Hebrew Scriptures. Each Catholic priest is ordained a priest forever in the line of Melchizedek, echoing this language. What this affirms is that the question of priestly lineage is very important to the biblical writers, and to the understanding of the church. Luther's view that such a link could be severed seems, to Catholics, to be a radical break with tradition.

The church is a Eucharistic community, and by becoming one with Christ through the sacrament of baptism, and partaking in his body and blood, we all share in his mission as prophet, priest, and king.[80] As we mentioned earlier, this is also true of the baptized laity. Bishops and priests, whose ordination shares in Christ's own ordination in a different way, consecrate the Eucharist in the service of Christ and his church. But

80. *CCC*, 901-13.

laypeople are sent from this celebration to consecrate the world itself.[81] So it is wrong to think that laity are only ministered *to* in the Catholic Church. Their task is indispensable for carrying out the ministry of Christ's church in the world. Yet the laity must be built up by the teaching and sacramental ministry of those who succeed Jesus in this unique office.

An apostle is one who is sent, and there can be no serious question among Christians of whether Jesus sent the apostles out for ministry in the Gospels. Indeed, he did so at many points and, after his resurrection, he commissioned them with a sacramental ministry (Matt. 28:19). Shortly thereafter, we know that the apostles went about the business of ordaining priests and deacons by means of the laying on of hands (Acts 6:6). St. Paul links St. Timothy's priestly status with the fact that he had received the laying on of hands from Paul himself (1 Tim. 4:14 and 2 Tim. 1:6). In the present day, the bishops are understood, as we have already noted in earlier chapters, as the successors to the apostles. But even in the scriptural record, we know that there was a need for priestly assistants. In Acts 6:1-7, the apostles selected seven men to be given a special commission to be these assistants for the apostles, and to devote themselves to works of charity. This has come down to us as the office of deacon.[82]

Holy orders itself is one sacrament, but there are three degrees of sharing in it: bishop, priest, and deacon. Only bishops, as successors to the apostles, can actually perform ordinations, whether of priests or deacons. Deacons are not ordinary ministers of the sacraments, though they can officiate at weddings, administer baptism, and bring communion to those who are homebound. They are not permitted to confirm, hear confessions, consecrate the Eucharist, or anoint the sick. Each degree of ordination brings with it an "indelible mark," just as we said that a priest is a priest "forever" in the line of Melchizedek. Priests can be forbidden to exercise certain functions but they can never again be a member of the laity in the strict sense.[83] This is an important lesson for us as we reflect on holy orders: a bishop, priest, or deacon is never simply reduced to the functions he performs. I often hear Protestant friends worrying about how the Catholic tradition regards its priests as different, in their very nature, from the laity. I think this worry is overblown. After all, if you don't think that there is something definitively changed in the person who is ordained, then it's

81. *CCC*, 901.
82. *CCC*, 1570.
83. *CCC*, 1583.

difficult to see why ordination is not merely a functional idea. But if ordination is merely a function, then why is one ordained a priest "forever" in the line of Melchizedek?

We should also briefly discuss the matter of celibacy in regard to ordination. It is important first to note that not all Catholic priests are celibate. Since the Catholic Church has more than one rite, in the Eastern rites, as in the Orthodox churches, many priests are married. A very small number of priests even in the Latin rite who have joined the Catholic Church from the Anglican tradition, for instance, can sometimes be given a dispensation to be readied for ordination as well. Bishops are always to be celibate, and one cannot be married after having received holy orders, but some married men can receive ordination. The diaconate allows a transitional or permanent form, the transitional for those men on the way to full priestly ordination, and the permanent form, for those men who seek only to be deacons. Married men can be ordained permanent deacons. Pope Benedict XVI, before he became pope, gave an interview in which he conceded that celibacy is not a dogma, but merely a discipline that developed on "good biblical grounds."[84]

But why? What are the biblical grounds? Here we must be very brief. In the Old Testament, the married state seemed especially privileged.[85] To depart from it seemed strange. Yet Jesus encouraged those who could renounce marriage for the sake of the kingdom of heaven (Matt. 19:12). He also noted that, in heaven itself, human beings will neither be married nor given in marriage (Mark 12:25). The discipline of celibacy was part of the new covenant in Christ, and it could only be understood as a practice of imitation of him.[86] It is also an anticipation of the kingdom of heaven. The magisterium, following St. Paul, has said that it is better, in some sense, to live the celibate life.[87]

It is important to understand what is meant here. St. John Paul makes it very clear that it is not because sex is bad.[88] To say that would be to succumb to a version of Gnosticism sometimes called Manicheanism, because it would separate the physical and earthly from the spiritual and heavenly.

---

84. Joseph Cardinal Ratzinger, *Salt of the Earth*, trans. Adrian Walker (San Francisco: Ignatius Press, 1997), p. 195.

85. St. John Paul, *Man and Woman He Created Them: A Theology of the Body*, 55:2, trans. Michael Waldstein (Boston: Pauline Books and Media, 2006), p. 417.

86. St. John Paul, *Man and Woman*, p. 422.

87. DH, 1810.

88. St. John Paul, *Man and Woman*, p. 430.

It is only because celibacy is an anticipation of the kingdom of heaven, and because it allows a person to be devoted to God with an undivided spirit (1 Cor. 7:34) that it would be better, *but only for those people who are genuinely called to it.* If one were himself called to marry and consistently rebelled against this calling on his life, then he would introduce division into his life despite the fact that he may be celibate. This would be counter-productive to say the least. St. Peter, as is well known, was married (Matt. 8:14), but since we can suppose he was genuinely called to this vocation, it was no doubt the best state of life *for him.* Nevertheless, the vocation to celibacy, if authentic, is a special dignity for a person.

Despite the fact that priests are different from the laity, they are nevertheless equal fundamentally because of their baptism.[89] Each Christian has his or her own role to play, and a distinctive contribution. Each has a special vocation, and each can, through God's grace, become a saint in his or her own way. Why, then, one might ask, are vocations doled out the way that they are? Why, in particular, may only men be priests? This is a deep and vexing question that must be analyzed calmly and carefully if we are to understand the church's teaching. At the same time, we cannot pretend to establish an answer in this brief treatment of the issue. All we can do is give some basic reasons for why the church sees the matter the way it does.

For one thing, some have contended that the New Testament allows women to be ordained. St. Paul mentions Phoebe as a minister or deacon (the root of the word for "deacon" means "to serve") and a person some have contended is a woman, Junia, is mentioned as well known to, or prominent among, the apostles (Rom. 16:1, 7). However, one of the difficulties in reading backwards across so many centuries is that it is not always easy to know if the capacity in which Phoebe served is the same office of deacon as it developed and came to be known in later centuries, and similarly in the case of Junia as apostle. As for the case of Junia, debates rage on to which there is no foreseeable resolution.[90] But even if Junia is grouped among the apostles in the text, the more interesting question is what that might mean. In our own day, women are welcomed to many leadership roles inside and outside of the church, including positions such as the chancellor of a diocese. An apostle, as we have said, is one who is

---

89. *CCC*, 872.

90. See Michael H. Burer and Daniel B. Wallace, "Was Junia Really an Apostle? A Re-examination of Rom 16.7," *New Testament Studies* 47 (2001): 76-91, and Eldon Jay Epp, *Junia: The First Woman Apostle* (Minneapolis: Fortress Press, 2005).

sent, and in serving the church, laypeople of all different backgrounds are exercising their apostolate. Vatican II devoted an entire decree to the lay apostolate.[91] It is difficult to say for certain, merely on the basis of reading the biblical text, whether Junia attained the office of apostle to which Jesus appointed the twelve (Matt. 10:2-3). As to the question of Phoebe's role, Susan K. Wood writes, "The historical evidence for women deaconesses is somewhat controverted, though clearly deaconesses existed to assist women [who would be naked] in the baptismal rites of the early Church."[92] Again, there is no question that women served and serve (again, this is what the root of the word for "deacon" means) the church in profoundly important ways. In regard to the New Testament, the question is narrower though. When the apostles elected seven men as deacons in Acts 6:3, did they have it in view that future holders of this office could be women?

Again, we cannot pretend to provide a resolution to these questions that will satisfy all parties. Our job is to explain how the Catholic Church has taught on these matters. The wrongful subordination of women has found its way into just about every institution at some point in history, and the church is no exception. But the question is not about women's equality, but rather whether men and women are sacramentally the same. That is a more complex question. As members of the church and recipients of the sacraments, of course they are equal, and here St. Paul's refrain rings loudly: "There is neither Jew nor Greek, there is neither slave nor free person, there is not male and female; for you are all one in Christ Jesus" (Gal. 3:28). The difficulty, however, is that we *are* male and female and this is how God created us (Gen. 1:27). We are all one in Christ, to be sure, but the Catholic Church does not think that our sex is merely an accident nor does it think that we are male and female because of sin.[93] Aquinas argued that we wouldn't need, or have, food, drink, or sex in heaven, but he did think we would continue to have all the organs that make a human being complete. That is to say, he thought we would continue to have sexual organs and continue to be male and female even in the resurrection.[94] Imagine how much of our earthly lives and the very infrastructure of our society are dominated by the concerns of what we will eat and drink, and when, where, and with whom we will sleep. Our lives in heaven will not

91. See Vatican II's *Apostolicam Actuositatem.*
92. Susan K. Wood, *Sacramental Orders* (Collegeville, MN: Liturgical Press, 2000), p. 180.
93. See St. John Paul, *Man and Woman*, p. 187.
94. Aquinas, *Compendium*, 157, pp. 178-79.

be animated by any such concerns, and yet we will continue to be male and female.

There are two main reasons that should be mentioned as to why the Catholic Church does not ordain women. When my sister-in-law asked my wife and me why the church does not, the first reason is the only one I had the sense to mention, though the second is perhaps more interesting. The first reason is that Jesus did not ordain women as apostles. This doesn't sound like a very good reason, but we need to keep in mind what we've already said about the person of Christ. As we noted in chapter 4, we cannot say of Jesus that there was some stage in the liberation of women to which he just couldn't see his way clear because of cultural circumstances. Christ did not become man to capitulate to oppression; he came in part to fight it. Jesus accorded women a far higher dignity throughout his ministry than the culture of his day would allow. Nor does Christ's decision to choose male apostles reflect poorly on the moral fitness of women. Mary is higher "in dignity and excellence" than the apostles, but she was not called as an apostle.[95] Meanwhile, St. Peter, the head of the apostles, denied Christ in his hour of extreme need. Given all of this, Jesus' decision not to choose female apostles, and the apostles' decision not to choose women as deacons, may be worth a closer look. Outside the Catholic tradition, C. S. Lewis once noted that the idea of considering "priestesses" would be to "cut ourselves off from the Christian past."[96] For more than 1900 years, the Christian tradition denied attempts to ordain women. Any change along these lines would be for the church to take into her hands the authority to overturn this tradition. This is why St. John Paul, in his 1994 apostolic letter, *Ordinatio Sacerdotalis,* declared, in a way that is binding for all Catholics, that the church does not have the *authority* to ordain women.[97]

The other main argument to consider when it comes to the question of ordaining women is the question of what a priest is. To better consider this, let's turn back to our earlier imagery of the Eucharist as wedding feast. If the priest is really *in persona Christi,* as we have said, and the Mass really is the wedding feast of the Lamb, then who is getting married? The New Testament is not silent on this point. St. Paul says that marriage is a "great mystery" but he is speaking primarily of the marriage between Christ and

95. See the Congregation for the Doctrine of Faith, *Inter Insignores,* 2, and St. John Paul, *Redemptoris Mater,* 26 and 41.

96. See C. S. Lewis, "Priestesses in the Church?," in Lewis, *God in the Dock,* ed. Walter Hooper (Grand Rapids: Eerdmans, 1994), pp. 234-39, at p. 235.

97. See St. John Paul, *Ordinatio Sacerdotalis,* 4.

the church (Eph. 5:32). Centuries of Christian reflection have spoken about how the church is not just the mystical body but the mystical bride of Christ. As Lewis points out, "One of the functions of human marriage is to express the nature of the union between Christ and the Church."[98] In our day the next question is "but why can't a marriage be between a woman and a woman or a man and a man?" We will have to save that question for the final chapter. For now the thing to emphasize is that a priest is an icon of Christ in the Mass. An icon is not merely a picture, but a sacred image. Recall from chapter 3 that Christianity sprang from a faith (Judaism) that was very nervous about speaking God's name or depicting God. The idea that we could pray before and reverence sacred images, even kiss them, was bitterly contested. The Catholic Church decided that it was legitimate to reverence icons as pictures of Christ and his followers because of his incarnation.[99] We are in a poor position to say what it is about our bodies that will and will not change in the resurrection. But we seem in a better position to say that our sex will not. If the Eucharist is a mystical marriage between the bride and Bridegroom, is it not fitting to see to it that the mystical marriage and the sacramental marriage between husband and wife agree? Clearly the Eucharist, ordination, and marriage are all linked. What then does that mean for marriage?

Marriage

Although marriage (or matrimony) can refer to a legal institution, it is ultimately a divine institution. Marriage was intended for human beings even before their fall (Gen. 2:24), but it is also a sacrament of God's new covenant in Jesus. In fact, because the church is founded on the mystical marriage of Christ and his bride, St. John Paul even calls marriage "the sacrament of the Church."[100] While we will treat issues of sexual morality that pertain to marriage in the final chapter, here we should discuss its characteristics as a sacrament.

Since most Protestant traditions recognize only baptism and Eucharist as sacraments, they do not admit that marriage is a sacrament. The technicalities of this debate are not important to engage here. Paul's

---

98. Lewis, "Priestesses in the Church?," p. 238.
99. DH, 600-603.
100. St. John Paul, *Man and Woman*, p. 222.

invocation of the marriage of husband and wife as an image of the marriage of Christ and the church is an important clue, though. How could being brought into a union that signifies Christ's self-sacrificing love for the church fail to impart a divine blessing? Jesus had in mind to renew marriage and to incorporate this renewal into his new vision of the covenant (Matt. 19:8-9; Mark 10:5-9). Some might wonder at how Jesus could institute the sacrament of marriage into the new covenant without actually "officiating" at a wedding. Such concerns seem to misunderstand the Catholic view of marriage. For Catholics, the matrimonial consent makes marriage, and the two parties are actually the ministers of the sacrament to each other. Unless it is not possible, this should be done in the context of the church's liturgy, and it is especially appropriate that it take place in the context of the Mass, the wedding feast of the Lamb — but at its deepest level, the man and woman are the ministers.[101]

So much is this the case that the church itself recognizes that marriages could be valid, in certain extreme exceptions, even if no priest or deacon can be present. It is important to recognize how this could work. Some Catholic writers give the example of a marriage in a concentration camp, or a situation where there may be danger of death, and a reasonable expectation that a priest will not be around for a long time.[102] There must be a distinction between the intent to marry and the actual consent. Pretended marital consent cannot be used as a pretext for premarital sex. Any real consent must be one that takes into account, with sober judgment, that marriage is permanent and exclusive. It must not be given under duress. It must also be between people who are of valid age and, in the ordinary case, should have the full knowledge and consent of the church.

Marriage is a complete gift of the self, in which nothing should be held back. Jesus indicates that even looking at another with a lustful gaze is adultery in the heart (Matt. 5:28). One cannot truly give oneself in marriage if one mentally makes the reservation: "until I find someone else more appealing." One also violates the gift of self that marriage involves by living even a portion of one's sexual life in a fantasy with another. In fact, St. John Paul, after careful analysis of adultery in the heart, argues that what is really evil about adultery in the heart is the fact that it fails to treat

101. Ludwig Ott, *Fundamentals of Catholic Dogma,* ed. James Canon Batible, trans. Patrick Lynch, 4th edition (1955; reprint Rockford, IL: Tan Books, 1960), p. 468.

102. See *CCL,* 1116, and Rev. Ronald Lawler, OFM, Joseph Boyle, and William E. May, *Catholic Sexual Ethics* (Huntington, IN: OSV, 1985), p. 187.

one's spouse with the dignity of which she or he is deserving.[103] To treat even one's spouse as a sexual object is to commit "adultery in the heart."

One also fails to give oneself fully if one agrees to marry another only if she or he avoids having children.[104] Marriage is said to be consummated only when the couple actually engages in noncontracepted intercourse that is open to the possibility of life.[105] Sexual intercourse is the physical union toward which marriage is ordered. Marital sex is holy and good. So much is this the case that if someone is perpetually impotent and could not consummate a marriage that person should not attempt one.[106] While we will have to save a discussion of the sexuality of the human person for the next chapter, for now, it is important to note that marriage is ordered both to the unity of the spouses and to procreation, though nothing about it depends on whether procreation is ever successful. Our very selves are created with a view to becoming one with another person, physically, emotionally, and spiritually. Even celibates and virgins, though they do not become sexually one with another, do honor marriage by their marriage to Christ as members of the church, and, in a certain way, especially for priests, a marriage to the church.[107]

You might say that all of this total and exclusive self-giving business sounds nice, but what about the Old Testament patriarchs? Didn't Jacob and even King David, for instance, have more than one wife? This is true, of course, but Jesus' attitude to the Old Testament is revealing (Matt. 10:5). The Genesis account of Adam and Eve sounds strongly monogamist, and Jesus intends to return marriage to what the Creator intended for it. Among the many things this means is that the Old Testament toleration of polygamy (Deut. 21:15) seems part of the old covenant that Jesus wants to change. Having more than one wife is not part of how the Catholic Church sees the Gospel's message on marriage. Having more than one faith in a marriage is permitted, but I know from experience that it can be difficult. My wife and I lived with her Catholic faith and my Protestant faith for several years before I grew to embrace the Catholic faith as my own.

Marriage for Catholics is a sacrament, and to receive any sacrament (though not necessarily to administer one) one must first be incorporated

---

103. St. John Paul, *Man and Woman*, pp. 297, 299.
104. DH, 827.
105. *CCL*, 1061.
106. *CCL*, 1084.1.
107. See St. John Paul, *Pastores Dabo Vobis*, 23, and St. John Paul, *Mulieris Dignitatem*, 20-21.

into the body of Christ through baptism. Marriage between a baptized Christian and an unbaptized member of another faith is possible, though it can bring with it the temptation for neither party to insist on the practice of her or his faith simply for convenience's sake. For Catholics, once a valid marriage with appropriate consent occurs and it is consummated sexually, it is ultimately indissoluble. This is in fidelity to Jesus' command that remarrying after divorce constitutes adultery (Matt. 19:9), but it also agrees with the sense that marriage is the gift of the self, both now and until death. For very serious reasons, like adultery, there can be separation. In certain cases, a civil divorce may be the only way to provide for certain legal matters including the care of children,[108] but a dissolution of valid, consummated, sacramental marriage is not possible. It is sometimes possible to obtain a declaration of nullity, which would indicate that some condition had been discovered according to which the marriage was never valid in the first place. Finally, what if two non-Christians marry and one is later baptized into the church as a Christian? If the other spouse cannot live peacefully with his or her spouse, then this marriage can be dissolved and both can remarry. This is on the basis of what St. Paul says in 1 Corinthians 7:12-15.[109]

The Catholic vision of marriage is a kind of earthly anticipation of the mystical marriage of Christ and the church. It is not just a legal matter, but a holy and sacramental matter. The Creator himself made Adam and Eve to complement one another, and to be gifts to each other. Since marriage is a full and complete gift, it cannot be withdrawn. Marriages promise to be until death, and spouses cleave to one another in sickness and in health. This can be extremely difficult, especially as the years go by and spouses grow old and ill. Some may require constant care, but this is the love that we pledge in marriage. It is also the love Christ manifested to the church when he even died for her sake.

Anointing of the Sick

I often wonder, when I talk to Christians who claim to practice nothing but the message they discern in the Bible, why they don't anoint the sick. "Is anyone among you sick?" asks the Epistle of James. Anyone who reads the Bible faithfully should be able to picture a sick member of the church

108. *CCC*, 2383.
109. *CCL*, 1143.

saying, "Why, yes, I'm sick!" The Epistle of James then tells us what to do. "He should summon the presbyters of the church, and they should pray over him and anoint [him] with oil in the name of the Lord, and the prayer of faith will save the sick person, and the Lord will raise him up. If he has committed any sins, he will be forgiven" (James 5:14-15). Early in his ministry, Jesus sent the apostles out to preach the kingdom of God and heal the sick, and the message they got was that it would be a good idea to do this by the anointing with oil (Mark 6:13). As with the rest of the sacraments, its effects are not magic; your sins may indeed be forgiven, but you'll need to be sorry. The sacrament can succeed in communicating the healing power of God, but only if God chooses, and God does not always choose this. The sacrament is, however, a gift to the church for the communication of grace and care of the sick.

This sacrament used to be called "extreme unction," which reflects the fact that it would be administered in extreme cases of those who seemed near death. Now it is more commonly used, and one can receive it even prior to a serious operation.[110] It should be reserved for cases of real and serious illness, but to refuse to give it to someone who is not literally on the point of death is missing the point. By then the illness has advanced where it is primarily a sacrament for those departing this life. The sacrament is that, and it can be used as that, but it need not be used only in that way. One enters into new life in Christ's body, the church, by the sacraments of initiation, which are baptism, confirmation, and Eucharist. One hopes to enter into eternal life in Christ with confession of one's sins, Eucharist before dying (called viaticum), and the anointing of the sick.[111]

The Catholic life is a sacramental life. The sacraments make the church, and, through Christ's redeeming grace, they make her holy. But holiness is only achieved through union with Christ, our light and life. The marriage of Christ and the church and his life and sacrificial death for her is the deepest sacramental reality into which the individual sacraments bring us forth. Christ did not need the sacraments to redeem us. Still less did he need seven of them. But the sacraments through their material reality confirm our creation and resurrection as spiritual, and yet material, beings. In the next chapter we will consider the eternal destiny to which Christ's redemption calls us, and in the final chapter we will close by considering how the Catholic Church understands the human person.

110. *CCC*, 1515.
111. *CCC*, 1525.

Chapter 7

Heaven, Hell, and Purgatory

A while ago a close friend of my sister, and of our family, died. The circumstances were tragic, and she was much too young. It had been a couple of years since I had joined the Catholic Church, and my family, while supportive, was still a bit confused as to why I had done so. After the funeral, my parents and my wife and I were having a meal at a local restaurant and, while we were sad, we were comforted by the warm meal and the company. As sometimes happens at such times, it's easy to talk about something else, though it's also appropriate to talk about the person we're mourning. My father, as I recall, broke one of these lighter conversations with some questions that were heartfelt and sincere. None of us had any difficulty believing that our departed friend would be welcomed into God's heavenly kingdom, but she had lived through many trials and had some maturing to do even as she passed from this life. My father confessed to us that he felt it somehow appropriate to pray for our friend even though she was no longer with us. This was not a prayer for us, or a prayer for her family or friends, however appropriate those would have been. It was somehow a prayer for our friend herself, and a prayer that she might experience some healing. This prayer was not part of the faith with which my father had been raised, but he somehow knew it was good and right. Then he looked at me and asked, "Is that what purgatory is about?"

Purgatory and Indulgences

The doctrine of purgatory begins with the conviction that it is good, right, and important to pray for those who have preceded us in death. This is not a judgment on their standing before God, as if they needed more help than we do. It is the compassionate response of a people that prays. We have an example of this in the Catholic Scriptures, though it is from a book that is part of the Catholic and Orthodox canons, but not part of the Protestant canon. Judas Maccabeus, in 2 Maccabees 12:38-46, discovered that some of his fallen warriors had been wearing amulets they should not have been wearing. Then, Judas and his men, "turning to supplication, . . . prayed that the sinful deed might be fully blotted out" (v. 42). Why would Judas do this if he thought they were beyond hope? To Catholics down through the ages, it has seemed clear that if his comrades had been beyond hope, then Judas's men would not have prayed in this way, but they did. But if these men were not beyond hope, neither were they beyond the reach of prayer. Purgatory is a doctrine that came about in part because the church needed a doctrine to explain certain practices that were deeply entrenched in the practice of the faithful. One of those practices was praying for the dead.

The Anglican C. S. Lewis, who was and is a darling to many evangelical Christians because of his *Chronicles of Narnia* and other works like *Mere Christianity,* also believed in purgatory. In fact, his main reason is exactly the one we are discussing here. He writes, "Of course I pray for the dead. The action is so spontaneous, so all but inevitable, that only the most compulsive theological case against it would deter me. And I hardly know how the rest of my prayers would survive if those for the dead were forbidden."[1] So, the argument goes, if we pray for the dead at all, then we need something like purgatory to answer the church's deeply felt need to pray for the dead. But what does the doctrine look like?

For starters, purgatory is not a place.[2] Purgatory is also not a cosmic rest area on the highway to heaven; it is not a limbo that is "not that bad" and "not that good," as one of my students once told me the satirical cartoon show *Family Guy* depicts it. Rather, as St. Catherine of Genoa put it, "There is no joy save that in paradise to be compared to the joy of the souls in purgatory."[3] Nor is purgatory a second chance to do something you had no intention of doing during earthly life. If there were any question of it being about a second chance, then it would be possible to choose to reject God's will just as it would be possible to accept God's will. But here's the

---

1. C. S. Lewis, *Letters to Malcolm* (New York: Harcourt, Brace & World, 1964), p. 107.

2. See Pope St. John Paul II, General Audience, 4 August 1999.

3. See St. Catherine of Genoa, *Purgation and Purgatory,* trans. Serge Hughes (New York: Paulist Press, 1979), p. 72.

good news about purgatory: there is no trap door. If you are "in" purgatory at all, you are going to heaven; that much is certain.

The reason this is certain is because what purgatory is, more than anything else, is the cleansing process we endure on our way to union with Christ. Pope Benedict XVI writes of purgatory that "[Christ's] gaze, the touch of his heart heals us through an undeniably painful transformation 'as through fire.' But it is a blessed pain, in which the holy power of his love sears through us like a flame, enabling us to become totally ourselves and thus totally of God."[4] This is why Catholics also see a suggestion of purgatory in 1 Corinthians 3:15, where St. Paul tells us that many will be saved but only "as through fire."

This metaphor of a purifying fire was common in the early church. In the writings of Pope St. Gregory the Great (pope from 590 to 604), we read that if we build upon the one foundation of Christ that Paul is telling us about with "wood, hay, or straw," the flames will consume that material, and the result will be our salvation. This purification will be painful at points, but it will also be pleasurable, because each movement of purification is a movement closer to the fullness of union with God. However, if a person were to build upon the one foundation of Christ with other materials like iron, bronze, or lead, this would be a way of saying that she has made her heart hard and has insulated herself from God's purifying love.[5] This is the situation of a person who will not let God reach her, and because we are creatures who are always restless until we rest in God, theology calls this hell. We will discuss hell a bit later in this chapter.

In the last chapter we discussed the distinction between venial and mortal sins. Venial sin is one thing that can be in some sense cleansed by the purification of purgatory, but the church also talks a good deal about what are sometimes called "temporal punishments" for sin.[6] To understand what is meant by this, we need to talk a bit about the nature of sin. If we think for a bit about what we do when we sin, I think we will find that we never sin except when we find something at least partially attractive in the sin. I may have promised my wife that I would clean the bathroom, but then a movie comes on TV that I would really like to see and I choose to watch the movie. I don't relish the discussion we'll have when my wife

4. Pope Benedict XVI, *Spe Salvi*, 47.
5. Pope St. Gregory the Great, *Dialogues* 4.41, trans. Odo John Zimmerman (New York: Fathers of the Church, 1959), p. 249.
6. *CCC*, 1472.

returns, but for the time being, let's say, I do enjoy the movie. If we're honest with ourselves, we can admit that some sins are at least partially attractive to us. But the reason we actually choose to go through with them is that we choose to give priority to the thing that, ultimately speaking, is less important. Sin is what happens when we value earthly things over and above things that will allow us to make progress in holiness. While there may not be anything wrong with watching the movie in itself, there is something wrong with breaking promises just because some fleeting enjoyment came your way. So, we sin by valuing transitory earthly things more than we value the things of God. In sinning, we sow the seed of an addiction to earthly things. Sin is itself a kind of addiction to such things over against our better judgment, and even when a person has already confessed her sins and received forgiveness for them, the addiction must still be gradually conquered with God's help.

This corresponds quite well to our ordinary understanding of addiction. Real addictions carry side-effects with them, and the symptoms of withdrawal, the desire for the drug, and the pain that accompanies it, cannot be done away with simply by an act of resolve. Is it possible for God to wipe away all the vestiges of such addictions in one fell swoop? Yes, of course; God can do abundantly more than we can ask or even imagine. But the fact that God can do whatever God should want does not mean that God will do whatever *we* should want. Certainly when we turn our lives toward God and seek the bliss that is inseparable from union with him, part of us would like very much for him to simply do away with the "growing pains" that come along with Christian maturity. But, generally speaking, this is not the experience of most Christians. God gives us grace, to be sure, but the grace helps us persevere through the difficulty. It does not do away with it entirely.

As we reflect on the nature of addiction, though, we can note that symptoms of withdrawal are often offset (even if only a little) by something as simple as a kind word, a gentle hand, or (as Christians think) even a prayer. Sometimes there are remedies (as in the case of nicotine addiction) that can help reduce the symptoms of withdrawal. Indeed, sometimes these are things that can be made available for one's own addiction, and sometimes there are remedies one can give to another. For all we know, perhaps it is possible to produce a medicine that can offset the symptoms of withdrawal entirely.

The idea that we can alleviate more, or even all, of our symptoms of withdrawal to earthly things through Christ's help in the church is one way to understand the basic idea behind what are called "temporal punishments" for sin. It is not just because God is angry, but because of the very nature of sin and the effect on our souls that sin carries with it an attachment to creatures that we cannot simply wipe away. But the grace Christ won for us that is dispensed to us through the church can help to offset this. This is the basic insight of indulgences. Indulgences are partial or plenary in the sense that they can help to alleviate a portion of our symptoms of withdrawal from addiction to earthly things, or, in rare cases, all of those symptoms in a plenary indulgence.[7] It is fair to note, though, that St. Catherine of Genoa says:

> Do not rely on yourself and say, "I will confess myself and receive a plenary indulgence, and with that be cleansed of all my sins." The confession and the contrition that is required for the plenary indulgence is such, and so demanding, that were you to realize it you would tremble in terror, more fearful of not having that grace than confident of being able to attain it.[8]

Indulgences are gifts of grace, but they are granted to those who are properly disposed. Thus, they are rooted in devotion, and this requires grace and holiness.

Martin Luther, who ultimately split from the Catholic Church, had many objections to the practice of indulgences, though he did not object to purgatory itself until after his reformation had begun.[9] Some of his complaints (though by no means all) were justified. Pope Leo X, whose excesses we have already mentioned in chapter 2, did in fact use funds from indulgences in his attempt to climb out of the debt he incurred because of his lavish spending. While ordinarily monetary gifts to the church from out of sincere faith and desire to further her mission could be quite good, Leo X's intentions were not. He and the bishops under him also made use of preachers who were little more than peddlers of indulgences. Johann Tetzel (1465-1519) was the most famous. Whether legend or not, the saying "as soon as the coin in the coffer rings, the soul from purgatory springs" is forever associated with his name. Thankfully, the saying does

---

7. *CCC*, 1471.

8. See Catherine of Genoa, *Purgation and Purgatory*, p. 84.

9. See Luther, *Defense and Explanation of All the Articles*, LW 32, p. 95, and *Table Talk*, LW 54, p. 259.

not reflect actual Catholic doctrine on indulgences. Still, when I became Catholic, many of my mentors and friends were concerned about just this saying.

The church's doctrine of indulgences is a stumbling block for many, but there are some important boundaries to keep in mind when it comes to this doctrine. First, it's important to keep in mind that a selfish and bookish sort of mentality in seeking out indulgences is out of place. One could easily pursue them so selfishly that they end up doing one no good at all. This is not an objection to indulgences; it is part of the Catholic doctrine of them. At the same time, many indulgences are for things that selfish people would have little interest in doing, such as helping those in need, fasting, praying the Rosary, and reading Scripture. In the movie version of *The Lord of the Rings: The Fellowship of the Ring*, Arwen is trying to get a dangerously wounded Frodo to safety and medicine. She prays "what grace is given me, let it pass to him." This is the attitude of someone who secures an indulgence for someone else, departed or alive, and there is not much for Christians to worry about here.

Second, one must be careful not to attack indulgences using arguments that would likewise be effective against prayer itself. In fact, the most interesting objections to indulgences (and most of Luther's) are not objections to indulgences as much as objections to the power of the papacy. For instance, if you think indulgences tamper with the individual's relationship before God, then this question should also be asked about prayer in general. But surely Christians of all sorts agree that prayer can make a real difference, both with regard to things like physical illnesses and even, at times, spiritual conversion. If this were not so, St. Monica's (331-387) famous prayers for her son St. Augustine and his conversion would have been useless. Finally, Luther was right to be concerned with the abuses of indulgences, and recent popes have confirmed that this abuse "humiliated" the power of the keys to the kingdom that Christ had given Peter and the papacy. Pope Paul VI deplored the idea that indulgences had ever been sold, calling it "blasphemous."[10] At the same time, indulgences pertain to people who are properly disposed to give and receive them, and sincere faith is required for both of those sorts of people. The worry that the unrepentant Mafioso will coast into heaven on the strength of indulgences is simply a misunderstanding.

Rather, most of the time, indulgences are ways to lighten the load

10. Pope Paul VI, *Indulgentiarum Doctrina,* 8.

of ourselves and others and they are also ways of spurring us on to do things that would give us the kinds of good habits that would help to alleviate our residual addiction to creaturely things anyway. We have to continue to wage this battle against our addiction to sin and the symptoms of withdrawal it brings. This is how the process works in our everyday life, quite apart from things like indulgences, and many Protestant thinkers are happy to agree. The Protestant reformer John Calvin noted that "by uninterrupted, sometimes even by slow, progress God abolishes the remains of carnal corruption in his elect, cleanses them from pollution, and consecrates them as his temples, restoring all their inclinations to real purity, so that during their whole lives they may practice repentance, and know that death is the only termination of this warfare."[11] St. Francis de Sales (1567-1622), a Catholic bishop of Geneva shortly after Calvin's death, also pointed out that, while the blood of Christ is the only real cleansing for our souls, Christ often makes use of various trials that cleanse us in this life.[12]

So the main difference between the Catholic and Protestant traditions on the question of purgatory is *not* that many Protestant traditions think that the blood of Christ cleanses us while the Catholic tradition thinks that we have to "work it off" in purgatory. Rather, both traditions agree that we are cleansed by the blood of Christ. The main difference is simply that most Protestants (though fewer now than in years past) think that God simply brings an end to this process upon death. Even if that's true, what does "bringing an end to this process" involve? We already noted that, for Pope Benedict XVI, the encounter with Christ is itself the refining fire that burns away the dross from our souls. We are taken *through* this process after death, says the church, not taken *away* to heaven only to find out later the ways that God transformed us without our knowledge. The idea that this transformation would happen after death (for those of us who will need it) is all that is meant by purgatory. Indeed, purgatory is itself temporary. As C. S. Lewis once noted, there are finally only two sorts of people, those who say to God "Thy will be done," and those to whom God says "thy will be done."[13] In the end, there will only be heaven and hell.

11. John Calvin, *Institutes of the Christian Religion,* I.3.3 (one-volume edition, from first volume), trans. Henry Beveridge (Grand Rapids: Eerdmans, 1989), p. 516.

12. Part III, Article II, Chapter 1 in *The Catholic Controversy,* p. 353.

13. C. S. Lewis, *The Great Divorce* (San Francisco: Harper, 1973), p. 75.

Heaven

The apostle Paul tells us that eye has not seen and ear has not heard what God has ready for those who love him (1 Cor. 2:9), and it's a good thing, too. God is infinite, and heaven is God, or at any rate, our heaven is enjoying God, who is infinite.[14] We as humans also have a nearly unlimited capacity to become bored. If we were to put down in finite terms what heaven is it would be all too easy to get bored with the idea and we would no longer long for it. That's not because heaven isn't worth our longing but because our minds aren't ready for it. Descriptions in Scripture of the New Jerusalem that tell us its streets are made of pure gold, and its twelve gates are each made from only one pearl (Rev. 21:21) should not be seen as ways of putting a stop to our imagination but as ways of allowing our imagination to soar upward, past whatever we can conceive.

Whatever heaven is, it will involve everlasting loving contemplation of, and communion with, God. If that sounds boring to you, then you might want to think a bit more about what that would be like. For instance, long hot baths are good, but they are not heaven. Baths cleanse, they relax aching muscles, they give warmth, and, ideally, they are quiet. If your life is as busy as my wife's is, it's often difficult to imagine something better. But the reason it's difficult to imagine something better is because it is difficult to find calm in everyday life. It's also difficult to keep clean in a house of young children, and it's difficult to ignore aches and pains. These are all symptoms of everyday life that are mostly unavoidable but not pleasant. A long hot bath can help take that away, but its power resides in its ability to take bad things away and restore equilibrium, not to raise us to new heights. Thus, long hot baths are not fundamentally activities. They are passivities. This explains why some associate such things with spas and being waited on. In these types of passivities, we want to be what philosophers would call the "patient" rather than "agent" of the activity. Sometimes we need that, but who would be proud of a life lived entirely in the bathtub?

Human beings were created for activity, and certain sorts of activities at that, even if sometimes we need to be restored before we can really find those activities appealing. Even our sports activities are things we engage in probably because we want to test ourselves and take ourselves beyond what we thought we could do in the past ("playing catch" is more

---

14. See Pope Benedict XVI's homily from August 15, 2008.

about social interaction than about excelling at an activity). Activity is not always especially physical, either. Some important activities are primarily mental. Pursuing knowledge is primarily mental. Prayer is, in some ways, a mental activity but it can, with God's grace, be a foretaste of the kind of contemplation of God we will only know in heaven. This is why prayer is ultimately neither entirely passive nor entirely active.[15] Heaven is ultimately an activity in which we transcend ourselves, which we cannot do *by* ourselves, by coming to know, love, and commune with God.

Sex, too, is good, and it is a unique activity, but heaven is not sex, at least not as we know it. At its best, sex is the desire for union with another person (body, soul, and spirit) who is deeply loved. Sex unites human beings as well as they can be united this side of heaven, but even sexual ecstasy is short-lived and extraordinary.[16] But the love of God is so powerful that in heaven it makes everything ordinary.[17] Again, that may sound boring, but it is far from it. The most extraordinary pleasure we experience on earth is just a shadow of what *normal* is in heaven. Also, in earthly sexual union we briefly transcend ourselves, whether in our desire to be one with another, or in the way that sex is linked with transcending ourselves in procreation.

But in heaven, we are always transcending ourselves. We are always growing out of our old selves and into our new selves, as we are continually being united to our infinite God in a process that, because of God's infinity, we will never become bored with or outgrow. Scripture describes heaven as a wedding feast (Matt. 22:1-14) and the church as the bride of Christ (Eph. 5:25-33). Heaven is union with Christ through the church and union with all others through our union with Christ. Thus, Peter Kreeft says that "in the Communion of Saints, promiscuity of spirit is a virtue."[18] This doesn't mean that heaven is an orgy; it means that committed, earthly, marital sex points forward to a heavenly unity that we will ultimately have with everyone, and most especially with God in Christ. From the heavenly point of view, earthly sex is a clumsy way to achieve this unity.[19] This

15. See, for instance, Book I, chapter 3 of St. John of the Cross, *The Dark Night,* in *The Collected Works of St. John of the Cross,* p. 303.

16. See St. Thomas Aquinas, *Aquinas's Shorter Summa (Compendium Theologiae),* section 156 (Manchester, NH: Sophia Institute Press, 2001), p. 178.

17. *The Cloud of Unknowing* (Mahwah, NJ: Paulist Press, 1981), p. 125.

18. Peter Kreeft, *Everything You Ever Wanted to Know about Heaven . . . But Never Dreamed of Asking* (San Francisco: Ignatius Press, 1990), p. 129.

19. Kreeft, *Everything You Ever Wanted to Know about Heaven,* p. 131.

seems to be why Jesus said that in heaven, they "neither marry nor are given in marriage" (Matt. 22:30). Heaven is not in the business of destroying families and relationships, but in heaven, our union with Christ will more perfectly express, and incomparably surpass what we long for in our earthly relationships.[20]

This, however, points to the fact that heaven is inextricably social.[21] Our lives are not lived in bubbles, but with much assistance from others. Nor are our bodies just vehicles for social interaction because, to a large extent, we are our bodies.[22] Catholic teaching specifies two things on this point. The first is that there is a real resurrection of the body, and the second is that, perhaps paradoxically, those whose bodies have not yet been raised at the present time can, after their purification, attain to the heaven of union with God even before their bodies are finally raised up again.[23] Theologians and philosophers will puzzle endlessly about how to maintain both of these beliefs, and this is not the place to go into those controversies. What we should say, however, is that if the body were not ultimately raised, this world would ultimately be an illusion. This world is not an illusion but a foretaste, a kind of shadow, of the world to come. To illustrate this, consider that in C. S. Lewis's *The Great Divorce*, the residents of heaven that come to meet the main characters in the story are described as "solid people" and the others become more solid, and larger, when they finally decide to enter into the joy of heaven.[24] This is merely a literary illustration of how heaven is more real, not less real, than earth. Nevertheless, God's creation of our physical world is very good (Gen. 1:31), which is why heaven is the renewing of creation, not the destruction of it.

Surely, though, this world is not all there is. Our bodies are not even in the truest sense bodies unless they are alive, and our lives are always shaped by our own unique perspective on what we experience. If my past were identical up to this moment, I could still choose to do something different than what I am now choosing. Our bodies and the physical world can certainly influence us, but they cannot determine us. This points us to the fact that there is something more, something spiritual, about us. Truly, I would not be saying all there is to say about me if I did not discuss

20. *ST,* II-II.26.13.
21. Pope Benedict XVI, *Spe Salvi,* 14.
22. St. John Paul, *Man and Woman He Created Them: A Theology of the Body,* 55:2, trans. Michael Waldstein (Boston: Pauline Books and Media, 2006), p. 346.
23. *CCC,* 990 and 1023.
24. Lewis, *The Great Divorce,* pp. 74, 78, 138.

my body. Nor, however, would I say all there is to say about me simply by talking about my body. At the last judgment, all bodies will be resurrected and, while we pray that all will experience the joy of heaven, after we are purified, some may not.[25] But even before then, each of us faces a particular judgment and (probably) purification. Does God have some halfway-house in store for those who, like St. Paul, are bound for heaven and just happen to die long before the last judgment? Ultimately, the church decided, after some controversy, that the answer to this question is no.[26] Such people experience the joy of heaven, which is the contemplation of, and communion with, God. At the same time, all creation awaits the consummation of creation in heaven, and the souls of the blessed are no exception. They enjoy God right now, and when they are united to their bodies, they will still enjoy God, but they will be more perfectly who they were meant to be, and their glory will increase because of this.[27]

Another facet of heaven that is distinctive about the Catholic vision of heaven, and that many find difficult to accept, is the view that the experience of heaven is not equal for all who enjoy it. Dante Alighieri (1265-1321), the famous author of *The Divine Comedy,* writes of heaven that "every where/of Heaven is Paradise, though there the light/of Grace Supreme does not shine equally."[28] *What* we experience in heaven (union with God) is the same, but *how* we experience it is not. Objectors will rightly be concerned about the parable of the vineyard (Matt. 20:1-16), which seems to suggest that rewards in the kingdom of heaven are equal. In one sense, this is certainly true, since God himself is our reward. But the parable of the talents (Matt. 25:14-30) must also be considered. There two servants are hailed as good and faithful, one servant who was given five talents (a large measure of money), and made five more, and another servant who was given two talents, and made two more. It's also worth noting that many in the early church saw the many mansions of heaven (John 14:2) as an indication that heavenly rewards would not be equal.

But there is another reason to take this doctrine seriously. Does anyone seriously believe that all humans have a factory-made "God-scope" that will allow each of them to know God in exactly the same measure as

25. *CCC*, 1038.

26. DH, 1002.

27. See Ludwig Ott, *Fundamentals of Catholic Dogma,* ed. James Canon Batible, trans. Patrick Lynch, 4th edition (1955; reprint Rockford, IL: Tan Books, 1960), p. 478.

28. See Dante Alighieri, *Paradise,* Canto III, lines 88-90, in *The Portable Dante,* ed. and trans. Mark Musa (New York: Penguin, 1995), p. 406.

everyone else? How could Mary, who was given the privilege of know-ing Jesus in his infancy in the most intimate way, have the union with Christ that everyone else has? Christ, too, is a human being, and human beings are different. Nor, at the end of the day, are the rest of us equal in all important respects. Some of the saints were providentially needed and appointed to carry the church through tumultuous times, and they coop-erated with God's grace heroically and longed for him desperately. Others of us can recall serious failings in our Christian life and yet we do long for God, however imperfectly.

Now you might object that purgatory was supposed to cleanse us, and so why wouldn't everyone, upon death, be brought up to speed with everyone else who had already entered heaven? After all, purgatory could be long or short for various people, but once it's done, shouldn't everyone be on the same footing? To answer this, consider an example drawn from our discussion of purgatory. St. Paul's imagery of a cleansing fire was used to suggest that some sins or after-effects of them would be like wood, hay, or straw, and would need to be burned off, and one would thus be saved "as through fire." Likewise, we noted that Gregory the Great said that we can obscure the one foundation of Christ by building upon it with materials like iron, bronze, and lead, and that this is the lot of those who perma-nently rebel against God in hell. However, Paul himself discusses some who build upon the one foundation of Christ with gold, silver, or precious stones (1 Cor. 3:12). This seems a fitting analogy for those who ornament their lives with acts of deep love for God and others.

To see what this might mean, consider an example. Suppose that my wife and I both have a friend and, when all three of us are out together, I close the evening by telling a joke that happens to offend our friend, even though, let us suppose, I told it more out of a momentary lapse in sensitiv-ity than out of positive spite. Now imagine that I need to leave our gather-ing early, but shortly after I do, my wife quickly apologizes for my rudeness and buys flowers for our mutual friend. Finally, suppose that, for whatever reason, all of our lives end abruptly shortly after that unfortunate dinner. I may need some purifying for my insensitive joke and may have some wood, hay, or straw that needs "burning" away because of it. On the other hand, my wife has ornamented her life with a jewel and has also deepened her relationship with our mutual friend. As our heaven is fundamentally about our relationship to God, were the friend in our analogy to stand in for God, he would have no intention of taking this ornament away from my wife, any more than our friend would return the flowers. It redounds to God's glory and the splendor of his kingdom. Precisely because of this, it increases my wife's joy and her ability to delight in that kingdom. If I were jealous because of this, all it would mean is that I didn't yet belong in God's kingdom, because that kingdom is concerned with our ability to participate in *God's* joy. During his vision of heaven, Dante talks to a soul in heaven known as Piccarda, who has one of the lowest positions in heaven. She notes to him, "If we desired to be higher up, / then our desires would not be in accord / with His will Who assigns us to this sphere."[29] The idea here is simply that each of us is given a share in God's kingdom. In God's providence, those shares are not equal, just as the parts of the body, though equally necessary for the whole, are not equal (1 Corinthians 14–26).

In heaven, we will also be perfectly free. That doesn't mean that we will be free to leave heaven and go to hell. This is somewhat counterintuitive for modern notions of freedom, so let's explain this a bit further. The difficult thing to understand about this view of freedom is that, while we often think that freedom is the ability to choose between things, on earth, as in heaven, freedom is ultimately the ability to choose the *good*. In life right now, most of us find doing the right thing difficult, at least some of the time. To borrow our earlier example, sometimes I know that keeping my promise to clean the bathroom is the right thing to do, but I would rather watch the movie (even at the expense of my promise). But even when we have only choices that we enjoy and that are morally acceptable, like whether to go to a movie or to a baseball game that is taking place at the same time, we don't always enjoy the experience of choice. Probably everyone knows the feeling of standing around with a few friends and saying "What do you want to do?" and having another person answer "I don't know — what do you want to do?" This often carries on for what seems like forever and sometimes the reason it carries on forever is because each person really does like both options and each person feels that the choice is not determined for her because she likes both options equally.

This is not the picture of real freedom. If these people were to keep going forever, they would miss out on both events. Real freedom is not the ability to choose between things, but the ability to choose, clearly, and with a sense of satisfaction, the right and the good, because it is right and good. That doesn't mean that good people never experience some indecision, but they don't experience indecision *about the good*. In fact, as St. Anselm of Canterbury (1033-1109) once argued, we are actually less

29. Dante, *Paradise,* Canto III, lines 73-75, p. 406.

free when we *can* choose evil than we are when we cannot.[30] In order to understand this, you need to understand that human beings have appetites that they don't directly control. I love candy. My appetite for my favorite candy (pear-flavored Jelly Bellies), if acted on constantly, would drain my family's income. It would also make me sick. When my family's income is drained, we are less able to contribute to our children's Catholic school tuition or to anything else that is important. If I am sick, I won't feel well enough to play with my daughter and son, or to enjoy a night out with my wife. Following the desires of our appetites (which we don't choose) makes us less able to enjoy more deeply valuable activities (which we often do need to choose). Acting constantly on desires, most of which we do not choose, is more like slavery than freedom. It is obeying your appetite and enslaving yourself to it. Choosing the good frees you for higher and better pursuits (like playing a musical instrument), even though the initial stages of learning are difficult.

Habits make choices easier. Doing the right thing is easier when you've developed a habit of doing it, though doing the wrong thing is also easier when you've developed a habit of doing it. But when an individual, through a series of choices, becomes capable of withstanding the attacks of temptation so that she is no longer driven about by her appetite, she won't even consider those temptations a serious threat to doing what she more deeply wants to do. When a person matures in this way to a point where she simply can't take a temptation seriously, then she is freer than she was when she still had to contend with those temptations. It may be psychologically impossible for her to take the temptation seriously, but she is freer to do what makes her most deeply happy because of it.

This is why purgatory comes before heaven. The self that is in heaven has matured through a process that makes her now totally incapable of taking temptation seriously. A soul in heaven simply cannot take seriously temptations to depart the everlasting bliss that she experiences in God. The sin that we talked about earlier that is at least partially attractive does not even make a dent on her appetite. Since she now knows that God is the crown of all her longings, and her deepest happiness, she loves other things through her love for God, or not at all. Whatever physical sensations might be associated with the resurrected body, they will be consistent with loving God above all. Remember, indifference is not freedom. We did not

---

30. See Anselm, *On Freedom of Choice,* chapter 1, in *Anselm: Basic Writings,* ed. and trans. Thomas Williams (Indianapolis: Hackett, 2007), p. 148.

create ourselves, and we can never change the fact that God is our highest good. If we actually were indifferent about God, that would signal that our ability to appreciate the good was seriously damaged. It would not signal freedom but captivity to foreign notions of goodness.

Hell

Habit, however, is a double-edged sword. As we said, making good choices gets easier the more you do it. Yet making bad choices also gets easier the more you do it. One can, by practice in life and purifying in death, grow to full maturity in Christ so that temptations do not even make a psychological dent on our choices. In a similar way, one can also, by practicing one's rejection of God in life and carrying that rejection through until death, make it psychologically impossible to be attracted to life in God after death. Even though we are all created to find our deepest happiness in God, the mystery of sin is that we can really make choices that are evil. As Josef Pieper puts it, "Sin is an act against reason, which thus means: a violation against one's own conscience, against our 'better' knowledge, against the best knowledge of which we are capable."[31] Indeed, that knowledge includes what is ultimately good and best for us, and yet we still choose it. It is difficult to understand how or why anyone really does evil, but when we are honest with ourselves, we know that the blame rests with us. This kind of choice has far-reaching effects. God's mercy is infinite, but it will not force our hand. We cannot dismiss the possibility that someone has forged a character so wrecked by sin that he or she will not accept God's rescue. It is important to note that the activity that makes hell possible is ours, not God's. Pope Benedict XVI counters the idea that God is the one actively condemning people to hell, noting that when Scripture talks about God's "wrath" it is really a way of explaining our own negligence in living in a way that is not right, best, and healthy for us.[32]

There are many texts in Scripture that appear to be addressing hell, though the picture is not always clear. Jesus' most common term for hell is Gehenna, which is a way of referring to the valley of Hinnom where, in

---

31. See Josef Pieper, *The Concept of Sin,* trans. Edward T. Oakes, SJ (South Bend, IN: St. Augustine's Press, 2001), p. 45.

32. See Joseph Cardinal Ratzinger, *God and the World,* trans. Henry Taylor (San Francisco: Ignatius Press, 2002), p. 104.

ancient times, child sacrifice was practiced (2 Kings 23:10). Later residents of Jerusalem would burn garbage there. By Jesus' time the name of this place was a popular way to refer to a place of punishment in the afterlife.[33] St. Jude seems to claim that it is characterized both by "eternal fire" (v. 7) and "darkness" (v. 13) and it's not obvious how the two attributes are consistent. Fire, after all, tends to bring light with it. Furthermore, St. John Paul, in reading the language of the "pool of fire" in Revelation 20:14, notes that this language is surely meant "figuratively."[34]

The church has never officially said that any particular person is in hell. Indeed, St. John Paul even goes so far as to say that Scripture does not determine whether Judas, Christ's own betrayer, is in hell.[35] So in recent years when evangelical leader Rob Bell came out with a book called *Love Wins*,[36] which only raises the possibility of everyone ending up in heaven, and never definitively claims that this will happen, controversy erupted in evangelical circles, but Catholics took very little notice. This had already occurred in Catholic circles with the publication of Hans Urs von Balthasar's *Dare We Hope That All Men Be Saved?*[37] and this book, while certainly controversial, did not provoke any official condemnation from the magisterium. The main point here is that, while Scripture does, at points, seem to point to a hell that some experience, we are in no position to know who those people might be.

The reason for this is rooted in the church's theology of sin. Mortal sin, the kind of sin that so destroys a loving relationship with God that it is a rejection, a decisive "no," was something we discussed in the last chapter under the sacrament of confession. Yet, it's worth remembering that a mortal sin would have to be about a "grave matter"; it would need to be committed with "full knowledge" and "deliberate consent."[38] Nowadays, most official Catholic documents use terms like "mortal sin" only sparingly, usually preferring terms like "serious sin." This is probably because we may know some sins that are serious, but we cannot know the heart

---

33. See William Crockett, "The Metaphorical View," in William Crockett, ed., *Four Views on Hell* (Grand Rapids: Zondervan, 1996), pp. 43-76, esp. p. 58.

34. See St. John Paul, General Audience, 28 July 1999, 3.

35. St. John Paul, *Crossing the Threshold of Hope*, trans. Jenny McPhee and Martha McPhee, ed. Vittorio Messori (New York: Alfred A. Knopf, 2003), pp. 185-86.

36. Rob Bell, *Love Wins* (San Francisco: Harper, 2011).

37. Hans Urs von Balthasar, *Dare We Hope That All Men Be Saved?*, trans. Dr. David Kipp and Rev. Lothar Krauth (San Francisco: Ignatius Press, 1988).

38. *CCC,* 1857.

of a person. Some may be in the grip of a bad theory about how to attain otherwise just ends, some may be shaken up by fearful circumstances, and some may simply have debilitating psychological or physical problems that make it impossible or at least very difficult (more difficult than for many of us) to get through ordinary life without lapsing into some form of sin. So we still reject the sin, but we should not be claiming that everyone we encounter is going to hell, whether he is someone whose concern for justice for the poor has wrongly gotten him involved in violent revolutionary tactics, whether she is an Afghani addict for whom heroin is cheaper than food, or whether a person may have taken his or her own life after many difficult psychological struggles.

I still encounter many people who believe that the Catholic Church is especially harsh when it comes to people who have committed suicide, since the common perception seems to be that the church condemns them to hell without further ado. This is not true, though the stereotype persists in places like Hollywood films. In the 2005 movie *Constantine,* a woman's brother was refused a Catholic funeral because, having committed suicide, it was presumed he must be in hell. What the church actually says is this: "We should not despair of the eternal salvation of persons who have taken their own lives. By ways known to him alone, God can provide the opportunity for salutary repentance. The Church prays for persons who have taken their own lives."[39] Our lives are gifts of God, along with all of our resources. If we squander our resources, not giving any thought to those in need, we can expect the judgment of Christ in Matthew 25:41-45. Similarly, if we squander our very lives, rejecting this gift that God has given us, with full knowledge, and deliberate consent, then surely this is a serious matter. But if you know people who have taken their own lives, as I do, you're surely aware that the reality is rarely like this. Many such people suffer from physical and psychological illnesses or even emotional distress and this is often a major factor in what is nevertheless a very regrettable decision. The church prays for these people, and, as we said when we talked about purgatory earlier, prayer is something we do for people who we presume are not beyond hope.

Another topic often persists in people's thinking about hell. Because of the way that original sin infects us even before we could be in a position to do anything about it, for a long time there was a common thought in the Catholic Church that if you died before you were baptized (i.e., cleansed of

39. *CCC,* 2283.

original sin) then you could not be in heaven, and so must be in hell. This is the idea that gave rise to "limbo," a word you'll often have trouble finding in contemporary official Catholic documents, which have, for some time, distanced themselves from this idea. The first thing to say about this is that taking original sin and the sacraments of the church seriously will require us to take seriously the question of infants who die without being baptized. Although we noted in the introduction to this book that one could experience "baptism of blood" and "baptism of desire" even without the ordinary sacrament of baptism, the fate of infants who die without being baptized raises some difficult questions, since they probably didn't stand firm in the face of persecution, and it's not obvious that they really desired baptism as a catechumen who died prematurely probably would have. In the Middle Ages, theologians like Aquinas taught that such infants did not really know what they were missing, in being excluded from the contemplation of God, and that they were given a kind of natural happiness.[40] So, even though they might have missed out on the supernatural happiness God intended for human beings, it was thought that God was nevertheless very merciful to them. Still, "limbo" was never a dogma of the church, and through the years many of the church's members have found this view deeply distressing. Although heaven's bliss is more perfectly found in the communion with God that it offers, it is a great comfort to us here on earth that we will see our loved ones in heaven, and it is difficult to reconcile the mercy of God with the view that an unbaptized infant will have drawn rather the short straw in missing out on the bliss of heaven because of factors quite beyond her control. After all, God really does desire the salvation of all (1 Tim. 2:4).

In 2007 the Catholic Church's International Theological Commission completed a report on this doctrine and concluded that there were good reasons to hope that unbaptized infants would be granted the bliss of heaven "precisely because it was not possible to do for them that which would have been most desirable," namely, baptize them into the faith of the church.[41] The document emphasized that this was a prayerful hope, and not certain knowledge.[42] Still, this hope seems supported by some good reasons. As we noted in the previous chapter, the Catholic Church under-

40. See Aquinas, *On Evil,* Question 5, Article 3 (Notre Dame: University of Notre Dame Press, 1995), pp. 218-20.
41. International Theological Commission, *The Hope of Salvation for Infants Who Die without Being Baptized,* prologue.
42. International Theological Commission, *The Hope of Salvation,* 102.

stands infant baptism to be an important way in which we are enveloped by and in the body of Christ before we are yet in a position to explicitly want this. Ultimately, the only real way to get outside of God's grace is to expel oneself from it; there is no forgetfulness in God's mercy. In the case of infants who die after their baptism, their parents and the community saw to it that they were cleansed by God's ordinary mechanism for cleansing. In the case of infants who die before this is possible or in the custody of parents or a community that did not see to their baptism, God knows of this discrepancy, and can see a certain artificiality in it. In the first case, many desired the baptism of the infant before she was in a position to desire it herself, and so they had her baptized. In the second case, many desired her baptism (because many share God's desire for the salvation of all), but as an accident, they could not secure it. It is difficult to see how this unfortunate accident will be in a position to hold a candle to God's almighty grace. Thus, although we are not ready to say just exactly how God manages to save unbaptized infants, we may trust that God can bring them to salvation.

So, what, finally, is hell? The church claims that "[t]his state of definitive self-exclusion from communion with God and the blessed is called 'hell.'"[43] I've often encountered people who claim that hell is "separation from God," and this is certainly right in one sense. Usually these people are trying to get away from a literal view of hell as fire and brimstone, and so forth. Certainly, as St. John Paul noted, we don't need to envision the "pool of fire" discussed in Revelation to be a literal pool or lake of earthly fire, and to that extent I think that people who want to get away from this excessive literalism are on the right track. But, as we learned in our discussion of God and humanity in chapter 3, God and humanity are not so easily parted. God sustains everything in existence. Without God's sustaining power, nothing would be at all. The Catholic tradition has generally thought that, just as rewards in heaven are unequal, so punishments in hell are also unequal.[44] That doesn't mean one needs to believe in Dante's graphic and sometimes disturbing accounts of various punishments fitted to various crimes in hell, but it does mean that God's mercy relents in various ways with various people.

In fact, the very existence of hell is a sign of God's mercy in this respect: if God had wanted to, God could have annihilated those who chose

43. *CCC*, 1033.
44. See Ott, *Fundamentals of Catholic Dogma*, p. 482.

to exclude themselves from heaven. Some recent theologians contend that we should think of hell as another way of referring to God's decision to annihilate those who separate themselves from the wedding feast of heaven.[45] It is often suggested that this is more merciful than everlasting conscious punishment. The difficulty here, though, is that it is precisely an expression of mercy that God continues to remain with those in hell by continuing to sustain their existence. God is still in them by his activity. The relationship is not harmonious, but that is because those in hell have refused to be reconciled to God. This is torment in the same way that one experiences the tearful phone messages of an estranged relative longing for reconciliation, when one wants nothing to do with this relative. God is the one who longs for reconciliation, and although in hell our character is fixed and reconciliation is psychologically impossible, by God's sustaining presence and mercy, those in hell know that God loves them. It may be difficult to endure, but what could be worse than if God were to stop calling? For us to be in existence at all is for God to love us by wishing us good.[46] God is goodness itself, and to exist will always be for some portion of God's will to be brought about in you. Being is always better than nonbeing. Hell is the decision to opt out of what is really best for you. But even hell is not what is worst for you; God's love does not cease so easily. Annihilation would be worse than the torment of God's spurned love. It would be for God to give up.

Purgatory is the merciful preparation God makes so that human beings are ready for the best God has to offer. Heaven is God's immeasurable goodness in inviting us to partake of his own unstoppable joy. The joy of the wedding feast continues on forever. Those who have refused to put on a wedding garment (Matt. 22:12) experience this as torment (hell), but the fact that the wedding feast goes on at all is a sign of God's deep and abiding love for all and his invitation to all to share his joy. C. S. Lewis once claimed that "it matters more that Heaven should exist than that we should ever get there."[47] The very fact that God invites us to his joy is an infinitely greater dignity to human beings than we could have ever expected. If some decide to reject this offer, that does not mean that it would be better for them that they pass out of existence.

---

45. See Clark Pinnock, "The Conditional View," in Crockett, ed., *Four Views of Hell,* pp. 135-66.

46. See *ST,* I.20.2.

47. See C. S. Lewis, *Surprised by Joy* (London: Geoffrey Bles, 1955), p. 209.

Chapter 8

The Human Person

In my own state of Michigan, in 2006, the state's Catholic conference (whose leaders are its bishops) openly opposed two distinct proposals. The first measure was one that sought to prohibit any state institution from exercising "affirmative action" in its policies. The second measure sought to increase state funding for embryonic stem-cell research. Thus, the church in Michigan supported affirmative action and opposed funding for human embryonic-stem cell research. It is not important right now to argue over whether the bishops were right to do this, though I think they were. What is important to understand at this point is that the reasons one might use in opposing the two measures, while distinct, to a Catholic mind are clearly related. Both have to do with the nature of the human person.

The human person, according to the Catholic Church, is bodily, spiritual, sexual, and social. The human person must also be free, equal in dignity, and able to engage in a system of law ordered to the common good of all. As we will see, to allow embryos to be discarded for the purpose of research fails to realize that human embryos are not less than human merely because they are not yet capable of exercising their reason. Also, to say that affirmative action is categorically unjust would be to lose sight of the fact that affirmative action, properly understood, can be an important tool in achieving something closer to the common good for all, especially in the wake of sex and race discrimination. It would be impossible to fully unpack the church's understanding of the human person in a short chapter like this. What we can do is discuss some of the basic contours of the church's understanding so that we are in a better position to understand how the church approaches some of the more controversial questions in our day.

Moral and Spiritual Foundations

Early in chapter 3 we discussed what is called the natural moral law, or the conviction that some important moral truths can be discerned without the need for special revelation by God in the Scriptures. It is important to recognize, however, a deep agreement between the natural law and divine revelation here, for the church understands certain passages in Scripture to be indicating the existence of something like the natural law. Thus, St. Paul writes that "[w]hen the Gentiles who do not have the law by nature observe the prescriptions of the law, they are a law for themselves even though they do not have the law. They show that the demands of the law are written on their hearts" (Rom. 2:14-15). Although there are moral truths that can be known without the need for divine revelation, this is ultimately because the natural law is the law that is written on our hearts by God. What that means is that human nature, as created by God, delights in God above all but thrives best in an environment that recognizes the unique way in which humans flourish.

Everything in us is created by and subordinated to God. It is natural that this is so. As we noted in chapter 3, the Catholic Church holds that the human being can come to know that there is a God even without divine revelation. Just as there is natural law, there is also natural theology. This just means that, however well-intentioned many individual atheists may be, atheism itself simply does not give us a workable understanding of our own human reality. Neither, it should be said, can we ever have a complete picture of human life without discussing the new creation we become in Christ, or the Trinitarian life into which we are caught up in the process, though these latter dimensions cannot be discussed without bringing Christian revelation into the picture. The same is true in morality. Our moral views will never be complete until they are integrated into a picture where God is the good toward which everything strives. Because God is the ultimate end of all things, even morality itself, God can command things that do not conform to the way natural law *usually* works, as when God commanded Abraham to sacrifice his son (Gen. 22:2).[1] Since God is the Lord of life and death, life itself is subject to his decree. The point of this is not to throw morality into upheaval. It is precisely the opposite. As Pope St. John Paul II argues, in a cultural climate without a sense of God's role, we can no longer really look on ourselves

---

1. *ST,* II-II.104.4, reply to objection 2.

as *persons*. Without acknowledging our existence as spiritual and related to God, we cannot truly understand our bodily existence. Our bodies would then become just a "complex of organs" whose functions we will figure out based on what we can get away with.[2] The reverse is also true; if we fixate on our souls at the expense of our bodies, we will quickly find our way to equally serious errors. Nevertheless, it is impossible to have a complete view of the human person without considering our relationship to God.

Part of acknowledging our whole human reality is acknowledging our human dignity. The *Catechism* notes that "only man is 'able to know and love his creator.'"[3] Everyone will find ways in which nonhuman animals can approach the cognitive capacities of human beings. Whether your favorite animal of comparison is the dolphin, the pig, or the monkey, we are always learning more about how amazing other creatures are. The whole creation is a marvel, and we should delight in it, and consider carefully how best to care for it. Yet there is a hierarchy in creation. Certainly, a single leaf from a maple tree is not equal in dignity to a dolphin. There is a reason why vegetation was part of the third day of creation and animals a part of the fifth day (Gen. 1:9-23). Still, human beings have a special dignity in that we can approach our existence as a question, and attempt to view it as a whole. We can go beyond the search for food, and search instead for God. We can turn to God and ask not just for rain for crops, but for a deeper union with him. We have the dignity of persons, and this dignity is the source for our moral and social existence.

The first principle of the natural law, which is so basic that no one could ever prove it, is that one should seek good and avoid evil.[4] It's difficult to imagine anyone seriously contesting this. What is not difficult to imagine are disagreements concerning what the good is. In our modern life we have that in spades. Some disagreements are not about fundamental moral principles but merely about their application in various contexts. We should always respect others' earnestly held views even if we disagree, but sometimes we don't even need to disagree. Sometimes a particular cultural context is better suited for one application of the natural law and sometimes another cultural context is better suited for another. For instance, the church opposes communism and looks favorably on forms of

2. See St. John Paul, *Evangelium Vitae*, 23.
3. *CCC*, 356.
4. *ST*, I-II.94.2.

government that encourage democratic participation.[5] But how exactly a particular state or nation puts together a representative system may admit lots of variation, and there is no need to suspect that there is something morally wrong about that. But how shall we understand morality itself? How do we know what is right and what is wrong?

There are basically three things that need to be evaluated in order to assess an act morally. The order is very important. First, let us talk about the object that is chosen. The words of St. Paul in Romans 3:8 seem rather harsh when it comes to those who would do evil that good may come of it, and this has been an important source for moral reflection within the Catholic Church. If it is bad that one do evil so that good may come of it, then presumably there must be a classification of moral evil and moral good before one chooses these things. At a very basic level, this means that moral decisions are not purely relative to the person who chooses them or to the society or culture that values them. I sometimes run into students who parrot this relativistic approach to ethics, but invariably no one really means it. If morality or ethics were simply a matter of arbitrary individual preference, then we could not say anything to any genocidal or homicidal maniac other than "what's right for you may not be right for me." That is foolish, because what we mean by right or good in this context is something that contributes to real human flourishing. But even atheists cannot get around the fact that we did not create ourselves. We don't just *decide* what we will value; sometimes we value it because we are *human.* I value not being tortured for some madman's brutal amusement, and that is not something I can just "choose" away. If there is even one principle by which, when all humanity obeys it, humanity is fundamentally *better off* than it would be if all humanity disobeyed it, then we must not be relativists. Here is one such principle: "It is morally wrong to torture innocent people for the fun of it."[6] If everyone obeyed this principle everyone would be better off than they would be if everyone violated it. Obeying this principle contributes to human flourishing.

The *Catechism* goes a step further, and argues that "there are concrete acts that it is always wrong to choose, because their choice entails a disorder of the will."[7] This is a step further because we might have been able to

<hr>

5. DH, 2786, and *Compendium of the Social Doctrine of the Church,* 190-91.

6. See Louis P. Pojman, "A Defense of Ethical Objectivism," in *Moral Philosophy,* 4th edition, ed. Louis P. Pojman and Peter Tramel (Indianapolis: Hackett, 2009), pp. 38-52, at p. 47.

7. *CCC,* 1761.

imagine someone agreeing that it is wrong to torture innocent people for the fun of it, because that principle specified a fairly trivial reason, namely, someone's amusement. But what about torturing someone you believe may have information about the location of a bomb that could detonate in the next few minutes, possibly killing hundreds of people? This would be to do evil (torture) so that good may come (obtaining the information). But why should we not do evil so that good may come? Here we need to discuss consequentialist theories (theologians sometimes call similar theories "proportionalist") of morality. A consequentialist theory holds that we should discern right from wrong based on weighing the benefits and harms each action promises now and in the future. One version of this kind of theory, the version held by philosopher John Stuart Mill (1806-1873), holds that we should always pursue the course of action that leads to the greatest amount of happiness in the long run. In this context, happiness is understood as "pleasure" and unhappiness means "pain" or the "privation of pleasure."[8] St. John Paul rejected these kinds of theories in his 1993 encyclical *Veritatis Splendor*.[9] Let's take a moment to consider why this kind of theory would have problems. I should say up front that, except where I say the church has endorsed some position or cite a source from the magisterium, in the rest of this section I am merely putting forward one way of looking at these matters that I have found helpful and that is consistent with Catholic teaching.

The philosopher Robert Nozick (1938-2002) once posed this thought experiment to his reader. Imagine that you are offered the opportunity to enter an "experience machine," in which you will be able to select any simulated pleasurable sensation and any time period in which to have it.[10] If you wanted to eat cotton candy, you wouldn't eat it so much as *feel* the pleasure you ordinarily would feel upon eating it. Nor would you know, at the moment in which you were "eating," that your simulated experience was a sham. Want the experience of writing a novel? No reason why the experience machine couldn't handle that. But would you get in? Nozick's intuition is that few people would ultimately want to get in, because something matters to us other than how our lives *feel* from the inside. We don't just want the sensations involved in writing a novel; we want to *write* a

8. See John Stuart Mill, *Utilitarianism*, ed. George Sher, 2nd edition (Indianapolis: Hackett, 2001), p. 7.

9. St. John Paul, *Veritatis Splendor*, 75.

10. Robert Nozick, *Anarchy, State, and Utopia* (New York: Basic Books, 1974).

novel. The pleasure that accompanies it is desired, yes, but not for its own sake so much as for what it accompanies.

There is another thing that the experience machine should be showing us. Mill's consequentialism (he called it Utilitarianism) held that the only foundational good was pleasure. Every good was a function of how much pleasure it provided. Actually, he tried to appeal to the idea of "higher" and "lower" pleasures,[11] but many people, including me, think that his appeal is a failure because of his view that pleasure is the one fundamental good. But if pleasure is the only fundamental good, then everyone should enter the experience machine, because pleasure is what it provides. Since we don't really want to enter the experience machine, or at least I certainly don't, we need to realize that what we want isn't just one thing under the sun. Ultimately, what we want *moves* the sun and the other stars. So the objects of our actions must be capable of being ordered to God. Another way to say this is that they must be worthy of the spiritual dignity for which God singled out human persons. Although God is the end of all our striving, there is no finite good at which all our efforts aim. We cannot develop a full ethical theory to cover every kind of evil here, but we can say that there are several unique goods, such as life, the integrity of a person, friendship, and so on.[12] But if there are several goods at which we aim, why not just take any particular action, and sum up the amount of goodness each option tended toward and choose that? This is how St. John Paul construes proportionalism, a view he rejects.[13]

One problem with this proportionalist view is that if we're going to determine where the greater proportion of good is in a particular choice, we need to be able to total up the good in its own separate column. That is, we still need a single good of which every other good is a function; we need one bucket in which to put all our separate goods. But the only single good at which we all aim is God, and God doesn't come in buckets. God's relevance in morality is determined by his will, not by "how much" of him one action accords us. The role for our reason in morality is to aim at real goods, which are good because God's creation is good and God himself is good (Gen. 1:31).

This means that the attempt to "add up" all of the goods and evils

11. Mill, *Utilitarianism,* p. 10.
12. See St. John Paul, *Veritatis Splendor,* 80, and John Finnis, *Natural Law and Natural Rights* (Oxford: Clarendon, 1980), chapter 4.
13. St. John Paul, *Veritatis Splendor,* 75.

that various courses of action would result in is impossible. The goods are incommensurable; they cannot be measured since to measure any two things one needs a unit of measurement that can be used for both items. One needs a scale to measure the weight of any two objects, but there is no such scale to measure the "amount" of good across diverse goods. How would you measure the good of a friendship over the good of life? Is one very good friendship worth the destruction of one life? What about two? What about three? What is the number? There is no number. What are we to do then in a world where evil often travels with good? A good way to think about this would be to say that we should never act directly against one of the foundational human goods. Subduing a violent aggressor to prevent him from harming one's life or someone else's is acceptable; it protects life. In the extreme case when an entire force is mobilized to do violence to a people the only way to defend one's nation is to use force that will likely be deadly, but even then *murder* is not one's intent. If it were, there would be no prisoners of war and no rules about how to treat them.[14] To directly intend to take someone's life is to violate the good of life. Certainly, plenty of the ordinary cases of this are pretty clear: murder, mutilation, slavery, and so on.

What we mean by directly intending to violate a basic good harkens back to our discussion of double effect in chapter 3. Sometimes we can intend to do something good even though we know that an evil accompanies it.[15] As long as we directly intend the good and not the evil, and the good is the kind of thing that can and should be sought, the action can be permitted. There are controversial cases on which Catholic teaching has not pronounced a judgment as of yet, but sometimes it is easy to spot obfuscation. Trying to excuse yourself from murder on the ground that all you wanted to do was rearrange your victim's molecules a bit, and that couldn't happen without his death, is silly. A murderer intends to kill.

This brings us to the second major component of moral assessment the *Catechism* recognizes, namely, the intention of the agent. The intention is important, but it is second in importance to the object of the act. James Bond may be able to gain important information by committing fornication or adultery with well-placed informants, but he shouldn't. He may even have the *intention* to gain information vital to national security and think the only way to do it is to commit such a sin, but that would be

14. *CCC*, 2313.
15. *CCC*, 2263.

to do evil so that good may come. An action with a good object should also have a good intention, such as love of God or neighbor or both.[16] One can perform an action with a good object but nevertheless have a bad intention. An example could be Jesus' own example of giving alms to the poor and vainly blowing a trumpet so that all will see you and think well of you (Matt. 6:2).

The circumstances in which an act takes place are a third element in the moral assessment of an action, but they are not a primary element. This condition works mostly to either enhance the good of an action or diminish the evil of an action. Spreading a false and damaging rumor about a friend with whom you are feuding is evil, and yet it does seem to involve a more cold and calculating evil to have the power and resources to mount a worldwide campaign falsely to defame someone's character. Circumstances in this case don't change the evil, but they do contribute to a heightening of it.

A final remark should be made here in discussing the moral foundations for a Catholic understanding of the human person, and it concerns the virtues. Although someone may choose a good action with the right intention in the right circumstances, she may not yet be very joyful in the performance of such an action. The moral life can be a struggle, but the virtuous person advances beyond the struggle so that she can choose what is right for the right reasons and do so with joy. The church makes a distinction between human virtues and theological virtues. Human virtues are "acquired by human effort,"[17] though of course there is no good human effort without God. All of these ultimately come to nothing, however, without the theological virtues, faith, hope, and charity (or love), and the greatest of these is love (1 Cor. 13:13).[18]

The Human Person as Bodily

The body is an indispensable component of what it means to be human in any Christian vision. Otherwise, the Apostles' Creed would not proclaim the resurrection of the dead. We do not swap species and become angels in heaven. Although we are not *just* bodies, we are bodily. Because of the

16. *CCC*, 1752-53.
17. *CCC*, 1804.
18. *CCC*, 1812-29.

special dignity of the human soul, God endows each of us with a spiritual soul at the moment we are conceived, but this unity of body and soul forms one human nature. The soul is the "form" of the body.[19] Thus, any time we have a living human body we have a soul. The human person is the body-soul composite entity, not something else that comes into being later.

It is important to emphasize this because some thinkers hold that the human person does not come onto the scene until the human being has developed some of the right capacities. For instance, philosopher Mary Anne Warren (1946-2010) argues that the fetus is not a "member of the moral community" until it is self-conscious, can reason, can communicate, and so on.[20] Warren carries this view to its logical conclusion, namely, that we should consider the fetus to have little more right to life than a "new-born guppy."[21] This view of personhood has its roots in the philosophy of John Locke (1632-1704). Locke held that a person was something different from a body or even a soul. He held that personal identity was dependent only on consciousness.[22] Thus, until a fetus develops a consciousness, a point some locate at between twenty-five and thirty-one weeks of development,[23] many of those who favor policies allowing abortion would claim that it cannot be considered a person.

The Catholic Church has opposed this view of personhood and the moral view of the fetus it implies, but it does not claim that to come to some understanding of this we must wait until Christian revelation confirms it. If we needed Christian revelation for all of our moral principles, how could we even formulate just laws in a pluralistic society? Rather, the *Catechism* argues that the right to life and legal protection must be given to the fetus from the moment of conception.[24] But if we can know this without revelation, why should secular thinkers hold this view? As regards the moral status of a human being, this is a subject for philosophy. All biological science can tell us is what organic conditions are present in the fetus, not what that means for its moral status. Here we should consider which

19. *CCC*, 365.

20. See Mary Anne Warren, "On the Moral and Legal Status of Abortion," *The Monist* 57 (1973): 43-61, at p. 55.

21. Warren, "On the Moral and Legal Status of Abortion," p. 58.

22. See John Locke, *An Essay Concerning Human Understanding*, ed. Alexander Campbell Fraser, 2 vols. (New York: Dover, 1959), vol. 1, pp. 450-51.

23. See David Boonin, *A Defense of Abortion* (Cambridge: Cambridge University Press, 2003), p. 127.

24. *CCC*, 2270, 2273.

view of the person is preferable. To do this, let's investigate the opposing view on its own terms.

If we held that consciousness is the criterion for a person, then there must be something that unites all of one person's conscious experiences (let's call the person Sally). Otherwise, there would be no reason to call those experiences Sally's. To say that it is simply the soul would not be very helpful in the debate, since many people who are not religious might be ill at ease with the concept of a soul. But to say that it is the consciousness of a person does not help matters much, either, because, especially for secular thinkers, consciousness is one of the most mysterious realities of our existence. But if consciousness is mysterious and not well-understood across religious and non-religious lines, why would we make it the basis of our laws regarding human personhood? Surely the answer cannot be that we want to justify abortion, because that would be circular. Instead, it seems best to just stick with the body, which we all interact with daily, and which makes more sense as the basis of legal policy, as the thing that houses and ensures the continuity of conscious experience. If we do that, then we can no longer say that we need to wait for some signs of *conscious* life to appear; we just need signs that the human organism is alive, period.

But what would constitute a sign of life in this regard? If I were to look for signs of life, I would look for signs that a thing can act as an entity. To be a little simplistic, if I'm looking for a sign of whether the dog lying on the floor is alive, I'd gently poke it to see if it moved or breathed differently, sought to defend itself, or generally did anything of which it was the subject. Turning to human reproduction, prior to conception, we have only gametes, sperm and ovum, and these are definitely not entities in their own right. I'm a little embarrassed to admit that when I was younger I saw the 1983 movie *The Meaning of Life* by the crass British sketch comedy act Monty Python's Flying Circus. I now consider this movie morally problematic, but in it, Catholics are ridiculed as holding that "every sperm is sacred." Although there is something mysterious and wonderful about the sexual act in its reproductive dimension, which we will discuss shortly, the idea that "every sperm is sacred" is a misrepresentation of the church's position. What is sacred is the new life that begins as a result of the uniting of sperm and ovum. The potential that exists in a sperm to unite with an ovum is different from the potential that exists in a newly fertilized zygote to develop into an adult human being. A sperm has only the former potential. But what kind of integrity as an organism would a zygote have? How about the integrity to protect itself against polyspermy, or the fertilization by more than one sperm, a potential threat to its existence? This seems to me, and to others, to be a time when we have a new organism.[25] This happens just prior to the lining up of the two gametes' chromosomes, after which the process of growth and maturation are on an entirely new course.

Now of course, the embryo is not yet the *moral* subject of action in the sense that it can be praised or blamed for, say, going down the fallopian tube and entering the uterus. We certainly don't blame even infants for dirtying their diapers. But they are organisms and we do interact with them. Likewise, the embryo interacts with its environment in such a way as to develop eventually into an adult human being. That kind of organic integrity seems to be what we're looking for, and yet to agree to that would be to recognize zygotes, embryos, and fetuses among the class of legal persons. Nor is this jeopardized by simply recognizing that a very young embryo can still "twin." That would just mean that it would either give rise to another like itself or (the less likely view) two new embryos took the old one's place.[26] This of course means that the life of the person has begun even if she is frozen as an embryo. For reasons like these, the Catholic Church has opposed human embryonic stem-cell research for failing to treat young human persons with the dignity they deserve. It is important to recognize that this worry of the church is based in a concern about unjust discrimination. Not only are embryos put to service without their consent, they are usually destroyed in the process, and for no other reason than that their adult capacities have not developed. It is for reasons such as these that St. John Paul declared, by an act of the ordinary and universal magisterium, that abortion is always morally wrong.[27]

It is a fashionable device to say that one holds this belief but is not ready to impose this belief on other people through political means. This could mean two things. On the one hand, it could mean that one simply lacks the will to insist that moral principles about something as serious as abortion, which St. John Paul defined as "the deliberate killing of an innocent human being," should be followed in the public square. If that is all it means it is simply a failure of nerve. Forms of contraception that do not destroy embryos can be legally tolerated even if they are morally wrong (as

25. See Robert P. George and Christopher Tollefsen, *Embryo: A Defense of Human Life*, 2nd edition (Princeton: Witherspoon Institute, 2011), p. 38.

26. George and Tollefsen, *Embryo*, p. 239.

27. St. John Paul, *Evangelium Vitae*, 62.

we will consider shortly), but the killing of the innocent cannot be legally tolerated. Any politician who said so would immediately be out of a job for being "soft on crime." On the other hand, if the claim that one is not willing to impose her belief about the wrongness of abortion on others means that one actually thinks that there are circumstances in which a woman should be allowed to have an abortion morally *even if* the fetus is a person, then it deserves a few more words.

Philosopher Bertha Alvarez Manninen defends the abortion right in this way. She argues that the woman cannot be under an obligation to protect the fetus even if it is a person.[28] To understand a Catholic perspective in response one must see that the unborn child is not an aggressor against the mother, and so no matter how serious the reasons, abortion is not a form of self-defense.[29] To abort the child even because of a danger to the mother (whether psychological or medical) is to act against the life of the child. But the child cannot be seen as a part of some campaign against the woman. Both are in their predicament together, and in the sphere of parenthood things are simply not equal. The mother unquestionably assumes a greater responsibility during the time of pregnancy, and for this the father must recognize a debt to the mother.[30] But this important responsibility of the mother to be the sole and intimate guardian of her child while she is pregnant requires that she not act against the child, even if she must make demanding sacrifices for her child. Of course, if, for example, a woman has a cancerous uterus that threatens her life *and* the life of the child inside of her, then it is permitted to use medical measures to treat the cancerous uterus even if the child will die in the process, so long as the death of the child is not what is intended.[31]

Life must be respected and legally protected from conception until natural death, and this applies not just to birth, but also to death. Thus, the church opposes the death penalty, since in modern penal systems, it is almost always possible to protect society from an individual aggressor

28. See Bertha Alvarez Manninen, "Rethinking *Roe v. Wade:* Defending the Abortion Right in the Face of Contemporary Opposition," *American Journal of Bioethics* 10 (2010): 33-46.

29. St. John Paul, *Evangelium Vitae*, 58.

30. See St. John Paul, *Mulieris Dignitatem*, 18.

31. See United States Conference of Catholic Bishops, *Ethical and Religious Directives for Catholic Health Care Services,* 5th ed., directive 47, at http://www.usccb.org/issues-and -action/human-life-and-dignity/health-care/upload/Ethical-Religious-Directives-Catholic -Health-Care-Services-fifth-edition-2009.pdf. Accessed 15 July 2014.

without killing him, and it may still be possible to help him.[32] On a larger scale, as we have said, when an entire nation presents a violent threat to the safety and security of another, and there is no other way to defend the innocent but to go to war, then war may be undertaken. Wars of aggression are wrong, and I will frankly admit that, like St. John Paul, I had grave reservations about the most recent war effort undertaken by the United States in Iraq. The Catholic Church does not teach pacifism, but indicates that war can be legitimate as long as other means of putting an end to conflict have been exhausted and the actual war effort is both realistic and restrained.[33]

In ordinary matters, life must be allowed to run its course, and just as there must be a time when we should give life in its beginning stages the respect of a person, there is a time when we must give a deceased person's body the respect it is owed. But when does a person die? The television program *Sesame Street* for years ran a song called "They're Not Alive" in which children discovered things that were not alive. The criteria were simple and obvious and were intended to separate rocks, chairs, and cars from spruce trees, turtles, and human beings. All that was asked was does the thing eat, breathe, or grow? If the answer was no, then the thing was not alive. Of course, this is simplistic. Rudimentary forms of life don't have lungs and don't eat in what we would consider an ordinary way. But if a thing is alive it will still take nourishment and will grow to some degree. If its growth and integrity are permanently at an end and it simply has not yet decomposed, then an organism can be said to be dead. That doesn't mean that everything on a living organism has to grow. I won't be growing taller, but parts of me still grow, and blood continues to pump through my veins and that happens because the body-soul entity that I am is still alive.

The thing to realize here, however, is that a turtle still grows if it is alive but not awake. In fact, if a turtle were under general anesthesia, it would still be alive. If a turtle were in a coma, it would still be alive. Not only would it be alive, it would be a *turtle*. This point is more important than it probably seems. Patients in a hospital setting sometimes reach what medicine generally calls a "persistent vegetative state." St. John Paul, however, in a 2004 address, argued that no human being can ever become a "vegetable" or a mere "animal" just because her capacities are lessened.[34]

32. *CCC,* 2266-67.
33. *CCC,* 2307-17.
34. See St. John Paul, *Address of John Paul II to the Participants in the International Congress on "Life-Sustaining Treatments and Vegetative State: Scientific Advances and Ethical Dilemmas,"* 3. Dated 20 March 2004.

Such patients remain *human*. The respect owed to a living human being is different from the respect owed to a deceased human body, but all living human beings are owed the same respect, regardless of their capacities. This is why, if a human person can still eat, breathe, and grow, then she must not be deprived of food or water. We would not withhold nourishment from a child too young to serve herself, nor would we hesitate to provide her with simple nourishment even if we needed to use technology to deliver it. Obviously, if you're in a remote location where the technology of a feeding tube is simply not available, then you can't be required to provide it, but when it is available, even a feeding tube should be provided, unless it is medically counterproductive or the patient is near death for some other reason.[35] However, there is a difference between the situation of a young child and the situation of someone who is very old. All of us will die, and while it is not right intentionally to end life or hasten death, it can be holy to accept death with serenity and faith. Providing food and water is not medical *treatment,* but some medical treatment can be "overzealous."[36] Costly and burdensome procedures make much more sense if they are being given to those who we have reason to think will live for a good while longer. But if the person is at the end of her life it is not necessary to undergo costly and difficult treatment if the realistic result will only be to gain just a few more hours or days of earthly life.

The Human Person as Sexual

Just as the person's bodily life must be respected, so must her bodily *integrity*. Deliberately to kill someone is evil, but deliberately to harm a person is also evil. One particularly grievous way in which a person can be harmed is by rape. Rape is a deliberate and terrible assault on someone's sexual identity and integrity. We think of it as one of the worst crimes against the person, and indeed, against humanity that can be imagined. We are surely right about this. But an important clue to understanding our sexuality is involved in this recognition. Our sexuality is tied very closely to our sense of who we are as persons. As Pope Francis's first encyclical *Lumen Fidei* has

35. See the Congregation for the Doctrine of Faith, *Responses to Certain Questions of the United States Conference of Catholic Bishops Concerning Artificial Nutrition and Hydration,* and especially the final two paragraphs of the *Commentary* on it. Dated 1 August 2007.
36. *CCC,* 2278.

it, "love aims at union with the beloved."[37] Rape attempts to *steal* bodily union with a person without any consideration of the importance of the whole person and her emotional and spiritual well-being. On the other hand, marriage, the proper context for sexual activity, is hard work. It takes time and care to know one's spouse well enough, and to care for her or him deeply enough, to give the whole gift of self that sex can be. As we noticed in the last chapter on heaven, in the life of the world to come we await deeper union with everyone in Christ than we can achieve in this life with even one person. Everyone longs for heaven, whether they realize it or not. A pure love on earth realizes that it can only experience a foretaste of heavenly love in a committed marital relationship, but some who are impatient for the promiscuity of spirit in heaven attempt to exchange it for the promiscuity of the flesh on earth.

God created us male and female (Gen. 1:27), and this arrangement was not a mistake. It was intended both for the future of the human race and for deep and intimate friendship between the two. These two become "one body" (Gen. 2:24) in marriage and sexual union. After the fall, various kinds of sexual immorality were introduced. In fact, when St. Paul writes to the Corinthians in the horror that Christians had been frequenting prostitutes (1 Cor. 6:15-20), he notes that visiting a prostitute involves becoming "one body" with her, the very thing that one is only supposed to become with one's spouse. This is a rich and interesting statement because it means that being "one body" is not about "being on the same page" emotionally, psychologically, or even spiritually. It seems safe to assume that people weren't frequenting prostitutes because they wanted emotional intimacy. They wanted union; a union of conquest, perhaps, but still union, and Paul thinks they got it.

This means that becoming "one body" is a physical fact.[38] This is why Paul thinks sex with a prostitute is bad: it is becoming one body with her without giving a whole gift of self to her. Sex *should* be bodily, but it should also be emotional, psychological, and spiritual. Marital union should be a union of two whole people and their entire lives.[39] Obviously, "one-night stands" are not going to be a union of two people's whole lives. But there are other ways in which an attempt at union can fail. Outside the biblical

---

37. Pope Francis, *Lumen Fidei*, 27.

38. See Alexander Pruss, "Christian Sexual Ethics and Teleological Organicity," *The Thomist* 64 (2000): 71-100, at p. 80.

39. See St. John Paul, *Familiaris Consortio*, 11.

text, the 1988 slapstick comedy *The Naked Gun* gives an obviously outlandish case for our discussion. The main character and his love interest are off to bed, but before they engage in intercourse, they fit themselves out with full body condoms. This of course is ridiculous, but the point it makes is anything but ridiculous. The union this couple hopes to foster in sex is belied by the equipment they've donned that makes their union impossible.

It's probably not difficult to see where I'm going with this. The Catholic Church thinks that sex should be a total gift of the self, and it is worried that reserving even one's fertility is a failure to bring forward a full gift. Nor is it just that sex with a condom (or any form of artificial contraception) isn't *as good* as sex without one, because sex is about union with another person, and that isn't something you *grade.* Love aims at union, and when it doesn't fully give itself, sex is not really union at all. Contraceptive sex aims at union with the mind, but doesn't give union with the body. This is why St. John Paul used the admittedly strong language of a "lie" to characterize sex in which there is not a total gift of the self in this way.[40] Protestant philosopher Caroline J. Simon disagrees. She worries that prohibitions against contraception "put the unitive aspects of marital sexuality at risk in real life."[41] I respect her work, but I believe that it is not the prohibition against contraception that threatens marital union, but contraception itself.

But how do the two become one body? What could that mean? Marriage is ordered to procreation and ultimately so is the sexual act. The fact that a given couple may not be fertile is not the point. The point is that they are united in this act, in which their bodies become one by aiming at the same thing, reproduction, whether their minds are consciously aiming at it or not.[42] This is why, in the Catholic tradition, marriages are only consummated "if the spouses have performed between themselves in a human fashion a conjugal act which is suitable in itself for the procreation of offspring, to which marriage is ordered by its nature and by which the spouses become one flesh."[43] Marriages, like love, aim at union. Marriage aims to express that union throughout the lives of the husband and wife, but it cannot do so without that union also being expressed concretely in the sexual act precisely because we are bodies. Sex is not merely a symbol of unity; it *is* marital unity. Married couples cannot pledge what they

40. St. John Paul, *Familiaris Consortio,* 11.
41. Caroline J. Simon, *Bringing Sex into Focus* (Downers Grove, IL: InterVarsity Press, 2012), p. 158.
42. See Pruss, "Christian Sexual Ethics," p. 77.
43. *CCL,* 1061.1.

do without uniting physically as the culmination of all the ways in which their lives are woven together. All that occurs in sex is ordered in some way to marital unity. For a man to intentionally ejaculate outside his wife's vagina, or through "oral sex" or "anal sex" would damage that unity, just as Onan's act in Genesis 38:9 did, when he interrupted his intercourse because he did not want his brother's widow to become pregnant. Insofar as complete sexual satisfaction is sought outside the context of heterosexual monogamous intercourse, there is something substituting for real unity. A female student of mine once had the courage to frankly and politely ask me during class what a traditional view might say about female orgasm. Female orgasm must still take place in the context of sexual union, but since it is not linked with new life in the same way that the emission of semen is, it needn't be during actual penetration.[44] Complete sexual satisfaction can only be understood as part of the love that aims at union. The point of the Catholic vision of sexuality is, as Pope Benedict XVI has said, not to "stifle" love but to make it "healthy, strong, and truly free."[45]

The unity of the couple and procreative possibilities go hand in hand. If a couple just happens to be infertile, they are still one flesh in intercourse, but if they deliberately work against procreative possibilities, then they also work against their unity. The same thing goes if couples attempt to procreate outside of marital unity. A child is a gift from God, and this gift should be given by God as the fruit of a couple's love. As a father of two children who are adopted, I certainly believe that my children are gifts from God and that they were given as the fruit of my wife's and my love. Anyone with a sense of the complexity and difficulty in the adoption process should be able to agree. Our children are the fulfillment of our longings for parenthood and we love them with all of our hearts. Indeed, we felt our longing for our children very deeply because of our experience of infertility. There is something important here to notice. The grief of infertility shows us that we want to be given the gift of children through marital union. This is not because of the nature of parental love, but because of the character of sexuality. Ultimately, it longs to transcend itself, be fruitful, and multiply (Gen. 1:28). Nevertheless, to seek to have children

44. See Christopher West, *Good News about Sex and Marriage: Answers to Your Honest Questions about Sex and Marriage*, revised edition (Cincinnati: Servant Books, 2007), pp. 90-91; and Rev. Ronald Lawler, OFM, Joseph Boyle, and William E. May, *Catholic Sexual Ethics* (Huntington, IN: OSV, 1985), pp. 172-73.

45. See Pope Benedict XVI, *Address of His Holiness Benedict XVI to the Participants at the Ecclesial Convention of the Diocese of Rome,* dated 5 June 2006.

by working *against* marital union seems a very strange posture to take. It again does evil so that good may come of it. This is why the church rejects artificial insemination and *in vitro* fertilization as ways to secure children: they intentionally separate the unity of the spouses and the procreation they hope to engender.[46] Insofar as some other methods merely *assist* the unity of the couple to conceive, they may be permitted.[47] What is not permitted is to obtain sperm in the fashion most medical facilities would regard as customary: through masturbation, since this is itself a major separation of sexuality from the context of marital union.[48]

It is only in the context of this overall view of human sexuality that we can say that homosexual activity cannot be condoned. This is not a question of pointing out that Jesus says nothing about homosexuality, since Jesus says a good deal about the marriage of husband and wife and intends to restore marriage to its original dignity as the unity of man and woman. It is in the context of appreciating what the scriptural writers understand by "one body" and how a married couple becomes one body that we can talk about homosexual activity. The Catholic Church wants us to discover how married love can be strong and free, and the deviations from this are many. Homosexual activity is, in its essence, one more way of closing off sexuality from the transmission of life.[49] At the same time, homosexual activity is unique in that some people have an inclination toward it that they most likely did not choose, and because of this, the mere possession of a homosexual inclination, tendency, or orientation, is not itself sinful.[50] What is sinful is the deliberate separation of the unitive and procreative elements in a given sexual act, and people of the same sex cannot unite in a way that preserves those two dimensions. That is why, if a person cannot be sexually attracted to a person of the opposite sex, the Catholic Church teaches that she should remain celibate. Reformed Protestant theologian Allen Verhey argues that if we permit heterosexual remarriage while a former spouse is still living, we should also permit homosexual unions in the church.[51] But

46. *CCC*, 2377.

47. See United States Conference of Catholic Bishops, *Ethical and Religious Directives for Catholic Health Care Services*, directive 38, and chapter three of William E. May, *Catholic Bioethics and the Gift of Human Life*, 2nd edition (Huntington, IN: OSV, 2008).

48. See DH, 3684.

49. *CCC*, 2357.

50. See the United States Conference of Catholic Bishops' document *Ministry to Persons with a Homosexual Inclination: Guidelines for Pastoral Care*, p. 5.

51. Allen Verhey, *Remembering Jesus* (Grand Rapids: Eerdmans, 2002), p. 239.

since the Catholic Church, in keeping with the way she understands Jesus'
teaching on marriage, rejects remarriage when both spouses are still living,
she also rejects homosexual unions. Nevertheless, it would be foolish to
deny that homosexual individuals have often been the target of hate and
even violence merely because of their sexual desires. This mistreatment is
itself a terrible failure to respect the human person.

The Human Person as Social

What can we say, then, about the proposal to legally recognize homosexual unions? To be sure, the church is not the state, nor should the church
attempt to replace the state.[52] At the same time, all states strive for some vision of justice, and the church has a duty to speak up when human dignity
is not being respected. We simply cannot pretend that politics is a morally neutral endeavor. Society has a responsibility to pursue the common
good of its citizens. Clearly different moral visions will understand "the
common good" differently. How does the Catholic Church understand it?
Vatican II said that it is "the sum of those conditions of social life which
allow social groups and their individual members relatively thorough and
ready access to their own fulfillment."[53] In order to pursue the common
good, then, we'll need an idea of what it would be for human beings to be
fulfilled. This will require a full view of the human person. While this does
not mean that everything that is immoral must be made legally punishable,
nor that everything that is religiously good for a person needs to be given
some special political privilege, it does mean that the state itself should not
go so far as to condone things that are positively immoral.

    To return to our question, then, should the state honor same-sex
marriage with the same legal status it gives to heterosexual monogamous
marriage? As difficult as I know these issues are, the Congregation for the
Doctrine of Faith has indicated that the answer is no, and I think this was
the right decision.[54] The first reason is simply that, for the reasons I have
discussed above, homosexual activity cannot be condoned. For Christians,
revelation certainly aids in the discovery of this moral truth, but it is not

---

    52. Pope Benedict XVI, *Deus Caritas Est*, 28.
    53. Vatican II, *Gaudium et Spes*, 26.
    54. See Congregation for the Doctrine of Faith, *Considerations Regarding Proposals to
Give Legal Recognition to Unions between Homosexual Persons*, dated 3 June 2003.

just a matter of reading the Bible. Marriage is not just a societal convention, in the church's teaching, but a reality that exists before a state ever came along with the idea that it should sanction marriage.[55] The family, as the ancient Greek philosopher Aristotle (384 BCE-322 BCE) recognized, is established by nature for the meeting of everyday needs and wants.[56] Marriage, according to a very ancient view, is not just a long-term relationship, but the founding of a family. In addition, all marriages have some erotic component. No one would call a living arrangement between two bachelor brothers or two celibate nuns a marriage. The trouble is that there is no possibility of consummating a relationship with an act of marital unity because two members of the same sex cannot become one body in the way we've discussed. Yet same-sex marriages are still built around the sexual intimacy of the partners.

Should the state take a positive step to encourage people to form those relationships? Lesbian feminist Claudia Card argues that the state should instead get out of the business of marriage altogether. She argues that the institution of marriage itself, as a permanent, exclusive, and economic arrangement recognized by the state, needs to go.[57] While I think her conclusion is mistaken, I think her argument shows that any effort by the state to recognize a romantic relationship, especially in economic terms, is an invitation for people to form those relationships. The only question is which invitations should the state extend? If you think that a romantic relationship between two members of the same sex cannot be morally condoned, then I think you should ask a morally good state not to condone it. It is quite a different matter to impose stiff punishments on people simply for engaging in homosexual activity, and it is well within the bounds of Catholic orthodoxy to hold that it would be a mistake to do so. Nor need the state deny that homosexual individuals could determine who may visit them in the hospital or inherit their property, since this kind of right is an individual right that anyone could have, and there is no need to legally commend homosexual relationships to do that.[58]

The church's opposition to same-sex marriage is also grounded in her belief that marriage is the foundation for the family, and the family is

55. *CCC*, 1603.

56. Aristotle, *Politics*, Book I, chapter 2, 1252b13-14 in *The Complete Works of Aristotle*, ed. Jonathan Barnes (Princeton: Princeton University Press, 1984), vol. 2, p. 1987.

57. See Claudia Card, "Against Marriage and Motherhood," *Hypatia*, 11 (1996): 1-23.

58. See Sherif Girgis, Robert P. George, and Ryan T. Anderson, "What Is Marriage?," *Harvard Journal of Law and Public Policy* 34 (2010): 245-87, at 281.

the foundation for society. Indeed, the family, not the state, is the image of the Trinity itself.[59] As the *Compendium of the Social Doctrine of the Church* claims, "The family . . . does not exist for society or the State, but society and the State exist for the family."[60] The family is built upon the marital communion of husband and wife, and the church is convinced that children flourish best in an environment in which the balance of husband and wife, father and mother, is established.[61] This last point is a controversial claim in our day, when many rush to use methods in the social sciences to establish that children are as well-placed with homosexual parents as they are with heterosexual parents. This is not the place to enter into this debate, but I do think it is worth pointing out that every claim that a child flourishes must be based on a conception of what it would mean for her to flourish. To a Christian, the full flourishing of a human being has to be about more than whether she has access to social goods, but whether she has access to transcendent goods, most importantly the presence of God in Jesus. I don't anticipate many studies based on those criteria, and in any case, this can only be a secondary issue when it comes to the morality of homosexual activity.

We've looked at a couple of things that the state should not do, but what should it do? What is the state competent to do for the flourishing of human beings? First, let us say something briefly about what the state is. Philosopher Thomas Hobbes (1588-1679) is famous for arguing that the state is what comes into being when human beings realize they cannot ensure their safety on their own.[62] In Hobbes's so-called state of nature, human beings are free to do anything. Indeed, there is no such thing as injustice in Hobbes's state of nature. But since there is nothing to appeal to for personal security, human beings make a social contract, and lay aside some of their liberties to form a state whose purpose is the protection of the most basic freedoms. The trouble with Hobbes's system is that it paints a very bleak picture of why the human being needs the state. In a more Catholic vision, the human being does not need a state because she is frightened of the alternative. Rather, the human being needs a state because she is a social and political animal by her very nature, and having a state contributes to her flourishing as a human being.

In 1891, Pope Leo XIII (pope from 1878 to 1903) issued the first en-

---

59. *CCC*, 2205.

60. *Compendium of the Social Doctrine of the Church*, 214.

61. Vatican II, *Gaudium et Spes*, 52.

62. See Hobbes, *Leviathan*, ed. Edwin Curley (Indianapolis: Hackett, 1994).

cyclical whose focus was on social doctrine, called *Rerum Novarum*. He was writing in the wake of the Industrial Revolution as well as socialist theories of the day that attempted to do away with private property. Pope Leo clearly rejected socialism and insisted upon the importance of private property for protecting the human dignity of workers. Part of this insistence has to do with the priority of the family in Catholic social thought. It is part of human nature to organize life into a social and political network, but it is also part of human nature, and even more deeply a part of human nature, to organize as a family. In addition to draining the worker's motivation to work, having an overarching state control all property takes away the competence and importance of the family for providing for children and making decisions about their welfare.[63] This is an instance of the principle of subsidiarity, which we mentioned in chapter 2, which claims that if there is a smaller organization on the social chain (like the family) competent to handle a particular matter, then it should be left to that organization and not assumed by some larger organization (like the state).[64]

The church offers some teaching about how to understand private property, however. One should not just take the right to private property as a license to pursue shamefully indulgent wealth. There are a few things to notice here. First, it is a duty of Christian charity to give to the poor out of what remains.[65] Second, it is not just a Christian duty but also a social virtue for us to realize and put into practice that we are all really responsible for each other. This is the principle of solidarity, which is a "firm and persevering determination to commit oneself to the common good."[66] The need for solidarity in our rapidly changing world is especially clear when we consider that one of the most obvious ways in which our world is changing is that we can interact virtually with people across the world in real time. But this also comes with a corollary: we can *fail* to interact with people across the world in real time. There are drastic inequalities in income and opportunity in our world, and we can perpetuate these, or we can ensure that we do not leave behind whole portions of our common human family. Another thing to notice is that, since work is necessary for life, the worker must not be given a wage that is unjust or insufficient for living. Employers are not simply at their liberty to throw workers a pit-

---

63. Pope Leo XIII, *Rerum Novarum*, 6-13, DH, 3265-66.
64. See *Compendium of the Social Doctrine of the Church*, 186.
65. DH, 3267.
66. *Compendium of the Social Doctrine of the Church*, 193.

tance because their job is the only one on offer.[67] While this imposes an obligation on the potential employer, it is also necessary to indicate that the state itself should not feel at its liberty to impose burdensome taxes on its citizens, thereby watering down to nothing what would otherwise be a sufficient wage for living.[68]

In this context, we must acknowledge Pope Francis's 2013 apostolic exhortation *Evangelii Gaudium,* and his call for a church "which is poor and for the poor."[69] Jesus has a special love for the poor. The church, like Jesus, holds what is called a "preferential option for the poor."[70] In Matthew's Gospel, Jesus calls blessed the poor in spirit, the meek, those who mourn, and those who hunger and thirst for righteousness (Matt. 5:3-10). In Luke's Gospel, Jesus calls blessed the poor, the hungry, those who are weeping, and those who are hated, and he warns the rich, the sated, and the jovial (Luke 6:20-26). I have often felt indicted by these two messages, but I have never felt them inconsistent. The atheist and communist philosopher Karl Marx (1818-1883) famously called religion "the opium of the people."[71] His idea was that the poor tend to project a heavenly kingdom in which they will have all the comforts they lack here on earth and that this is the source of the religious impulse. Here is another idea. In our increasingly consumerist societies, it may well be that the poor and the oppressed understand better than the rich and powerful just how deeply all people need God and his loving grace. Suffering can be a way to identify with the sufferings of the crucified Lord of Christianity. Jesus did not come to rule in our sinful world. He came to live and teach, yes, but he also came to be rejected, spat upon, and killed so that through his sacrifice we could be redeemed and live with him when he comes again to make all things new. The church loves the poor for two major reasons. First, because she loves Jesus and wants to be like him and Jesus was poor. Second, because she wants to be like Jesus and Jesus loved the poor.

If you follow political debates at all, you might be noticing something. The Catholic Church's teaching does not line up neatly with any one political party's economic or even moral agenda. Employees have du-

---

67. DH, 3270.

68. DH, 3271.

69. Pope Francis, *Evangelii Gaudium,* 198.

70. *Compendium of the Social Doctrine of the Church,* 182-84.

71. See Karl Marx, "A Contribution to the Critique of Hegel's Philosophy of Right: Introduction," in *The Marx-Engels Reader,* ed. Robert C. Tucker, 2nd edition (New York: Norton, 1978), pp. 53-65, at p. 54.

ties and rights, but so do employers and even the state itself. The church teaches against viewing the human person as a mere individual, since she is a social being. But the church also teaches against subsuming the individual under some overarching collective state.[72] Likewise, if by "capitalism" one means a system of private property and a free economy, then the church can endorse it; but if that system does not put economic freedom at the service of human freedom and flourishing, then the church cannot fully endorse it.[73] Although the family is the first and most important sphere of education for children, the state can play an important role in this task as well.[74] Pope Benedict XVI spoke strongly of the need for basic healthcare for all people, but he also indicated that this healthcare must not violate the dignity of the person in areas such as abortion, euthanasia, and sterilization.[75] The church champions equality and dignity for all people and rejects discrimination on the basis of "sex, race, color, social conditions, language, or religion."[76] Indeed, that conviction led my state's bishops to oppose a proposal against affirmative action. At the same time, the church privileges the traditional family structure and resists efforts to include same-sex marriage under this rubric of equality. At least in the American context, a "Catholic political party" doesn't exist.[77] We all, of course, need to make our best judgments as to which candidates to vote for in an individual situation. In this judgment, not all issues are equal. A low minimum wage may be evil, but it is not as grievous an issue as the systematic destruction of unborn human life, along with the puzzling suggestion that access to abortion is a "right." An economy should be adequately free, and we should work to ensure this. Nevertheless, the freedom and equality of entire populations that have been historically marginalized through racism and other structural evils is often a more pressing concern.

I never feel very excited about the prospect of voting. I also prefer not to post signs in my yard for political candidates, because I usually have difficulty finding a candidate whose moral and political vision lines up very closely with mine and those of my Catholic faith. I do vote and I

---

72. DH, 3726.

73. DH, 4909.

74. CCC, 2223 and 1908, 1910.

75. See Pope Benedict XVI, *Message of His Holiness Benedict XVI to Participants in the 25th International Conference Organized by the Pontifical Council for Health Care Workers,* dated 15 November 2010.

76. Vatican II, *Gaudium et Spes,* 29.

77. See Charles J. Chaput, *Render unto Caesar* (New York: Image, 2008), p. 4.

try to discern which options seem most promising, but I also think that partisan politics may well be a symptom of humanity's fall from grace. This is especially clear to me when often enough party platforms endorse only a portion of the moral teaching of my Catholic faith, sadly leaving other portions for the other party to take up. In 2006, however, I happily voted against the proposal to block affirmative action and the proposal to increase embryonic stem-cell research, and I was happy to have the church guide my conscience to that decision.

The human person is spiritual, bodily, sexual, and social. These are not passing realities but deep truths about who we are as persons that in some sense will never leave us. Without our spiritual dignity, we have nothing. Creation itself must be cared for and not neglected, but creation itself was created for us as human beings.[78] Our clearest link with the rest of the creation is through our bodily existence. This, too, is a permanent feature of who we are. Whether in our own person or in the person of another, our bodies must be honored and never directly killed or harmed for any reason. This comes strongly to the fore with such controversial topics as abortion and euthanasia. Our sexual existence will ultimately be revealed as an anticipation of communion in heaven, but here on earth, we can become one in marriage with another. This is a holy and good gift from God and we must respect it and work against the evils that objectify all of us, but especially women, for our sexuality. Pornography and prostitution are especially insidious evils whose far-reaching effects we are only beginning to understand.[79] The human person is also social. She is born into a family where she should be nurtured by a mother and father. She is also born into a society where she should have the same rights and opportunities that all possess, regardless of race, sex, color, or creed. Society has an obligation to care for the human person in all of these dimensions and to see to it that she has the opportunity to live a faithful Christian life. There will never be a society that overcomes all ills. As Pope Benedict XVI has put it, "Love — caritas — will always prove necessary, even in the most just society. There is no ordering of the state so just that it can eliminate the need for a service of love."[80] Christians, however, have a duty to respect the human person and to love others with the special grace of Christian charity while we wait in joyful hope for the coming of our Savior, Jesus Christ.

78. *CCC*, 358.
79. *CCC*, 2354-55.
80. Pope Benedict XVI, *Deus Caritas Est*, 28.

Conclusion

I remember going to a priest some time before I became a Catholic to ask him what kinds of things Catholics really believed. I didn't want him to persuade me. I just wanted to understand what was distinctive about a Catholic way of looking at the world. He was a good and knowledgeable priest, but I was giving him a very difficult task. He gave me St. Francis de Sales's *Introduction to the Devout Life,* a wonderful book, some pointers that I no longer remember, and some encouragement. A little while later, I became a Catholic and a faculty member at a largely Protestant college in the same year. My colleagues have always been kind and generous, but over the years I have been asked many questions about Catholicism. My experience in RCIA (the Rite of Christian Initiation for Adults) was the best the good people who led it could muster, but it did not prepare me for the kinds of challenges I would confront. I still have much to learn, but because I have continually returned to Scripture, Catholic sources, and prayer, I think I can say a bit about what makes a Catholic worldview distinctive.

There are many ways in which Catholicism can and must be distinguished from other Christian views, whether they are Orthodox, Reformed, Lutheran, Episcopalian, and so on. Contrary to what many Catholics have been told, the church really does still teach the reality of purgatory, and when one properly understands it, that teaching is a blessing! The same is true of other distinctive doctrines, like the role of the pope, and the communion of saints, especially the Blessed Virgin Mary's role as mother, the presence of Christ in the Eucharist, and so on. As anyone knows who really considers the term, what flies under the flag of "nondenominationalism" in the United States is, of course, not really that. Such communities are merely forms of evangelical Protestantism that have made familiar Protestant decisions about what is "essential." All Christians want the Gospel essentials, but we understand them differently, and there is no getting around that. To ask of the Catholic Church that it shy away from its distinctiveness is to deny it its beauty. There is a spiritual fullness to the Catholic Church's vision of salvation, and I have tried to present a bit of that vision without shying away from what makes it distinctive.

I also wanted the chance in this book to imagine the Catholic faith in ways that are anchored to the tradition. From experience, I know that it is difficult to find concise explanations of Catholic doctrine that actually acknowledge that what the church teaches remains distinctive and beautiful. Catholic apologetical works often succumb to anti-Protestant prejudices, and many Catholic theologians either leave controversial stones unturned, or hurry to clarify what they regard as optional for Catholics. Many a curious reader walks away puzzled about why the church bothers to teach such things at all. I am convinced that hiding the controversy does little good, precisely because I think all of the church's teaching is an authentic expression of her spiritual devotion to Jesus. This is not to say that I wish to highlight what makes the Catholic Church different from other traditions merely to congratulate myself, or anyone else, on being a Catholic. There is much about which Christians agree, and it is important to emphasize that as well. But Christian ecumenism, the drive for unity, can only succeed when those involved in it have been deeply formed in their own traditions. Without articulating what has brought about our separation in the past, Christians cannot hope to achieve anything more than a cowardly and superficial unity. This is not the unity for which Jesus prayed (John 17:21).

What I have tried to do is to say what I believe as a Catholic and why I believe it, in the space allowed by a single manageable book. I believe everything that I have written, and plenty that I haven't written. This book is not an introduction in which I have no stake. Yet, I cannot claim that I could have come to these beliefs, or even very many of them, without the church in her role as teacher. As far as their historical genesis is concerned, many of my beliefs were formed *because* I came to understand that I should believe them as a Catholic. Since that time, to be sure, I have tried to investigate what reasons there might be for these beliefs so that I could offer a reason for the hope within me (1 Pet. 3:15); but many of my Catholic beliefs did not begin with reason but with faith, or at least in submitting my intellect and will to Christ's church. I have often been in the role that St. Thomas Aquinas describes when he observes that, although the truth that God exists is a truth that reason can demonstrate, nothing prevents someone from accepting this through faith.[1] Indeed, if many Catholic beliefs are things I now think have the better warrant of reason or Scripture, I am grateful for the church's guidance in helping me to see this. In this way, I have sought shelter in the Catholic Church, which I embraced as my spiritual home over ten years ago. But I do not think that there is anything shameful about taking refuge in the bosom of the church, which the earliest Christians understood as a mother, as long as one intends to die there.

I have had two students work with me in the writing of this project. Both were talented and bright Reformed Protestant Christians, and I think they might have been a little curious as to why I asked for their help and not for the help of Catholic students. The reason is that I wanted to write a book not to persuade in the manner of a book in apologetics but to explain the Catholic faith in the way I have outlined above. One of them has now read the full text. What I hope he does is take the explanations of Catholic belief I have developed and consider the resources in his own tradition for developing responses and treatments of the same issues. Do I think that ultimately the Catholic Church gives the best explanation of what faith in Christ amounts to? Of course! I became a Catholic because I became convinced that Catholicism is true. But I hope for careful dialogue that moves closer and closer to the real unity for which Jesus prayed, even though I am under no illusion about Christians finally achieving that unity this side of heaven. So I hope that non-Catholic readers of this book enjoy it, but I also want to invite them to challenge its conclusions if they disagree. Christians really do disagree, and for unity to progress, Christians must first understand why we are *not* one. Only then can we really long for unity, because only then can we fully experience the longing of Christ's own Sacred Heart.

---

1. *ST,* I.2.2, reply to objection 1.

Index of Subjects and Names

Index of Scripture References